AF708956

COMPUTER SCIENCE, TECHNOLOGY AND APPLICATIONS

VIRTUAL ENVIRONMENTS

DEVELOPMENTS, APPLICATIONS AND CHALLENGES

COMPUTER SCIENCE, TECHNOLOGY AND APPLICATIONS

Additional books in this series can be found on Nova's website under the Series tab.

Additional E-books in this series can be found on Nova's website under the E-book tab.

COMPUTER SCIENCE, TECHNOLOGY AND APPLICATIONS

VIRTUAL ENVIRONMENTS

DEVELOPMENTS, APPLICATIONS AND CHALLENGES

STEPHANIE TRAUTMAN
AND
FRANCHESCA JULIEN
EDITORS

nova publishers
New York

Copyright © 2013 by Nova Science Publishers, Inc.

All rights reserved. No part of this book may be reproduced, stored in a retrieval system or transmitted in any form or by any means: electronic, electrostatic, magnetic, tape, mechanical photocopying, recording or otherwise without the written permission of the Publisher.

For permission to use material from this book please contact us:
Telephone 631-231-7269; Fax 631-231-8175
Web Site: http://www.novapublishers.com

NOTICE TO THE READER

The Publisher has taken reasonable care in the preparation of this book, but makes no expressed or implied warranty of any kind and assumes no responsibility for any errors or omissions. No liability is assumed for incidental or consequential damages in connection with or arising out of information contained in this book. The Publisher shall not be liable for any special, consequential, or exemplary damages resulting, in whole or in part, from the readers' use of, or reliance upon, this material. Any parts of this book based on government reports are so indicated and copyright is claimed for those parts to the extent applicable to compilations of such works.

Independent verification should be sought for any data, advice or recommendations contained in this book. In addition, no responsibility is assumed by the publisher for any injury and/or damage to persons or property arising from any methods, products, instructions, ideas or otherwise contained in this publication.

This publication is designed to provide accurate and authoritative information with regard to the subject matter covered herein. It is sold with the clear understanding that the Publisher is not engaged in rendering legal or any other professional services. If legal or any other expert assistance is required, the services of a competent person should be sought. FROM A DECLARATION OF PARTICIPANTS JOINTLY ADOPTED BY A COMMITTEE OF THE AMERICAN BAR ASSOCIATION AND A COMMITTEE OF PUBLISHERS.

Additional color graphics may be available in the e-book version of this book.

Library of Congress Cataloging-in-Publication Data

ISBN: 978-1-62618-090-1

Published by Nova Science Publishers, Inc. † New York

CONTENTS

PREFACE

Virtual environments simulate a physical presence in places in the real world, as well as in imaginary worlds. Most current virtual reality environments are primarily visual experiences, displayed either on a computer screen or through special stereoscopic displays, but some simulations include additional sensory information, such as sound through speakers or headphones. In this book, the authors discuss the new developments, applications and challenges of virtual environments. Topics include measuring brain activation during spatial navigation in virtual reality; spatial representation of a multilevel building; user experience in a virtual art gallery; virtual environments in education; social networks and virtual environments from an adolescent point of view; and bringing skin observations to a higher level with 3D immersive virtual environments.

Chapter 1 - Upcoming virtual reality (VR) technology brings new interest in studying spatial knowledge, navigation and its neural basis in virtual environments. In VR spatial cognition can be assessed under controlled and realistic conditions. Compared to real world navigation tasks, it is no problem to assess brain activation patterns during spatial navigation in VR. The number of brain imaging studies investigating neuronal underpinnings of spatial cognition in VR is rising. Several studies using positron emission tomography (PET), functional magnetic resonance imaging (fMRI), or electroencephalography (EEG) determined key regions for navigation and spatial processing in the human brain. However, these neurophysiological methods are associated with some disadvantages as well, such as high costs, inflexibility, or the injection of radioactive tracers. To reduce costs and increase accessibility and portability we used near-infrared spectroscopy (NIRS) to assess cortical correlates of spatial navigation in VR. NIRS is a relatively new non-invasive optical neuroimaging technique that measures concentration changes of oxygenated hemoglobin (oxy-Hb) and deoxygenated hemoglobin (deoxy-Hb) in the cerebral vessels. For the first time, we performed a combined NIRS-EEG study to validate and correlate the results of the NIRS measurement with well-established EEG outcomes. Twenty-seven participants performed a spatial navigation task in a virtual maze, in which they had to learn the shortest way to the exit of the maze after a short learning period. Based on their navigation performance in the virtual maze, participants were split up in good and bad performers. During the navigation task, brain activation was assessed with NIRS and EEG in combination. In accordance with results of prior EEG studies, we found increased fronto-central EEG theta oscillations (4-7 Hz) during spatial navigation in VR, which were more pronounced in good compared to bad performers. The results of the NIRS measurement indicated increased activation at parietal sites during VR navigation, what is in accordance with prior fMRI studies examining neuronal underpinnings of spatial navigation. Oxy-Hb over parietal areas was significant higher in bad performers compared to good performers. In addition, a significant relationship between the NIRS and the EEG signal was found. EEG theta power was negatively correlated with oxy- and deoxy-Hb over parietal areas. These findings indicate that NIRS is an adequate method to measure brain correlates of spatial navigation in VR. Furthermore, they demonstrate for the first time that NIRS and EEG can be successfully assessed in combination during interacting in VR and that these brain signals correlate with each other. The practical impact of our findings is discussed, especially the impact on the potentially usefulness of VR in neurologic rehabilitation.

Chapter 2 - The present study aimed to provide suggestions for designing a three-dimensional (3D) map of a multilevel building by investigating spatial representation acquired in complex real and virtual multilevel buildings. The virtual buildings were augmented with either a 3D floor map, a 3D building map, or neither. After navigation in these buildings, participants made the judgment of spatial horizontal and vertical directions between objects. The results indicated that participants generally estimated directions more accurately when objects were on the same level than on different levels, when the target object was below than above the test plane, and when they imagined facing forward than backward. Participants with a 3D floor or building map spent less time on judging the spatial direction than those without a map aid, and participants with the 3D floor map performed best despite the increased degree of building complexity. There was no significant difference between spatial representations acquired in the virtual building augmented with a 3D floor or building map and in the real building. Potential applications of the study include the design of a navigational aid for navigation in a complex multilevel building.

Chapter 3 - One recent application of virtual reality technology is the creation of virtual art galleries. These allow artists and enthusiasts to showcase works in an accessible, online environment and are usually free to access. The aim of this research project is to analyze virtual art representations in an online, three-dimensional graphic environment. Specifically the research aims to discern how viewing art through these environments relates to the user experience. The representation of art in virtual environments is also examined to increase our understanding of the spectrum of reality/virtuality in media presentations.

This chapter describes a series of experiments involving 24 participants who experienced virtual artworks in multiple gallery environments and utilizing different viewing perspectives. Key terms are initially defined and introduced during a discussion of virtual worlds. The chapter then provides and analysis of the data recorded and gathered during user-testing and experimentation within a specific virtual art gallery in the online virtual world *Second Life*. Demographic data is linked to the user experience focusing on the use of first person (egocentric) and third person (exocentric) screen perspectives. An examination of the user's perception of both two-dimensional and three-dimensional virtual artifacts is also provided. The chapter concludes with an insight into the usability and effectiveness of designing, presenting and experiencing art in a three-dimensional virtual environment.

Chapter 4 - As computer-driven display technology becomes more powerful and accessible, the online, virtual art gallery may provide a new platform for artists to exhibit their work. Virtual exhibits may afford opportunities for both the artist and the patron to display, view and perhaps purchase various digital art forms.

The aim of this chapter is to examine user interaction with digital artworks inside a virtual gallery space along a metric based on a virtuality continuum. The chapter describes a number of experiments where users interacted with a virtual art gallery and were then extensively interviewed and surveyed. The gallery is a three-dimensional graphic digital construction within the RMIT University virtual campus in Second Life. Users take on the form of online avatars to access the Second Life online environment and experience various colourful art objects in a simulated gallery environment.

The experiment initially employs the taxonomy of Milgram and Kishino (1994) to assist the discussion of real, virtual and mixed-reality media. The chapter describes and delineates the user's navigation of space and compares their perception of art objects in the virtual environment to digital objects in a 'real world' gallery.

The data collected in this study provide the basis for a discussion of how the user may perceive and navigate virtual objects and spaces in the virtual art gallery environment. We observe levels of what Manovich (2002) describes as 'immersion' and what Slater (1994) would term 'presence' in relation to the user experience.

Chapter 5 - Recent advances in Collaborative Virtual Environments (CVEs) have attracted noted research efforts in using it for assisting design and facilitating design collaboration.

This paper proposes a CVEs framework for design research that focuses on practicability of each variable for providing design assistances in specific projects. Although previous work in CVE in design has properly addressed the variables in an isolated manner, comprehensive issues in terms of CVE effectiveness in design assistance need to be further developed. The comprehensive CVE framework consists of three dimensions and thirteen categories, which further address the variables for theory and implementation. The paper further critically reviews each of the variables in its implication of design assistance based on the findings from representative literature. This framework provides a basis for evaluating potential and important research areas and identifying driving factors for future CVE research in design assistance.

Chapter 6 - Virtual environments have witnessed a considerable growth over the past decade. They have been applied in diverse domains and for a variety of purposes. While they have been shown to enhance learning and performance in educational contexts, the landscape of virtual environments in terms of developments, applications, and challenges still remains relatively unexplored. The purpose of this study is to address this lack by exploring how far virtual environments in the educational sphere have come over the past 11 years. Data were collected from peer-reviewed journal articles in the ERIC database, which claims to be the "world's largest digital library of education literature." The database was searched on the basis of keywords "virtual environments." The time span of the publications reviewed ranged from 2001 to 2011. There were 155 articles identified in the search. These were then grouped into four categories based on the purpose of this study: patterns of yearly publications; fields of applications; themes of research; and challenges of applications of virtual environments in education. The qualitative data were analyzed through content analysis. Results are discussed and suggestions proposed for future research.

Chapter 7 - The importance of virtual spaces has been revealed in all the orders of the life and has concerned, in one way or another, to all groups and ages. However, young people, especially adolescents, are those who have received this impact to a greater extent, to the point that on some occasions have been raised a negative impacts. This work is based on research conducted among young teens that were enjoying their vacation in southern of the province of A Coruña (North West of Spain), during the summer of 2012. They have been asked about their relationship with virtual environments and their assessment of them in two respects: its usefulness as a means of acquiring knowledge and the utility as way to make friends, special attention has been paid to the relationship of teenagers with social networks and the purposes for using them. We have developed an quantitative research using structural equation method. The results suggest that age and educational level are essential variables in assessing internet reliability.

Chapter 8 - Sectioning biopsies for confocal microscopy observation poses various difficulties to the user in the 3D volumetric reconstruction model such as distortions and warping during the cutting with cryostat and the labeling of sections with antibodies. It results in a misalignment between sections which corresponds to the major challenge that needs to be solved with accuracy and efficiency.

Computer-based visualization of large volume has led to the creation of 3D virtual skin models near to microscopic reality. To be at micrometer level and use a microscope system for observing histological sections automatically reduces the field of view.

Virtual environment (VE) enhances the user capacities and gives to him a skin interpretation. Most of the time, VE is developed for training tasks but, in cosmetic research the immersive SkinExplorer™ platform has been set up for observing 3D reconstructed data.

The aim of the platform is to give to the user the ability to reconstruct the 3D model intuitively, effectively and accurately and finally to explore the architectural organization of the 3D model components. The skin observation by virtual environment provides appropriate insights, allows exploration and understanding of the spatial arrangement and structural characteristics of complex serial histological sections.

The overall goal is to propose a novel approach for construction, display, manipulation, interaction and scientific visualization of skin components with volumetric data from confocal microscopy acquisitions.

The innovative immersive platform already permits researchers to visualize cutaneous structural changes in elastic fibers network during chronological aging and premature photo aging or after stretch marks formation. Some investigations also show the effect of cosmetic treatment. In this chapter, the SkinExplorer™ platform proposes to "enter" into the spatial organization of specific cells such as melanocytes responsible for skin pigmentation.

In: Virtual Environments
Editors: Stephanie Trautman and Franchesca Julien
ISBN: 978-1-62618-090-1
© 2013 Nova Science Publishers, Inc.

Chapter 1

MEASURING BRAIN ACTIVATION DURING SPATIAL NAVIGATION IN VIRTUAL REALITY: A COMBINED EEG-NIRS STUDY

Silvia Erika Kober[1,*], Guilherme Wood[1,†] and Christa Neuper[1,2,#]
[1]Department of Psychology, University of Graz, Austria
[2]Laboratory of Brain-Computer Interfaces,
Institute for Knowledge Discovery, Graz University of Technology, Austria

ABSTRACT

Upcoming virtual reality (VR) technology brings new interest in studying spatial knowledge, navigation and its neural basis in virtual environments. In VR spatial cognition can be assessed under controlled and realistic conditions. Compared to real world navigation tasks, it is no problem to assess brain activation patterns during spatial navigation in VR. The number of brain imaging studies investigating neuronal underpinnings of spatial cognition in VR is rising. Several studies using positron emission tomography (PET), functional magnetic resonance imaging (fMRI), or electroencephalography (EEG) determined key regions for navigation and spatial processing in the human brain. However, these neurophysiological methods are associated with some disadvantages as well, such as high costs, inflexibility, or the injection of radioactive tracers. To reduce costs and increase accessibility and portability we used near-infrared spectroscopy (NIRS) to assess cortical correlates of spatial navigation in VR. NIRS is a relatively new non-invasive optical neuroimaging technique that measures concentration changes of oxygenated hemoglobin (oxy-Hb) and deoxygenated hemoglobin (deoxy-Hb) in the cerebral vessels. For the first time, we performed a combined NIRS-EEG study to validate and correlate the results of the NIRS measurement with well-established EEG outcomes. Twenty-seven participants performed a spatial navigation task in a virtual maze, in which they had to learn the shortest way to

* Corresponding author: Silvia Erika Kober, Dr. Department of Psychology, Karl-Franzens University Graz, Universitätsplatz 2/III, A-8010 Graz, Austria. Phone: +43 (0) 316 / 380 – 8497. Fax: +43 (0) 316 / 380 – 9808. E-Mail: silvia.kober@uni-graz.at.

† Phone: +43(0)316/380–8503. Fax:+43(0)316/380–9808. E-Mail: guilherme.wood@uni-graz.at.

Phone: +43(0)316/380–5133. Fax: +43(0)316/380 – 9808. E-Mail: christa.neuper@uni-graz.at.

the exit of the maze after a short learning period. Based on their navigation performance in the virtual maze, participants were split up in good and bad performers. During the navigation task, brain activation was assessed with NIRS and EEG in combination. In accordance with results of prior EEG studies, we found increased fronto-central EEG theta oscillations (4-7 Hz) during spatial navigation in VR, which were more pronounced in good compared to bad performers. The results of the NIRS measurement indicated increased activation at parietal sites during VR navigation, what is in accordance with prior fMRI studies examining neuronal underpinnings of spatial navigation. Oxy-Hb over parietal areas was significant higher in bad performers compared to good performers. In addition, a significant relationship between the NIRS and the EEG signal was found. EEG theta power was negatively correlated with oxy- and deoxy-Hb over parietal areas. These findings indicate that NIRS is an adequate method to measure brain correlates of spatial navigation in VR. Furthermore, they demonstrate for the first time that NIRS and EEG can be successfully assessed in combination during interacting in VR and that these brain signals correlate with each other. The practical impact of our findings is discussed, especially the impact on the potentially usefulness of VR in neurologic rehabilitation.

Keywords: Virtual reality, spatial navigation, EEG, near-infrared spectroscopy NIRS, virtual rehabilitation

INTRODUCTION

In 1979, the perceptual psychologist J.J. Gibson exclaimed that "It is not true that the laboratory can never be like life. The laboratory *must* be like life!" (as cited in [1], p. 1089). Virtual reality (VR) technology can assert this claim due to the possibility of simulating real world scenarios in the laboratory. The VR technology developed rapidly in the last years. Recent improvements in computer speed, immersive visual displays, and wide-area tracking systems have made VR attractive for both research and real-world applications in neuroscience, cognitive science and psychology [1]. One big advantage of VR technology is that it affords ecological validity without compromising experimental control [2]. Hence, it is possible to simulate natural settings while precisely controlling stimuli and conditions in VR. Additionally, with VR technology it is easy for investigators to implement and conduct experiments. VR is not only an ideal tool for studying human behavior and recording behavioral data exactly, it is also possible to examine brain correlates of human behavior in VR using neurophysiological measures such as electroencephalography (EEG), positron emission tomography (PET), functional magnetic resonance imaging (fMRI), or near-infrared spectroscopy (NIRS). Consequently, new and exciting applications for VR technology have emerged in different fields such as research, training, rehabilitation, or teleoperation [1].

Examining brain correlates of natural behavior in real world settings, such as spatial cognition in real environments, is difficult. Spatial navigation is a complex behavior that requires multi-sensory processing and the integration and manipulation of information over time and space [3]. When learning the layout of an environment through navigational experience, the developing spatial knowledge undergoes qualitative as well as quantitative changes. The qualitative changes are characterized by a progression through three levels of knowledge constitutive on each other: landmark knowledge, route knowledge and survey knowledge [4]. The explosion in the development of computer simulation and VR technology facilitated the study of spatial cognition and navigation enormously [5]. When using VR to study spatial cognition, it is possible to examine each level of spatial knowledge separately by manipulating for instance the number of available spatial cues that can be used as navigational aids or providing a mapping view for spatial orientation. One has full control over the design of a virtual environment, which is not always possible in real environments. There are various behavioral studies showing that spatial performance in real and adequate virtual environments is comparable, giving rise to the assumption that VR is a valid assessment method for spatial cognition [6–15].

Making meaningful inferences from observing brain activation patterns while people navigate around complex real world environments is almost impossible. Ever-more realistic VR environments have made it possible that simulated real-world settings are no longer out of bounds for neuroscientific experimentalist [5]. Consequently, the number of brain imaging studies investigating neuronal underpinnings of spatial cognition in VR is rising. In these neuroscientific studies, participants mainly navigate through a virtual environment while positron emission tomography (PET) or functional magnetic resonance imaging (fMRI) scanning [16]. There are also some electroencephalography (EEG) studies examining electrophysiological correlates of spatial cognition in virtual worlds [17–20]. From these neuroscientific studies, a consistent pattern of brain activity associated with navigation has emerged in the past years, though there are still some disagreements about the exact functions of particular elements of the navigation system. From recent imaging studies using VR it seems clear that key regions for navigation and spatial processing in humans include the hippocampus, the medial and right inferior parietal cortex, parts of the basalganglia, the posterior cingulate cortex, the bilateral medial temporal region (including the parahippocampal gyrus), and the left prefrontal cortex [16, 21]. An allocentric (world-centered) representation of space or cognitive maps is provided by the hippocampus. Activation in the right hippocampus is strongly associated with navigational accuracy [21]. Animal studies as well as human studies could show that so called *place cells* in the hippocampus are crucial for spatial navigation. For instance, different place cells fire in different places and the firing of place cells is often anchored to visual landmarks in an environment [22]. The parahippocampus plays a role in object-location associations, but not in more complex cognitive mapping [16, 23]. Parts of the basalganglia, e.g. the nucleus caudatus, are associated with the rapidness of navigation to a defined destination [21]. The parietal lobe provides an egocentric (body-centered) representation of space and is involved in visuo-motor control. Different functional imaging studies found a relationship between the activation in the right inferior parietal cortex and the accuracy of navigation through VR [16, 21, 24, 25]. There is evidence that an inferior navigational performance in VR is associated with stronger activation in parietal brain regions [25]. Furthermore, increased EEG theta oscillation with a frequency range between 4 and 7 Hz have been frequently observed during various spatial navigation tasks in virtual environments [17–20]. In the literature, two types of theta rhythms are distinguished: the hippocampal theta rhythm and the frontal-midline theta (FM-theta). The first one was initially discovered in the hippocampus of animals, mainly in rats, during active motor behavior such as walking or exploratory sniffing, with a frequency range between 6 and 10 Hz. In recent studies, the role of hippocampal theta in spatial exploration in rodents was extended to human memory and self-directed learning [26]. The characteristic FM-theta rhythm is clearly visible in the human EEG with a frequency range between about 4 and 7 Hz [27]. FM-theta is generally maximal at fronto-central brain areas [28]. It has been frequently linked to spatial navigation, sensorimotor integration, memory functions, and language processing [17, 27, 29, 30]. Prior studies consistently show performance-related theta power increases during spatial navigation [26, 31, 32]. In the present study we focus on FM-theta, which will be henceforth referred as theta.

In summary, brain correlates of spatial cognition in VR are well examined. However, the neurophysiological methods used in these prior studies such as EEG, fMRI, or PET are associated with some disadvantages as well, such as high costs, inflexibility, the injection of radioactive tracers, or that they obstruct the sense of being in the computer-simulated environment. A major problem in utilizing fMRI or PET to study the neural correlates of VR experiences regards the "immersion" within the VR. The extend of immersion or presence experienced in a virtual environment, that means the degree to which the VR user treats it as he/she does the real world and behaves in a comparable manner, is obviously an important concern [5]. MRI and PET scanners are huge machines, produce disturbing noise, and electro-magnetic interferences with other instrumentations such as VR equipment, which constrains the formation of a feeling of immersion in VR. Furthermore, the horizontal and unnatural position of the participant during scans' acquisition limits the use of fMRI and PET to examine brain correlates of realistic VR interaction, too [33]. Some participants even experience discomfort while lying in a MRI scanner because of the noise and the narrow scanner, which also diminish immersion in VR. Beside these negative effects on the level of immersion, fMRI and PET are expensive neuroimaging methods, locally bounded to the installation site and restricted in study design due to the limitation of the participant's free moving [34].

To reduce costs and increase accessibility and portability we used near-infrared spectroscopy (NIRS) to assess cortical correlates of spatial navigation in VR. NIRS is a relatively new non-invasive optical neuroimaging technique that measures concentration changes of oxygenated hemoglobin (oxy-Hb) and deoxygenated hemoglobin (deoxy-Hb) in the cerebral vessels based on their different absorption spectra for light in the near-infrared range [35]. NIRS represents an adequate alternative to measure the blood oxygenation level dependent (BOLD) effect in cortical areas [34]. The typical hemodynamic response to mental activation is the measurement basis of NIRS, such as for fMRI. When a specific area in the brain is activated, neural metabolism is supported through a localized vascular response that causes an inflow of oxygen-rich blood to the active brain area and its surrounding tissue. Consequently, this leads to an increase in oxy-hemoglobin (oxy-Hb) and a decrease in deoxy-hemoglobin (deoxy-Hb) in the active brain region [36]. Deoxy-Hb decreases are the major source of the BOLD contrast as measured with fMRI [37]. Compared to EEG, the montage of the NIRS optodes is very fast. Repeated NIRS measurements are also more comfortable for participants as no abrasive gel is needed, which could lead to skin irritations. Compared to fMRI, it has lower costs, is more flexible and portable. Furthermore, NIRS has a higher temporal resolution than most commonly used fMRI scanners [38, 39]. Recently, also wireless and portable instruments are available [39, 40]. Compared with both fMRI and EEG, NIRS has a lower sensitivity to motion-artifacts and can accommodate a higher degree of movement, allowing measurements of brain activation also in natural and realistic environments [41, 42]. There is evidence that NIRS could be adequately used to measure brain activation patterns during playing a dance video game, where participants had to move extensively [43]. Therefore, NIRS is the only appropriate brain imaging method that can be used during active navigation through an environment to study spatial cognition in more realistic conditions.

Although NIRS has advantages over other neuroimaging methods, there is a lack of studies examining brain correlates of VR experience using NIRS. Seraglia et al. (2011) investigated cortical correlates of a virtual line bisection task using functional NIRS [33]. They found a significant hemodynamic activity with respect to the baseline in the right parietal and occipital areas during the virtual line bisection task. Hence, they could show that NIRS is an adequate method to study neural correlates that subtend VR experiences for the first time. In an exploratory study by Ayaz et al. (2011) two participants performed a navigation task in a virtual maze while measuring fNIRS [44]. They compared the mean oxy-Hb concentration changes between different task difficulties (low interference and high interference practice order). However, Ayaz and colleagues (2011) did not pursue the goal to examine brain correlates of spatial cognition in VR using NIRS, they aimed at providing a guideline for future studies for the design, implementation, data acquisition, and analysis phases of combined NIRS-VR studies [44]. Shimizu et al. (2011) investigated human spatial perception, especially right and left perception, by measuring brain blood flow using NIRS when participants performed driving tasks in VR. They partly observed hemoglobin density change in the frontal lobe during their driving tasks [45, 46].

Summing up, virtual reality technique allows for the exact measurement of brain activation patterns underlying VR interaction. To date, the majority of brain imaging studies applied only one single neuroimaging technique to assess brain activity during interacting in VR. The relationship between different neurophysiological signals is not clear yet. In this context, VR offers the best opportunity to study different brain signals, such as the BOLD-signal and changes in electrical brain activity, in combination. In the present study, we seized the chance and used the full potential of VR to measure different types of brain signals in combination during a spatial navigation task in VR. We developed a custom made grid to measure EEG and NIRS in combination and to evaluate the relationship between the EEG signal and hemodynamic responses, since the BOLD-signal is equivalent to changes in deoxy-Hb as assessed with NIRS [37]. Because neuroscientific studies assessing NIRS and EEG in combination are lacking, on the closest reference are the results of combined EEG-fMRI studies. Although there are recent studies trying to acquire EEG and fMRI data simultaneously, the relationship between the BOLD-signal assessed with fMRI and electrophysiological brain activity assessed with EEG is unclear. The biggest problem in combining fMRI and EEG is the compromised EEG quality due to the strong magnetic field of the MR scanner [47–50]. Therefore, a further advantage of NIRS is that this optical imaging method has no negative effects on the EEG data quality when assessed in combination. The constant finding of increased EEG theta power during diverse memory paradigms, such as spatial learning tasks, has intriguing parallels in the human fMRI literature, related to BOLD changes in the hippocampus and parahippocampus in similar memory tasks [47, 51]. It is assumed that EEG theta activity may serve as a window into hippocampal function explaining the parallelism between EEG theta oscillatory activity and hippocampal BOLD activation in memory tasks [47]. However, prior studies revealed heterogeneous relationships in these signals. For instance, Ekstrom and colleagues (2009 and 2010) have shown that parahippocampal and hippocampal BOLD increases were accompanied by significant EEG theta band increases, and that parahippocampal BOLD decreases were accompanied by decreases in the theta band during a spatial navigation task in a virtual city [52, 53]. But there is also evidence that the fMRI BOLD-signal and EEG theta activity correlate negatively elsewhere in the brain [47]. Mizuhara et al. (2004) performed simultaneous EEG and fMRI measurements during a mental calculation task. EEG-related negative BOLD response was dominant over anterior medial regions, corroborating the existence of a major association between negative BOLD to FM-theta [54–56]. Meltzer et al. (2007) also demonstrated that theta increases in medial prefrontal brain areas correlated negatively with BOLD during a working memory task [57]. However, theta oscillations have traditionally been viewed as indexing an active state of cognitive demand, and thus it is somewhat surprising that these prior studies found negative correlations with BOLD, which is also well-established as an indicator of neuronal activity of cognitive relevance [57]. Summing up, beside recent studies trying to clarify the relationship between electrophysiological activity and hemodynamic responses in the brain their exact relationship remains unclear.

The aim of the present study was to examine whether NIRS is an adequate method to measure brain correlates of spatial navigation in VR and to validate the NIRS results with established neurophysiological methods. Therefore, we performed a combined NIRS-EEG study, in which participants navigated through a virtual maze. We compared neuronal responses of good and bad navigators. Generally, we expect increased EEG theta oscillations during spatial navigation in VR compared to a static condition [17–20]. In relation to prior EEG studies we expect increased EEG theta power in good compared to bad performers. According to prior fMRI studies, we expect changes in hemodynamic responses in parietal brain areas during spatial navigation, which should be stronger in bad compared to good performers [16, 21, 24, 25]. Furthermore, we correlated for the first time the EEG and NIRS signals with each other. Prior neuroimaging studies examining the relationship between the BOLD- and the EEG-signal revealed heterogeneous results. In these prior studies the BOLD-signal was assessed using fMRI. Positive as well as negative correlations between the BOLD-signal in deep brain structures such as the hippocampus or parahippocampus and EEG theta oscillations at the scalp were found. Although activation in such deep brain structures cannot be assessed with NIRS, we expect a relationship between EEG theta power and changes in NIRS signals, though we cannot specify the direction of the relationship based on the literature.

METHODS

Participants

Twenty-seven right-handed, healthy adults (15 male, 12 female) took part in this study. All participants were paid for their participation and gave written informed consent. According to their performance in the VR navigation task, participants were split up in two groups: Good performers, participants that made no errors in the VR navigation task (9 male, 6 female, mean age = 24.07 yrs; *SE* = 0.71); Bad performers, participants that made navigational errors in the VR task (6 male, 6 female, mean age = 28.17 yrs; *SE* = 1.51). A non-significant chi-square $X^2(1) = 0.27$, $p = 0.60$ revealed that the number of men and women in the good and bad performer group was comparable. All volunteers had normal or corrected-to-normal vision and prior experience to three-dimensional computer games. During the experiment no sickness symptoms due to the VR paradigm were observed.

Spatial Navigation Task in VR

Participants performed a spatial navigation task in a virtual three-dimensional maze. The maze comprised a series of corridors, each leading to a junction with three turnoffs. The participants had to make a decision on direction at these junctions, which were used for subsequent EEG and NIRS analyses.

The participants were instructed to navigate as quickly and accurately as possible from a starting point to a goal point. All participants used a computer keyboard to navigate through the virtual maze in a ground-level, first-person view. Therefore, they used their right hand to operate specified keys to move forwards, backwards, and to turn left or right. During the whole spatial navigation task, continuous electroencephalogram (EEG) and near-infrared spectroscopy (NIRS) were obtained.

The spatial navigation task was subdivided in two parts, a learning phase and a testing phase. In the initial learning phase, arrows were placed at the junctions indicating the correct path through the maze (see Figure 1). Participants traversed the maze three times by means of following the arrows in the learning phase.

In the subsequent test phase, the arrows were removed. Hence, participants had to rely on a learned spatial representation of the maze. The participants had to navigate through the same maze repeatedly until they traversed it three times consecutively without errors. For statistical analyses of the behavioral data, three dependent variables were determined to assess navigational performance: (1) number of trials participants went through during the test phase (minimum three trials), (2) time on task, separately for the test (sum of the last three correct test trials) and learning (sum of the three learning trials) period and (3) the ratio of the sum of absolute travelled distance in all test trials to shortest possible distance. The shortest possible distance in the navigation task was 873 virtual meters, which could only be reached if the maze was traversed three times consecutively without errors in the test phase. A ratio of 1 corresponds to optimal performance and ratios >1 indicate increasingly sub-optimal navigational performance. All participants in the good performer group reached a ratio of 1. Participants in the bad performer group showed ratios >1 (mean ration = 2.53; *SE* = 0.19; see Table 1).

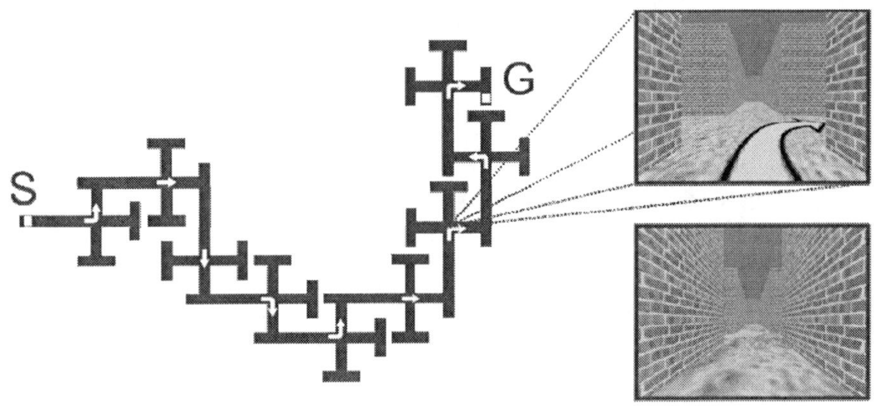

Figure 1. Blueprint of the virtual maze. "S" marks start position, "G" marks goal position. Arrows indicate the correct path. Two sample pictures of the virtual maze, such as a participant would see when traversing the maze in the learning phase (upper panel) and test phase (lower panel).

Before the spatial navigation task in the virtual maze, a 10 second resting period was implemented in which participants already saw the virtual maze but could not move through it. During this resting period participants were instructed to relax themselves.

Participants performed the spatial navigation task either in a Desktop-VR-condition (conventional 21-inch computer screen, monoscopic vision) or in a Single-Wall-VR condition (2x2 meter projection screen, stereoscopic vision). There were no differences in navigational performance between these two VR systems. Therefore, the reported results refer to both VR systems. A non-significant chi-square $X^2(1) = 0.01$, $p = 0.93$ revealed that the number of participants using the Desktop-VR and Single-Wall-VR system was comparable between the good and bad performer groups.

EEG Recordings and Analysis

EEG signals were recorded and amplified using a 32 channel BrainAmp Standard amplifier (Brain Products GmbH, Munich, Germany). Silver-silver-chloride-electrodes (Ag/AgCl) were used. The EEG was recorded from 21 electrode positions according to the extended 10–20 electrode placement system against a left mastoid reference and a right mastoid ground (see Figure 2).

It was recorded in combination with near-infrared spectroscopy (NIRS). Therefore, a custom-made grid of limited size was used. The grid was placed over frontal and parietal brain regions of the right hemisphere (see Figure 2). Vertical and horizontal EOG was recorded with three electrodes. Brain Vision Recorder (Brain Products GmbH, Munich, Germany) was used to record the EEG data (electrode impedances < 5 kΩ, 0.5-70 Hz, 50 Hz notch filter, 500 Hz sampling rate).

Brain Vision Analyzer software (version 2.01, Brain Products GmbH, Munich, Germany) was used for EEG data pre-processing and analysis. Ocular artifacts were automatically corrected using a regression method [58].

Automated rejection of other EEG artifacts (e.g. muscles) was performed according to the following criteria: Criteria for rejection: > 70.00 µV voltage step per sampling point, absolute voltage value > ±100.00 µV. All epochs with artifacts were excluded from further EEG analysis (5.49% of all trials).

For the EEG data analysis, absolute theta (4–7 Hz) band power was extracted by means of complex demodulation [59]. The junctions with three turnoffs, where the participants had to make a decision on direction, were used as active navigation determination. The averaged time window for the active navigation interval started 3 s before reaching a junction with three turnoffs in the maze and lasted for 2 s. This time window was chosen for statistical analyses because the psychophysiological data (NIRS and EEG) reached its maximum amplitude shortly before reaching a junction.

To aggregate the data, electrode sites were collapsed into four topographical regions of interest (ROI): F (Fz, F2, F4), FC (FCz, FC2, FC4), CP (CPz, CP2, CP4), P (Pz, P2, P4). For the learning phase, all three learning trials were averaged, whereas for the test phase only the last three correct test trials were taken into account. Hence, the number of averaged trials is equal for the learning and test phase, which increases their comparability. Additionally, only correctly responded test trials are included in the analyses to ascertain that a stable performance was analyzed.

NIRS Recordings and Analysis

NIRS recordings during the spatial navigation task in VR were performed using a 52-channel optical topography system (ETG-4000, Hitachi Medical Co., Japan). Ten light-emission and eight light-detection probes were arranged in a custom made grid comprising two 3×3 rectangle lattices (24 channels) and placed 3 cm apart from each other. Probes were placed on the scalp overlying the frontal and parietal lobes of the right hemisphere. The center of the grid corresponded to the Cz position of the international 10–20 system for EEG (see Figure 2). Two near-infrared laser beams (695±20 nm and 830±20 nm) were emitted and reflectance beams sampled at 10 Hz were used to calculate relative concentration changes in oxy-Hb and deoxy-Hb. To prevent crosstalk, its frequency is modulated for wavelengths and channels [60, 61]. Because continuous wave systems, such as the ETG-4000, cannot measure the optical path length [62], the scale unit is molar concentration multiplied by the unknown path length (mM/mm) [61].

For offline analyses of the NIRS signal, we focused on changes in oxy-Hb and deoxy-Hb over frontal and parietal areas (frontal F: average channels around EEG positions Fz, F2, F4; fronto-central FC: average channels around EEG positions FCz, FC2, FC4; centro-parietal CP: average channels around EEG positions CPz, CP2, CP4; parietal P: average channels around EEG positions Pz, P2, P4). Before statistical analyses, the NIRS raw signal was preprocessed. Specifically, the raw data were corrected from artifacts (criterion for rejection: amplitude of Hb-signal > +/- 3 SD; motion-induced artifacts characterized by sudden and sharp signal changes were detected by visual inspection of the data) and filtered with a 0.01 Hz high pass filter to remove baseline drifts and a 0.90 Hz low pass filter. The time courses of oxy-Hb and deoxy-Hb were averaged task-related (second -3 to -1 before reaching a junction in the maze). Task-related concentration changes of oxy-Hb and deoxy-Hb were referred to a 2-s baseline interval (second -10 to -8 before reaching a junction).

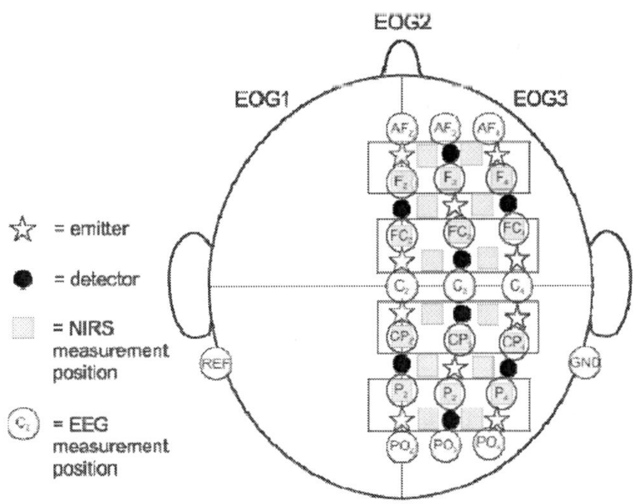

Figure 2. Details of the combined EEG and NIRS setup. EEG was recorded from 21 scalp positions according to the international 10–20 system (GND = ground, REF = reference). The 24 NIRS measurement positions for assessing the vascular response by near-infrared spectroscopy are represented by all available emitter-detector pairs. The four Regions of Interest (ROIs) for the NIRS analyses are indicated with rectangles (F, FC, CP, P).

RESULTS

Behavioral Data

To investigate performance differences in the virtual navigation task between the good and bad performer group, independent samples t-tests with the factor GROUP (good vs. bad performer) were applied for the dependent variables (1) number of trials participants went through during the test phase (minimum three trials), (2) time on task, separately for the test (sum of the last three correct test trials) and learning (sum of the three learning trials) period and (3) the ratio of the sum of absolute travelled distance in all test trials to shortest possible distance. The results of the t-tests are shown in Table 1. Participants of the bad performer group needed significant more trials to perform the navigation task in the testing phase without any errors than good performers. Good performers completed the three learning trials faster than bad performers. Furthermore, good performers also completed the last three correct trials during the test phase faster than bad performers although this difference did not reach significance. Additionally, participants of the good performer group made no errors during the test phase. Therefore, their resulting ratio of the sum of absolute travelled distance in all test trials to shortest possible distance is 1. The performance ratio of bad performers was significant higher than the ratio of good performers.

EEG

Theta Power

To assess whether EEG theta power was increased during the whole spatial navigation task compared to a 10 second static resting period before the navigation task, independent sample t-tests were applied comparing the EEG theta power between the 10 seconds resting period and the whole navigation task, separately for each ROI (F, FC, CP, P) and the learning and test phase. Theta power was significantly increased at frontal (F) and fronto-central sites (FC) during spatial navigation in VR compared to the resting period before the navigation task in both learning and test phase.

Table 1. Means and standard errors of the behavioral data and the results of the statistical analyses (t-tests). Significant results are marked with asterisks (p* < 0.05, ***p* < 0.01)**

	Good Performer	Bad Performer	
	Mean (SE)		*t-value (df)*
Number of trials participants went through during the test phase (minimum three trials)	3.00 (0.00)	6.75 (0.43)	-9.83 ** (25)
Time on task, learning phase (sum of the three learning trials) [s]	421.80 (5.54)	447.58 (12.57)	-2.01 * (25)
Time on task, test phase (sum of the last three correct test trials) [s]	403.93 (3.82)	418.92 (10.43)	-1.47 (25)
Ratio of the sum of absolute travelled distance in all test trials to shortest possible distance	1 (0.00)	2.53 (0.19)	-8.94 ** (25)

Table 2. Means and standard errors of EEG theta power during a 10-second static resting period before the navigation task in VR and the whole spatial navigation task, separately for the learning and test phase, and the results of the statistical analyses (t-tests). Significant results are marked with asterisks (*$p < 0.05$, **$p < 0.01$)

		Resting Period	Active Navigation	
		Mean (SE)	*Mean (SE)*	*t-value (df)*
EEG theta power during learning phase [μV^2]	F	4.77 (0.42)	5.24 (0.54)	-2.11 (26) *
	FC	5.20 (0.45)	5.75 (0.57)	-2.29 (26) *
	CP	4.50 (0.44)	4.73 (0.46)	-1.23 (26)
	P	4.17 (0.44)	4.40 (0.44)	-1.32 (26)
EEG theta power during test phase [μV^2]	F	4.77 (0.42)	5.47 (0.53)	-2.34 (26) *
	FC	5.20 (0.45)	5.81 (0.50)	-2.48 (26) *
	CP	4.50 (0.44)	4.87 (0.43)	-2.01 (26)
	P	4.17 (0.44)	4.58 (0.44)	-2.32 (26) *

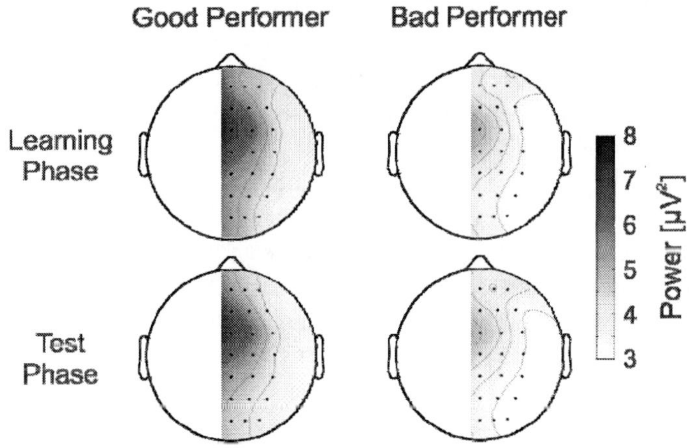

Figure 3. Topographic maps of EEG theta (4-7 Hz) power, presented separately for good and bad performers and the learning and test phase.

Hence, EEG theta oscillations significantly increased during spatial navigation mainly at fronto-central sites in both groups. The results of the t-tests are illustrated in Table 2.

For further statistical analyses, the EEG theta power during the navigation task was averaged for a time window starting 3 s before reaching a junction with three turnoffs in the maze and lasted for 2 s. Hence, for the NIRS and EEG analyses the same time window was averaged for better comparability of both neurophysiological signals.

To investigate differences in electrical brain activity between good and bad performers during the spatial navigation task in VR, we applied a 2x2x4 univariate repeated measures analyses of variance (ANOVA) with the between-subject factor GROUP (good vs. bad performers) and the within-subject factors TIME (learning vs. test phase) and ROI (F, FC, CP, P) for the dependent variable absolute theta band power during navigation in VR.

The ANOVA revealed a significant main effect of ROI ($F(3,75) = 37.46$, $p < 0.01$; $\eta^2 = 0.60$). Posttests showed that theta Power was highest over fronto-central electrodes (FC: $M = 5.04\ \mu V^2$, $SE = 0.43$), second highest over frontal electrode sites (F: $M = 4.70\ \mu V^2$, $SE = 0.43$), and lowest over centro-parietal and parietal areas (CP: $M = 4.19\ \mu V^2$, $SE = 0.39$; P: M

= 3.86 μV^2, *SE* = 0.37). The main effect of GROUP was significant by trend ($F(1,25) = 3.52$, $p = 0.07$; $\eta^2 = 0.12$). Good performers (*M* = 5.20 μV^2, *SE* = 0.53) showed higher EEG theta power during navigating in VR than bad performers (*M* = 3.70 μV^2, *SE* = 0.60). In Figure 3 the topographic maps of EEG theta power are illustrated separately for good and bad performers and the learning and test phase. In these plots one can clearly see a fronto-central maximum of EEG theta power (FCz) in all groups and conditions. Theta power was more pronounced in good compared to bad performers. No further main- or interaction effects reached statistical significance.

NIRS

For statistical analyses, 2x2x4 univariate repeated measures ANOVAs with the between-subject factor GROUP (good vs. bad performers) and the within-subject factors TIME (learning vs. test phase) and ROI (F, FC, CP, P) were applied, separately for the dependent variable oxy-Hb and deoxy-Hb during the navigation task in VR. The ANOVAs revealed the following significant results:

For *oxy-Hb*, the ANOVA revealed a significant main effect of ROI ($F(3,75) = 16.59$, $p < 0.01$; $\eta^2 = 0.40$). Oxy-Hb was higher over parietal areas (P: *M* = 0.029 m(mol/l)*mm, *SE* = 0.004; CP: *M* = 0.026 m(mol/l)*mm, *SE* = 0.004) than over frontal areas (F: *M* = 0.019 m(mol/l)*mm, *SE* = 0.003; FC: *M* = 0.022 m(mol/l)*mm, *SE* = 0.004) during spatial navigation in VR. The interaction effect between GROUP*ROI was significant as well ($F(3,75) = 3.53$, $p < 0.05$; $\eta^2 = 0.12$). Posttests showed that bad performers showed higher activation thoroughly over parietal (P) and centro-parietal (CP) areas than over frontal (F) and fronto-central (FC) areas, whereas good performers only showed differences in oxy-Hb between parietal (P) and frontal (F) brain areas (see Figure 4). Furthermore, in parietal (P) and centro-parietal (CP) areas bad performers showed significant higher oxy-Hb values than good performers (see Figure 4).

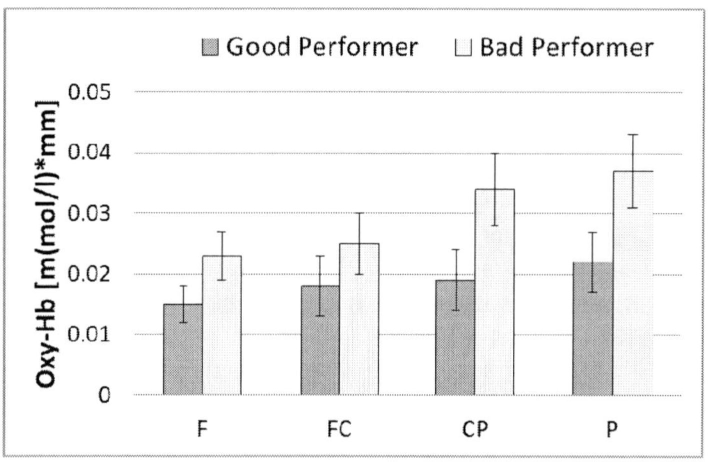

Figure 4. Bar graphs show significant interaction effect of GROUP*ROI (means and standard errors) in oxy-Hb, which is qualified by increased activity at centro-parietal and parietal sites in the bad performer compared to the good performer group.

Furthermore, the interaction effect between TIME*ROI was significant ($F(3,75) = 4.36$, $p < 0.05$; $\eta^2 = 0.15$). Oxy-Hb was higher over parietal (P) and centro-parietal (CP) brain areas during the test phase than during the learning phase (see Figure 5).

For *deoxy-Hb*, the ANOVA revealed a significant main effect of ROI ($F(3,75) = 11.65$, $p < 0.01$; $\eta^2 = 0.32$). Deoxy-Hb was lowest over fronto-central (FC) sites (M = -0.006 m(mol/l)*mm, SE = 0.001), and higher over parietal (P) compared to frontal (F) sites (F: M = -0.003 m(mol/l)*mm, SE = 0.001; P: M = -0.001 m(mol/l)*mm, SE = 0.001; CP: M = -0.002 m(mol/l)*mm, SE = 0.001).

The interaction effect between TIME*ROI was significant ($F(3,75) = 3.60$, $p < 0.05$; $\eta^2 = 0.13$). Deoxy-Hb was lower over parietal (P) brain areas during the test phase than during the learning phase (see Figure 6).

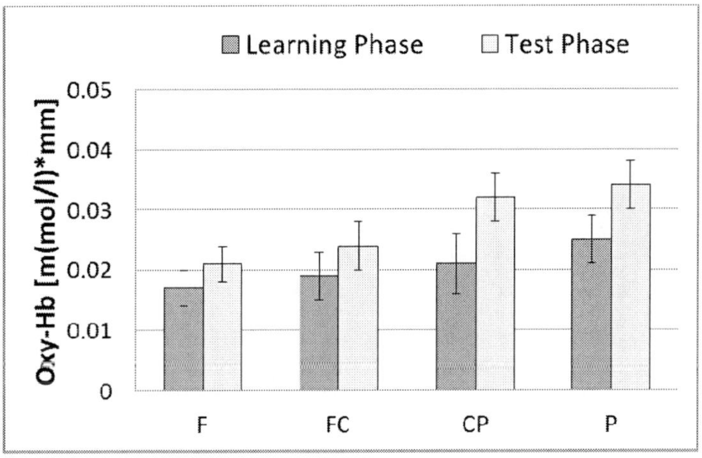

Figure 5. Bar graphs show significant interaction effect of TIME*ROI (means and standard errors) in oxy-Hb, which is qualified by increased activity at centro-parietal and parietal sites in the test compared to the learning phase.

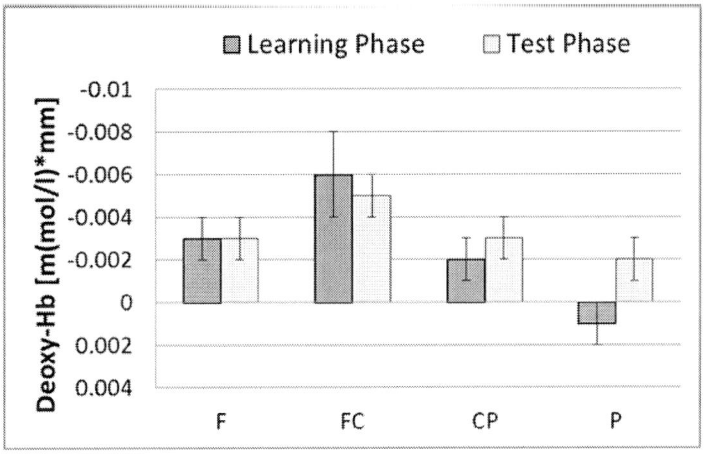

Figure 6. Bar graphs show significant interaction effect of TIME*ROI (means and standard errors) in deoxy-Hb, which is qualified by decreased deoxy-Hb at parietal sites in the test compared to the learning phase.

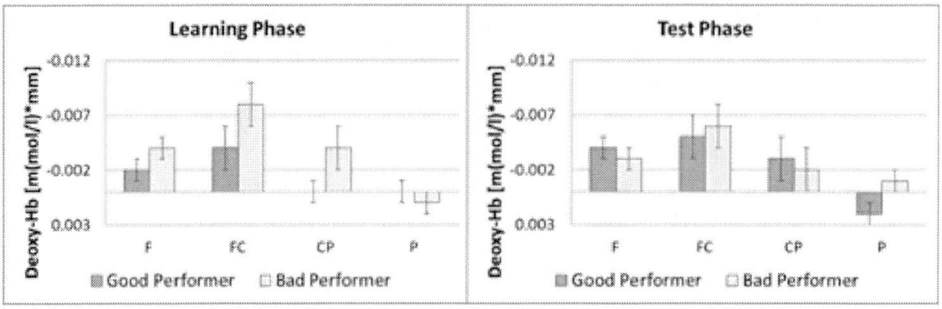

Figure 7. Bar graphs show significant three-way interaction effect of GROUP*TIME*ROI (means and standard errors) in deoxy-Hb, which is qualified by slightly decreased deoxy-Hb at FC in the bad compared to the good performer group during the learning phase.

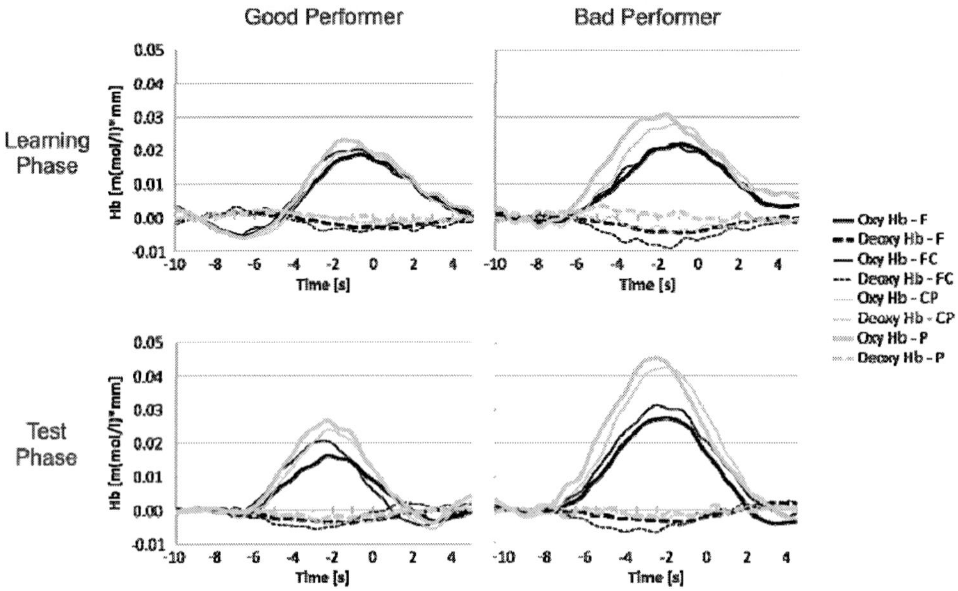

Figure 8. Time course of oxy- and deoxy-Hb during the spatial navigation task in VR. For statistical analyses second -3 to -1 was averaged. Second 0 indicates the time when participants reached a junction in the VR maze.

Furthermore, the three-way interaction effect GROUP*TIME*ROI was significant ($F(3,75) = 3.06$, $p < 0.05$; $\eta^2 = 0.11$). Posttests indicate that bad performers showed by trend ($p = 0.07$) lower deoxy-Hb values at fronto-central (FC) brain areas than good performers during the learning phase (see Figure 7). This indicates a stronger activation in fronto-central brain regions in bad compared to good performers. Additionally, good performers show higher deoxy-Hb at centro-parietal sites (CP) during learning compared to testing spatial knowledge in VR (see Figure 7). No other main- or interaction effects reached statistical significance.

In Figure 8 the time course of oxy- and deoxy-Hb during the spatial navigation task in VR is illustrated, separately for good and bad performers and the learning and test phase. It is clearly visible that oxy-Hb is most pronounced over parietal brain regions, especially in the bad performer group.

NIRS x EEG

To investigate possible relationships between hemodynamic changes (oxy- and deoxy-Hb) and electrical brain activity (EEG theta power) during spatial navigation in VR, we applied correlation analyses (Spearman's correlations). The correlation analyses between these two neurophysiological signals assessed during the test phase revealed significant results.

We do not report the results of the correlation analyses of these signals assessed during the learning phase because all coefficients failed to reach statistical significance. For the test phase, the results of the correlation analyses between oxy-/deoxy-Hb and EEG theta power are illustrated in Table 3. Deoxy-Hb at parietal sites (P) was negatively correlated with theta power. Hence, a higher cortical activation at parietal sites, as indicated by decreased deoxy-Hb values, was accompanied by increased EEG theta oscillations indicating increased cognitive processing as well. Furthermore, theta power at centro-parietal (CP) and parietal (P) brain areas was negatively correlated with oxy-Hb.

CONCLUSION

In the present study we assessed brain activation patterns during spatial navigation in VR using a relatively new and innovative optical imaging technique, the near-infrared spectroscopy. Furthermore, to validate our findings we performed a combined NIRS-EEG measurement and correlated the results of the different neurophysiological methods with each other. In accordance with prior brain imaging studies, we found an increased hemodynamic responses over parietal brain areas during spatial navigation in VR using NIRS. The EEG results are also in line with prior studies. Participants showed increased fronto-central EEG theta oscillations (4-7 Hz) during spatial navigation in VR compared to a resting period before the navigation task. Furthermore, we compared brain activation patterns between good and bad performers during spatial navigation in VR. Oxy-Hb over parietal areas was significant higher in bad performers compared to good performers. EEG theta oscillations were more pronounced in good compared to bad performers.

Table 3. Spearman's correlations between oxy-/deoxy Hb and EEG theta power assessed during the spatial navigation task in the test phase

		EEG Theta Power			
		F	FC	CP	P
Oxy-Hb	F	-0.09	-0.14	-0.34 +	-0.37 +
	FC	-0.13	-0.21	-0.42 *	-0.46 *
	CP	-0.14	-0.22	-0.43 *	-0.45 *
	P	-0.10	-0.16	-0.33 +	-0.34 +
Deoxy-Hb	F	0.03	0.08	0.23	0.21
	FC	0.04	0.03	0.14	0.14
	CP	-0.16	-0.15	-0.07	-0.08
	P	-0.34 +	-0.40*	-0.51 **	-0.55 **

$^{+}p < 0.10$, * $p < 0.05$, ** $p < 0.01$.

Additionally, correlation analyses revealed significant relationships between hemodynamic responses assessed with NIRS and electrophysiological signals (EEG). In the following, these results will be discussed in more detail.

During the spatial navigation task in VR, EEG theta oscillations with a frequency range between 4-7 Hz increased significantly compared to a static baseline resting condition. Theta Power was highest over fronto-central electrode sites. This result is in line with prior EEG, intracranial EEG and Magnetoencephalography (MEG) studies showing that theta oscillations in the human brain play an essential role during spatial navigation tasks in virtual environments [17, 19, 20, 28, 63–67]. Recordings from hippocampal depth electrodes measuring hippocampal theta rhythm and recordings from scalp electrodes measuring frontal-midline theta rhythm revealed similar results: theta activity increased during different spatial navigation tasks in different virtual environments confirming the results of the present study [17, 19, 28, 63–65]. One possible explanation for the increase in theta power during spatial navigation is the so called "sensorimotor integration hypothesis" proposing that theta oscillations coordinate sensory information with a motor plan to direct way-finding behavior to known goal locations. Hence, the motor plan is updated on the basis of incoming sensory information. For instance, the emergence of a spatial cue or landmark leads to a change of direction [19, 20, 68]. Generally, an increased theta power is associated with a variety of memory paradigms such as episodic, semantic, short-term memory, or spatial tasks [69–71].

Moreover, theta power was more pronounced in good than in bad navigators during the learning and test phase of the spatial navigation task in the virtual maze. Recent studies also demonstrated a positive relationship between navigation performance in VR and theta activity with a frequency range between 4-8 Hz [26, 31, 32]. Hence, our findings support previous research that emphasizes a predominant role of theta oscillations in spatial cognition. There is evidence from different EEG studies that increased theta activity during cognitive processing indicates more active task-related processing, whereas a decreased theta power indicates a weaker task processing in various cognitive paradigms [19, 27, 72]. In particular, theta power is related to encoding of new information. Increased theta power during encoding of new information leads to better performance during subsequent memory retrieval. Furthermore, theta power is also increased during successful memory retrieval [27]. In the present study, participants who made no errors during searching for the shortest way through the maze probably showed a more intense task-related spatial processing during the learning or encoding phase indicated by an increased theta power during spatial learning compared to the bad performer group. Consequently, spatial memory retrieval was also superior in the good performers accompanied by increased EEG theta oscillations compared to bad performers in the test phase.

The analyses of the NIRS recordings revealed that relative changes in oxy-Hb were most pronounced over parietal areas, especially during the test phase. This confirms results of prior brain imaging studies showing that the parietal cortex plays a crucial role in spatial navigation [16, 21, 24]. Significant topographical activation differences were found in deoxy-Hb as well. Deoxy-Hb showed the strongest decrease over fronto-central areas, which is associated with increased activity in this brain area. Van Horn and colleagues (1998) also found that the regional cerebral blood flow assessed with PET was activated in the right frontal lobe during spatial navigation through a virtual maze [73]. Moreover, the bad performer group showed a stronger activation over parietal brain regions than the good performer group. Interestingly, bad performers showed by trend a stronger decrease in deoxy-Hb values at fronto-central brain areas than good performers only during the learning phase. This is indicative of stronger task demands over frontal areas in bad compared to good performers. In this context, Grön and colleagues (2000) found stronger parietal activation in female participants showing inferior performance when navigating through a virtual maze compared to men. Furthermore, women also showed stronger activity at prefrontal brain areas than men. In contrary, male participants with a good navigation performance showed distinct activation of the left hippocampus [25]. The authors linked the differences in brain activation patterns associated with good and bad spatial performance to different navigational strategies. Behavioral studies provide evidence that women rely more on spatial cues, so called landmarks, whereas men use both geometric and landmark cues during spatial orientation [74]. These differences in processing of spatial information may lead to differences in brain activation patterns during spatial navigation. Grön et al. (2000) argue that this male-specific hippocampal activation reflects the males' reliance of the use of episodic memory information in navigation, leading to increased navigation performance. In contrast, increased activity in prefrontal brain regions in women have been interpreted as a sign of the working-memory demand to hold the landmark cues "on-line", keeping track of their navigational performance [25]. The results of the present NIRS study are in line with results of these former fMRI studies that found increased parietal and frontal brain activation during spatial navigation in VR in bad compared to good performers. However, in the present study we did not detect any gender differences. In both, the good and the bad performer group, the number of men and women was comparable. Statistical comparison of the behavioral performance between male and female participants revealed no significant performance differences as well. Probably, we did not find any performance differences between male and female participants because our sample was homogeneous, including only university students with a small age range. Furthermore, there is evidence that the prominent gender differences in spatial performance tasks disappear when tested in VR [20, 75, 76]. However, the usage of different navigational strategies may also explain the differences in parietal and frontal brain activation between good and bad performers in the present study. Probably, the good performer group showed a stronger activation in deeper brain structures, such as the hippocampus, due to more elaborated navigational strategies, which cannot be assessed using NIRS. The penetration is the main limitation of optical imaging methods such as NIRS, because one can only measure changes in oxy- and deoxy-Hb a few centimeters (0.5 – 2 cm) from the surface of the head, with a relatively low signal-to-noise ratio [38]. Hence, only the stronger activation in the surface of the brain as shown by bad performers could be disclosed using NIRS.

Additionally, we tried to validate the NIRS results by correlating the NIRS results with the EEG results. Hence, we investigated possible relationships between hemodynamic changes (oxy- and deoxy-Hb) and electrical brain activity (EEG theta power) during spatial navigation in VR. The applied correlation analyses between oxy-/deoxy-Hb and EEG theta power revealed significant relationships between the two neurophysiological signals: Theta power at centro-parietal and parietal brain areas was negatively correlated with oxy-Hb over the whole cortex. Furthermore, deoxy-Hb at parietal sites was negatively correlated with theta power in all assessed brain regions.

As discussed in the introduction, prior fMRI studies found positive as well as negative correlations between the BOLD-signal and EEG theta power. Our findings support the results of Ekstrom and colleagues (2009) who found that the fMRI BOLD-signal and EEG theta activity correlate positively during a spatial navigation task in VR since a positive BOLD-signal as assessed with fMRI corresponds to a decrease in deoxy-Hb assessed with NIRS [37, 52]. A relative deoxy-Hb decrease is associated with increased cortical activation. Increased EEG theta oscillations have often been linked to spatial cognition and spatial processing [17, 19, 20]. In the present study, we could also confirm that EEG theta power increases during a spatial navigation task in VR compared to a baseline period. Additionally, a positive BOLD response was frequently reported in spatial navigation tasks in VR mainly in deeper brain structures such as the hippocampus or parahippocampus but also in parietal areas [21–23]. Consequently, it makes sense that increased EEG theta oscillations are negatively correlated with deoxy-Hb assessed with NIRS. Although NIRS can only measure activity in the surface of the brain, a negative relationship between changes in deoxy-Hb and theta power is in line with findings of prior fMRI studies. In other fMRI studies that found a negative correlation between the BOLD-signal and EEG theta power, various cognitive tasks were used such as standard memory paradigms or mental arithmetic tasks restricting the comparability with the present study [54–57]. Beside the negative correlation between EEG theta power and deoxy-Hb, we also found a negative relationship between theta power and oxy-Hb. In contrast to deoxy-Hb, a decrease in oxy-Hb is associated with cortical deactivation. Hence, an increase in EEG theta power over centro-parietal and parietal brain areas was accompanied by a decrease in oxygen-rich blood over the whole cortex. As mentioned in the introduction, EEG theta oscillations which have been frequently linked to memory functions are most prominent over fronto-central brain areas, giving rise to the designation as "FM-theta" [28]. Probably, an increase in EEG theta oscillations at more posterior sites is associated with lower brain activation as indicated by the decreased oxy-Hb assessed with NIRS. However, changes in oxy-Hb are not directly linked to changes in the BOLD-signal as assessed with fMRI constraining the comparability of the present study with prior fMRI studies. Hence, further studies are needed to evaluated and validate the correlation between the NIRS and EEG signal using different cognitive paradigms.

To the best of our knowledge, this is the first study on navigation performance directly comparing NIRS and EEG signals assessed in combination. A few studies measured these two brain signals in combination but did not correlate them among each other [37, 77, 78]. For instance, Telkemeyer et al. (2011) successfully performed a combined NIRS and EEG study to investigate functional networks of speech perception in infants. But the authors did not correlate the results of the NIRS and EEG measurement among each other [37]. Hence, we could show that there is a relationship between hemodynamic responses assessed with NIRS and electrophysiological activity during a spatial navigation task in VR and that our results are in line with other brain imaging studies using fMRI.

Our findings give rise to the assumption that NIRS is an adequate method to measure brain activation patterns during spatial navigation in VR. The non-invasive NIRS technique represents an innovative method of real time mapping hemodynamic processes in the brain that is both relatively inexpensive and that can be employed even under extreme conditions. Most important for using NIRS in combination with VR technology is the fact that the NIRS measurement does not constrain the formation of a feeling of immersion in VR and movement related interaction within virtual worlds does not influence the NIRS data quality. The possible combination with EEG opens up the possibility of following the electro-cortical processes underlying spatial cognition with a finer temporal resolution as well as with deeper localization [78]. In the past years, there is growing interest in the use of VR in neurologic rehabilitation [12, 79–82]. Virtual rehabilitation is associated with several advantages. For instance, patients with brain damage show a reduced ability to interact with their physical environment, which is assumed to be counterproductive in terms of rehabilitation objectives. In this context, VR offers the possibility to develop specific and appropriate opportunities for environmental interaction, tailored for the individual patient, which makes VR to a useful tool in rehabilitation [80]. Because VR allows for the creation of individualized and/or natural environments, the ecological validity of training tasks and the generalization of learning improve [83]. One further advantage is the "economy of scale", which means that the same VR technology can be used for different types of exercises and also for different types of patients. For instance, the same VR technology such as a 3D projector can be used for a virtual navigation training with patients with neurological disorders, and it can also be used for a therapy to desensitize phobic patients. Additionally, there is evidence that virtual rehabilitation can spur the patient's motivation, especially in connection with video game-based therapeutic approaches [79]. Holden (2005) quoted three key concepts relevant to rehabilitation: repetition, feedback about performance and motivation [81]. VR provides the patients with all three of these key concepts. Furthermore, the data gathered during VR rehabilitation is stored transparently and objectively. In the case of telerehabilitation, where the patient is remote from the clinic and the therapist, it is possible to continue rehabilitation at the patient's home with low health care costs after the inpatient treatment. In the context of virtual rehabilitation, it is important to find useful neuroimaging techniques such as NIRS to measure brain activation patterns of neurologic patients during VR interaction. One major aim of virtual rehabilitation is to restore activations in damaged brain areas. Therefore, it is important to examine cortical correlates of VR interaction in neurologic patients and to determine which brain activation patterns change due to VR rehabilitation. Zeller et al. (2010) showed that NIRS has advantages over other neuroimaging methods in measurements situations and that it is suitable for investigating psychiatric/neurologic patients [84]. Hence, compared to fMRI, PET, and EEG, NIRS seems to be a good alternative to measure cortical correlates of VR interaction in neurologic patients. In this context, our results provide evidence that NIRS might be a useful tool to assess changes in the brain due to VR training, such as spatial navigation training in VR with patients with brain lesions.

ACKNOWLEDGMENT

This work was partially supported by the Neuro Center Styria (NCS) in Graz, Austria and the European Community Seventh Framework Programme (FP7/2007 2013), Grant Agreement nr. 258169. The authors are grateful to M. Lancelle, V. Settgast and D. Fellner of the Institute of Computer Graphics and Knowledge Visualization (Graz University of Technology) for technical assistance.

REFERENCES

[1] Tarr MJ, Warren WH. Virtual reality in behavioral neuroscience and beyond. *Nat. Neurosci.* 2002; 5:1089–92.

[2] Loomis JM, Blascovich JJ, Beall AC. Immersive virtual environment technology as a basic research tool in psychology. *Behavior Research Methods, Instruments, and Computers* 1999; 31(4):557–64.

[3] Wolbers T, Hegarty M. What determines our navigational abilities? *Trends Cogn. Sci.* 2010; 14(3):138–46.

[4] Siegel AW, White S. H. The Development of Spatial Representations of Large-Scale Environments. In: Reese HW, editor. *Advances in Child Development and Behaviour.* New York: Academic Press; 1975, p. 9–55.

[5] Maguire EA. Spatial Navigation. In: Parasuraman R, Rizzo M, editors. *Neuroergonomics: The Brain at Work.* Oxford: University Press; 2007, p. 131–145.

[6] Ruddle RA, Payne SJ, Jones DM. Navigating buildings in "desk-top" virtual environments: Experimental investigations using extended navigational experience. *Journal of Experimental Psychology: Applied* 1997; 3(2):143–59.

[7] Lloyd J, Persaud N, Powell T. Equivalence of real-world and virtual-reality route learning: a pilot study. *Cyberpsychology and Behavior* 2009; 12(4):423–7.

[8] Koh G, Wiegand TE von, Garnett RL, Durlach NI, Shinn-Cunningham B. Use of Virtual Environments for Acquiring Configurational Knowledge about Specific Real-World Spaces: I. Preliminary Experiment. *Presence: Teleoperators and Virtual Environments* 1999; 8(6):632–56.

[9] Kearney JK, Rizzo M, Severson J. Virtual Reality and Neuroergonomics. In: Parasuraman R, Rizzo M, editors. *Neuroergonomics: The Brain at Work.* Oxford: University Press; 2007, p. 253–274.

[10] Kalová E, Vlček K, Jarolímová E, Bureš J. Allothetic orientation and sequential ordering of places is impaired in early stages of Alzheimer's disease: corresponding results in real space tests and computer tests. *Behavioural Brain Research* 2005;159(2):175–86.

[11] Cushman LA, Stein K, Duffy CJ. Detecting navigational deficits in cognitive aging and Alzheimer disease using virtual reality. *Neurology* 2008; 71(12):888–95.

[12] Brooks BM, Rose FD. The use of virtual reality in memory rehabilitation: current findings and future directions. *Neuro Rehabilitation* 2003; 18(2):147–57.

[13] Wallet G, Sauzèon H, Rodrigues J, N'Kaoua B. Transfer of spatial knowledge from a virtual environment to reality: Impact of route compelity and subject's strategy on the cxploration modc. *Journal of Virtual Reality and Broadcasting* 2009;6(4).

[14] Morganti F. Virtual interaction in cognitive neuropsychology. *Stud. Health Technol. Inform.* 2004; 99:55–70.

[15] Livingstone S, Skelton R. Virtual environment navigation tasks and the assessment of cognitive deficits in individuals with brain injury. *Behav. Brain Res.*2007;185(1):21–31.

[16] Maguire EA, Burgess N, O'Keefe J. Human spatial navigation: cognitive maps, sexual dimorphism, and neural substrates. *Current Opinion in Neurobiology* 1999; 9(2):171–7.

[17] Kahana MJ, Sekuler R, Caplan JB, Kirschen M, Madsen JR. Human theta oscillations exhibit task dependence during virtual maze navigation. *Nature* 1999; 399:781–4.

[18] Kahana MJ, Seelig D, Madsen JR. Theta returns. Current Opinion in *Neurobiology* 2001; 11(6):739–44.

[19] Caplan JB, Madsen JR, Schulze-Bonhage A, Aschenbrenner-Scheibe R, Newman EL, Kahana MJ. Human theta oscillations related to sensorimotor integration and spatial learning. *J. Neurosci. (The Journal of neuroscience)* 2003;23(11):4726–36.

[20] Kober SE, Neuper C. Sex differences in human EEG theta oscillations during spatial navigation in virtual reality. *International Journal of Psychophysiology* 2011;79(3):347–55.

[21] Maguire EA, Burgess N, Donnett JG, Frackowiak RSJ, Frith CD, O'Keefe J. Knowing Where and Getting There: A Human Navigation Network. *Science* 1998;280:921–4.

[22] Dudchenko PA. *Why People Get Lost: The Psychology and Neuroscience of Spatial Cognition.* New York: Oxford Univ. Press; 2010.

[23] Janzen G, van Turennout M. Selective neural representation of objects relevant for navigation. *Nat. Neurosci.* 2004; 7(6):673–7.

[24] Wolbers T, Weiller C, Buchel C. Neural foundations of emerging route knowledge in complex spatial environments. *Brain Res. Cogn. Brain Res.* 2004; 21(3):401–11.

[25] Grön G, Wunderlich A, Spitzer M, Tomczak R, Riepe M. Brain activation during human navigation: gender-different neural networks as substrate of performance. *Nature Neuroscience* 2000; 3(4):404–8.

[26] Kaplan R, Doeller CF, Barnes GR, Litvak V, Düzel E, Bandettini PA et al. Movement-Related Theta Rhythm in Humans: Coordinating Self-Directed Hippocampal Learning. *PLoS Biol.* 2012; 10(2):e1001267.

[27] Klimesch W. EEG alpha and theta oscillations reflect cognitive and memory performance: a review and analysis. *Brain Res. Brain Res. Rev.* 1999; 29(2-3):169–95.

[28] Mitchell D, McNaughton N, Flanagan D, Kirk I. Frontal-midline theta from the perspective of hippocampal "theta". *Prog. Neurobiol.* 2008; 86(3):156–85.

[29] O'Keefe J, Recce ML. Phase relationship between hippocampal place units and the EEG theta rhythm. *Hippocampus* 1993; 3(3):317–30.

[30] Bastiaansen M, Hagoort P. Oscillatory neuronal dynamics during language comprehension. *Prog. Brain Res.* 2006;159:179–96.

[31] Cornwell BR, Arkin N, Overstreet C, Carver FW, Grillon C. Distinct contributions of human hippocampal theta to spatial cognition and anxiety. *Hippocampus* 2012; 22(9):1848–59.

[32] White DJ, Congedo M, Ciorciari J, Silberstein RB. Brain Oscillatory Activity during Spatial Navigation: Theta and Gamma Activity Link Medial Temporal and Parietal Regions: *Journal of Cognitive Neuroscience. Journal of Cognitive Neuroscience* 2012; 24(3):686–97.

[33] Seraglia B, Gamberini L, Priftis K, Scatturin P, Martinelli M, Cutini S. An exploratory fNIRS study with immersive virtual reality: a new method for technical implementation. *Front. Hum. Neurosci.* 2011;5.

[34] Weiskopf N. Real-time fMRI and its application to neurofeedback. *NeuroImage* 2012; 62(2):682–92.

[35] Villringer A, Chance B. Non-invasive optical spectroscopy and imaging of human brain function. *Trends Neurosci.* 1997; 20(10):435–42.

[36] Matthews F, Pearlmutter B, Wards T, Soraghan C, Markham C. Hemodynamics for Brain-Computer Interfaces. *IEEE Signal Process. Mag.* 2008; 25(1):87–94.

[37] Telkemeyer S, Rossi S, Nierhaus T, Steinbrink J, Obrig H, Wartenburger I. Acoustic Processing of Temporally Modulated Sounds in Infants: Evidence from a Combined Near-Infrared Spectroscopy and EEG Study. Front. *Psychology* 2011;1.

[38] Huppert TJ, Hoge RD, Diamond SG, Franceschini MA, Boas DA. A temporal comparison of BOLD, ASL, and NIRS hemodynamic responses to motor stimuli in adult humans. *NeuroImage* 2006; 29(2): 368–82.

[39] Sitaram R, Caria A, Birbaumer N. Hemodynamic brain–computer interfaces for communication and rehabilitation: Brain-Machine Interface. *Neural Networks* 2009; 22(9):1320–8.

[40] Muehlemann T, Haensse D, Wolf M. Wireless miniaturized in-vivo near infrared imaging. *Optics Express* 2008;16(14):10323–30.

[41] Lloyd-Fox S, Blasi A, Elwell CE. Illuminating the developing brain: The past, present and future of functional near infrared spectroscopy. *Neuroscience and Biobehavioral Reviews* 2010; 34(3):269–84.

[42] Nambu I, Osu R, Sato M, Ando S, Kawato M, Naito E. Single-trial reconstruction of finger-pinch forces from human motor-cortical activation measured by near-infrared spectroscopy (NIRS). *NeuroImage* 2009; 47(2):628–37.

[43] Tachibana A, Noah JA, Bronner S, Ono Y, Onozuka M. Parietal and temporal activity during a multimodal dance video game: An fNIRS study. *Neuroscience Letters* 2011; 503(2): 125–30.

[44] Ayaz H, Shewokis PA, Curtin A, Izzetoglu M, Izzetoglu K, Onaral B. Using MazeSuite and Functional Near Infrared Spectroscopy to Study Learning in Spatial Navigation. *JoVE* 2011(56).

[45] Shimizu S, Hirai N, Miwakeichi F, Kikuchi S, Yoshizawa Y, Sato M et al. Fundamental Study for Relationship between Cognitive Task and Brain Activity During Car Driving. *Proc. the 13th International Conference on Human-Computer Interaction* 2009: 434–40.

[46] Shimizu S, Takahashi N, Nara H, Inoue H, Hirata Y. Fundamental Study for Human Brain Activity Based on the Spatial Cognitive Task. In: Hu B, Liu J, Chen L, Zhong N, editors. *Brain Informatics*: Springer Berlin Heidelberg; 2011, p. 218-225.

[47] Meltzer JA, Fonzo GA, Constable RT. Transverse patterning dissociates human EEG theta power and hippocampal BOLD activation. *Psychophysiology* 2009; 46(1):153–62.

[48] Debener S, Ullsperger M, Siegel M, Engel AK. Single-trial EEG–fMRI reveals the dynamics of cognitive function. *Trends in Cognitive Sciences* 2006; 10(12):558–63.

[49] Debener S, Strobel A, Sorger B, Peters J, Kranczioch C, Engel AK et al. Improved quality of auditory event-related potentials recorded simultaneously with 3-T fMRI: Removal of the ballistocardiogram artefact. *Neuroimage* 2007; 34(2):587–97.

[50] Herrmann CS, Debener S. Simultaneous recording of EEG and BOLD responses: A historical perspective. *International Journal of Psychophysiology* 2008; 67(3):161–8.

[51] Hanslmayr S, Volberg G, Wimber M, Raabe M, Greenlee MW, Bauml KT. The Relationship between Brain Oscillations and BOLD Signal during Memory Formation: A Combined EEG-fMRI Study. *Journal of Neuroscience* 2011; 31(44):15674–80.

[52] Ekstrom A, Suthana N, Millett D, Fried I, Bookheimer S. Correlation Between BOLD fMRI and Theta-Band Local Field Potentials in the Human Hippocampal Area. *Journal of Neurophysiology* 2009; 101(5): 2668–78.

[53] Ekstrom A. How and when the fMRI BOLD signal relates to underlying neural activity: The danger in dissociation. *Brain Research Reviews* 2010; 62(2):233–44.

[54] Mizuhara H, Wang L, Kobayashi K, Yamaguchi Y. A long-range cortical network emerging with theta oscillation in a mental task. *Neuroreport* 2004; 15(8):1233–8.

[55] Scheeringa R, Bastiaansen MC, Petersson KM, Oostenveld R, Norris DG, Hagoort P. Frontal theta EEG activity correlates negatively with the default mode network in resting state. *International Journal of Psychophysiology* 2008; 67(3):242–51.

[56] Scheeringa R, Petersson KM, Oostenveld R, Norris DG, Hagoort P, Bastiaansen MC. Trial-by-trial coupling between EEG and BOLD identifies networks related to alpha and theta EEG power increases during working memory maintenance. *Neuroimage* 2009; 44(3): 1224–38.

[57] Meltzer JA, Negishi M, Mayes LC, Constable RT. Individual differences in EEG theta and alpha dynamics during working memory correlate with fMRI responses across subjects. *Clinical Neurophysiology* 2007; 118(11): 2419–36.

[58] Gratton G, Coles MG, Donchin E. A new method for off-line removal of ocular artifact. *Electroencephalogr. Clin. Neurophysiol.* 1983; 55(4): 468–84.

[59] Brain Products GmbH. *BrainVision Analyzer* 2.0.1 User Manual, (3rd ed.). Munich, Germany; 2009.

[60] Uludag K, Steinbrink J, Villringer A, Obrig H. Separability and cross talk: optimizing dual wavelength combinations for near-infrared spectroscopy of the adult head. *Neuroimage* 2004;22(2):583–9.

[61] Wriessnegger SC, Kurzmann J, Neuper C. Spatio-temporal differences in brain oxygenation between movement execution and imagery: A multichannel near-infrared spectroscopy study. *International Journal of Psychophysiology* 2008; 67(1):54–63.

[62] Hoshi Y, Tamura M. Near-infrared optical detection of sequential brain activation in the prefrontal cortex during mental tasks. *Neuroimage* 1997; 5(4 Pt 1):292–7.

[63] Nishiyama N, Yamaguchi Y. Human EEG theta in the spatial recognition task. *Presented at the 5th World Multi-Conference on Systemics, Cybernetics and Informatics,* Orlando, Florida (2001) 2001.

[64] Bischof WF, Boulanger P. Spatial navigation in virtual reality environments: an EEG analysis. *Cyberpsychology and Behavior* 2003; 6(5):487–95.

[65] Ekstrom AD, Caplan JB, Ho E, Shattuck K, Fried I, Kahana M. Human hippocampal theta activity during virtual navigation. *Hippocampus* 2005; 15(7):881–9.

[66] Araújo DB, Baffa O, Wakai RT. Theta Oscillations and Human Navigation: A Magnetoencephalography Study. *Journal of Cognitive Neuroscience* 2002; 14(1):70–8.

[67] Cornwell BR, Johnson LL, Holroyd T, Carver FW, Grillon C. Human Hippocampal and Parahippocampal Theta during Goal-Directed Spatial Navigation Predicts Performance on a Virtual Morris Water Maze. *Journal of Neuroscience* 2008;28(23):5983–90.

[68] Bland BH, Oddie SD. Theta band oscillation and synchrony in the hippocampal formation and associated structures: the case for its role in sensorimotor integration. *Behav. Brain Res.* 2001;127(1-2):119–36.

[69] Bastiaansen M, Hagoort P. Event-induced theta responses as a window on the dynamics of memory. *Cortex* 2003;39(4-5):967–92.

[70] Bastiaansen MCM, Posthuma D, Groot PFC, Geus EJC. Event-related alpha and theta responses in a visuo-spatial working memory task. *Clinical Neurophysiology* 2002;113(12):1882–93.

[71] Klimesch W, Doppelmayr M, Stadler W, Pollhuber D, Sauseng P, Rohm D. Episodic retrieval is reflected by a process specific increase in human electroencephalographic theta activity. *Neurosci. Lett.* 2001; 302(1):49–52.

[72] Kamarajan C, Rangaswamy M, Chorlian D, Manz N, Tang Y, Pandey A et al. Theta oscillations during the processing of monetary loss and gain: a perspective on gender and impulsivity. *Brain Res.* 2008; 1235:45–62.
[73] van Horn J, Gold J, Esposito G, Ostrem J, Mattay V, Weinberger D et al. Changing patterns of brain activation during maze learning. *Brain Research* 1998(793):29–38.
[74] Sandstrom N, Kaufman J, Huettel SA. Males and females use different distal cues in a virtual environment navigation task. *Cognitive Brain Research* 1998;6(4):351–60.
[75] Parsons T, Larson P, Kratz K, Thiebaux M, Bluestein B, Buckwalter J et al. Sex differences in mental rotation and spatial rotation in a virtual environment. *Neuropsychologia* 2004;42(4):555–62.
[76] Neubauer AC, Bergner S, Schatz M. Two- vs. three-dimensional presentation of mental rotation tasks: Sex differences and effects of training on performance and brain activation. *Intelligence* 2010; 38(5): 529–39.
[77] Jaušovec N, Jaušovec K. Do women see things differently than men do? *NeuroImage* 2009; 45(1):198–207.
[78] Brümmer V, Schneider S, Vogt T, Strüder H, Carnahan H, Askew CD et al. Coherence between Brain Cortical Function and Neurocognitive Performance during Changed Gravity Conditions. *JoVE* 2011(51).
[79] Burdea GC. Virtual Rehabilitation - Benefits and Challenges. *Methods Inf. Med.* 2003;42(5):519–23.
[80] Rose F, Brooks B, Rizzo A. Virtual reality in brain damage rehabilitation: Review. *Cyberpsychology and Behavior* 2005; 8(3): 241–62.
[81] Holden MK. Virtual environments for motor rehabilitation: review. *Cyberpsychology and Behavior* 2005; 8(3): 187–211.
[82] Kober S, Wood G, Hofer D, Kreuzig W, Kiefer M, Neuper C. Virtual reality in neurologic rehabilitation of spatial disorientation. *Journal of NeuroEngineering and Rehabilitation* 2012; in press.
[83] Schultheis MT, Rizzo AA. The application of virtual reality technology in rehabilitation. *Rehabilitation Psychology* 2001;46(3):296–311.
[84] Zeller JBM, Herrmann MJ, Ehlis A, Polak T, Fallgatter AJ. Altered parietal brain oxygenation in alzheimer's disease as assessed with near-infrared spectroscopy. *American Journal of Geriatric Psychiatry* 2010; 18(5): 433–41.

In: Virtual Environments
Editors: Stephanie Trautman and Franchesca Julien
ISBN: 978-1-62618-090-1
© 2013 Nova Science Publishers, Inc.

Chapter 2

Spatial Representation of a Multilevel Building: Bias, Complexity and the Role of a 3D Map

Zhiqiang Luo[1,*] and Wenshu Luo[2]
[1]Nanyang Polytechnic, Singapore
[2]Nanyang Technological University, Singapore

Abstract

The present study aimed to provide suggestions for designing a three-dimensional (3D) map of a multilevel building by investigating spatial representation acquired in complex real and virtual multilevel buildings. The virtual buildings were augmented with either a 3D floor map, a 3D building map, or neither. After navigation in these buildings, participants made the judgment of spatial horizontal and vertical directions between objects. The results indicated that participants generally estimated directions more accurately when objects were on the same level than on different levels, when the target object was below than above the test plane, and when they imagined facing forward than backward. Participants with a 3D floor or building map spent less time on judging the spatial direction than those without a map aid, and participants with the 3D floor map performed best despite the increased degree of building complexity. There was no significant difference between spatial representations acquired in the virtual building augmented with a 3D floor or building map and in the real building. Potential applications of the study include the design of a navigational aid for navigation in a complex multilevel building.

Keywords: Spatial representation, 3D map, Multilevel building, Complexity, Virtual environment

* Corresponding author: Zhiqiang Luo. E-mail: luo.peter@gmail.com.

1. INTRODUCTION

People often navigate in multilevel buildings, such as subway stations, shopping malls and even virtual museums. To effectively navigate in these real and virtual buildings, it is critical that people can build an accurate mental representation of such buildings. Mental representation refers to the internalized reflection and reconstruction of space in thought, including the structure, entities, and relations of space. The process of building the mental representation of environment is affected by effective learning experiences (e.g. with or without an aid, Hölscher, Büchner, Meilinger and Strube, 2007), environment characteristics (e.g. complexity, Weisman, 1981), and human cognitive ability (e.g. gender, Waller, Knapp and Hunt, 2001), where the learning experience and environment characteristics receive the attention in the present study. The main question addressed is how to build the accurate mental representation of a complex multilevel building by supplying the appropriate navigational aid.

1.1. Spatial Bias with the Mental Representation of a Built Space

Previous studies reveal that there are biases with the mental representation of a built space. The finding of spatial bias is important as it sheds light on understanding navigation strategy in a building (Hölscher, Meilinger, Vrachliotis, Brösamle and Knauff, 2006) and designing the training methodology to improve people's navigation performance in their daily life (Wilson, Foreman, Stanton, and Duffy, 2004b). Three spatial biases were focused on in the present study: vertical same level bias (Montello and Pick, 1993; Richardson, Montello, and Hegarty, 1999), downward bias (Wilson, Foreman, Stanton, and Duffy, 2004a; 2004b), and preferred orientation (Shelton and McNamara, 1997; 2004).

The vertical same level bias means that the mental representation of spatial layout is more accurate when spatial objects are on the same level than on the different levels. In a two-level real building, Montello and Pick (1993) required their participants to point out the object's direction after navigating two routes on different levels, each route with several objects. They found that the pointing performance was faster and more accurate (less direction error) when the target object and the reference object lay on the same level than on different levels.

The downward bias refers to the superiority of downward over upward spatial representations in spatial memory. Participants in the study of Wilson, et al. (2004a) explored a symmetrical three-level virtual building with two objects on each level, and then judged the directions between objects in this building. The more accurate judgments were observed when they judged the direction of target objects located below, rather than above, the test plane. The result was explained to reveal the influence of the vertical asymmetry of both human body axes and the environment on spatial memory (Bryant and Tversky, 1999).

The preferred orientation means that spatial relations of objects stored in spatial memory are retrieved faster or more accurately from one specifically preferred orientation than from others. Phenomena demonstrating this bias are evident in our daily life. For instance, imagining a space looking forward as we enter it is easier than imagining it as we exit it. Recalling the design of spatial layout is more accurate and faster from the direction previously faced in that space than from novel directions. Participants in the study of Shelton and McNamara (1997) learned the spatial layout in a room-sized space from one direction and then made the judgments of relative direction between objects (JRD, "Imagine you are standing at object A and facing object B, point to object C") (Easton and Sholl, 1995). The accuracy of direction judgments indicated that participants judged the relative directions between objects more accurately when imagining facing the direction aligned with the view direction than when imagining facing other novel directions. Their later study observed this bias by measuring the response time to perform the JRD task (Shelton and McNamara, 2004).

1.2. Building Complexity

It should be noted that the environmental context where the above three spatial biases were observed was limited in the previous studies. For example, the building layout was simple with the restriction of two routes (Montello and Pick, 1993); the virtual three-level building in the study of Wilson, et al. (2004a) was elegant with the carefully designed building structure and the geometry scale of the building was small; the preferred orientation was observed in mental representation of spatial layout in a room space or on one level (Shelton and McNamara, 2004), whereas few studies found this bias in the mental representation of spatial layout among multiple levels. It is well known that the environmental characteristics can greatly affect navigator's wayfinding strategy and the mental representation of a built space (Passini, 1984). Thus it is interesting to know whether the three spatial biases can be observed in the environment with different characteristics.

One dimension of environmental characteristics, the building complexity, was investigated in the present study. Two multilevel buildings with different degrees of building complexity were studied, one three-level building and one subway station (with three levels too). Specifically, the geometry and shape of each level of the two buildings were the same with each other. But the subway station was much more complex than the three-level building in twofold. First, the horizontal configuration on each level was more complex in the subway station than in the three-level building. The number of spatial objects is largely increased in the subway station comparing with the three-level building, and the distribution of spatial objects on each level is inconsistent in the subway station. Second, the vertical configuration was also more complex in the subway station than in the three-level building, including multiple connections among levels (e.g. elevator, escalator and staircase). Weisman (1981) found that participants experienced more difficulty in remembering and integrating the successive views as the complexity of spatial layout on a level is increased. Hölscher et al., (2006) found that wayfinding was difficult in a complex multilevel conference center because of identifying inconsistent floor layouts and disorienting staircases.

It should be noted that the present three-level building was even more complex than the building in previous studies (e.g. Luo, 2008; Shelton and McNamara, 2004; Wilson, Foreman, Stanton, and Duffy, 2004a) due to the changed geometry size and the added vertical connections. For example, participants in our previous study (Luo, 2008) navigated a vertically aligned three-level building (called the previous building). Each level of this previous building was a room-sized space (8m× 6 m), and there were three objects on each level. One elevator was designed to help participants take elevation inside the previous building. Participants were required to navigate all three levels to remember the locations of objects. The experiment results indicated that the above three spatial biases were observed in the mental representation of the previous building. The present three-level building, however, was much larger (with the smallest level size: 118 m × 10 m) than the previous building. Sovrano and Vallorigara (2006) pointed out that in a small-scale space spatial orientation mainly relied on the geometric information while in a large-scale space it relied on the landmark information. Besides one elevator connecting three levels, there were also two escalators introduced in the present three-level building, each connecting two levels (see Figure 1). Moreover, the present three levels were not aligned with each other.

1.3. The 3D Map Aid

Meanwhile, the above there spatial biases indicate that although people possess the cognitive ability for three-dimensional (3D) spatial processing, they need the navigational aid to counteract these biases and the building complexity and thus to assist the acquisition of spatial knowledge in the complex multilevel building. Traditional building maps, such as You-Are-Here (YAH) (Levine, 1982) map and floor plan (Werner and Long, 2003), are normally two-dimensional (2D) and omit the verticality connection between building levels. Hölscher, et al. (2007) found that the 2D floor plan had no positive impact on wayfinding performance in a complex multilevel building.

Recently, the 3D map, also called the exocentric map, has received much attention from researchers (e.g. Wickens, Vincow and Yeh, 2005). The 3D map refers to the exocentric view of space displayed on a computer screen or a paper. Compared with the 2D map, the 3D map preserves features of objects and integrates all three dimensions into a single rendering, thereby enhancing the shape understanding (St. John, Cowen, Smallman, and Oonk, 2001). Evidence for the benefits of the 3D map comes from the research on aviation display for navigation in the unconstrained 3D natural space (e.g. Hickox and Wickens, 1999) and the research on learning the building structure in the constrained building (e.g. Fontaine, 2001). For example, Fontaine (2001) found that compared with their counterparts using the 2D floorplan, participants using a 3D map which illustrated spatial layout across levels could better elaborate the vertical relations between levels of a subway station. Luo (2008) found that the use of a 3D map improved the accuracy of mental representation of a simple three-level building. Thus, it is expected that the above three spatial biases would be attenuated, or even be eliminated, when a 3D map is provided during navigation in a complex multilevel building.

A key concept in designing a map aid is the distinction between route knowledge and survey knowledge — a distinction that closely relates to the egocentric and exocentric representations of space (Montello, Hegarty, and Richardson, 2004; Siegel and White, 1975). Thorndyke and Hayes-Roth (1982) found evidence that people tend to acquire route knowledge from the navigation in a building while tend to acquire survey knowledge from the map study of a building. Navigating an environment provides a horizontal view from within the environment (that is, an egocentric perspective). Maps provide a vertical view from the outside looking in (that is, an exocentric perspective). Using a 3D map can mediate the costs to transfer from the exocentric perspective with the map study to the egocentric perspective with the direct navigation, which improves the acquisition of both route and survey knowledge (Wickens, Vincow and Yeh, 2005). Route knowledge and survey knowledge, however, are not exclusive of each other (Burgess, 2006). With the acquisition of survey knowledge, people can find an alternative route (such as a shortcut) rather than the traveled route to the destination (Montello, 1998), whereas survey knowledge can be acquired from the learned route knowledge as more navigation experiences are gained in space (Moeser, 1988; Thorndyke and Hayes-Roth, 1982).

Previous studies (Koh, et al., 1999; Olmos, Wickens and Chudy, 2000; Ruddle, Payne and Jones, 1999) recommend that the effective way of using a map aid during navigation is to integrate the (exocentric) map into the front view seen from the egocentric perspective. For example, participants in Ruddle et al. (1999) study were assisted by a global map, a local map, or both when searching objects in large-scale virtual environments. The global map was an overview map drawing the whole environment in a relatively small amount of detail, whereas the local map was an overview map only drawing the environment surrounding participants but in relatively great amount of details. The map was shown on the screen which also displayed the front view seen from within the environment. The results found that participants with the maps searched more efficiently than their counterparts without any maps.

The similar approach was adapted by the present study to design two types of the 3D map: the 3D floor map and the 3D building map (see the example in Figure 2). The 3D floor map illustrated the 3D spatial layout on each floor while the 3D building map illustrated the 3D spatial layout across all three floors into one rendering. Thus, compared with the 3D building map, the 3D floor map illustrated spatial layout on each level in greater amount of details and thus preserved more spatial fidelity of the building layout. But the 3D building map can better preserve the global structure information of this building layout than the 3D floor map. The 3D floor or building map would be embedded in the 3D immersive view seen from the egocentric perspective. This method was based on the split-screen technique used in the design of the aviation display (e.g., Olmos, Wickens and Chudy, 2000). This design allowed participants to switch back and forth easily and quickly between exocentric views of maps of spaces and egocentric views derived from being in that space, which was effective for remaining oriented and learning the space.

1.4. Aims and Hypotheses with the Present Study

The present study aimed to find the optimal way of designing a 3D map of a multilevel building by investigating spatial representation acquired in complex virtual and real multilevel buildings with two experiments. Specifically, in Experiment 1, participants navigated in a virtual three-level building and in Experiment 2, participants navigated in the real and virtual subway station. The geometry and shape of two building were the same with each other whereas the spatial configuration was more complex in the subway station than in the virtual three-level building. The virtual three-level building and the virtual subway station were augmented with either a 3D floor map, a 3D building map, or neither.

In order to measure the mental representation of the multilevel building, participants were asked to make judgments of relative directions between objects (JRD) (Easton and Sholl, 1995; Shelton and McNamara, 1997; 2004). To perform JRD tasks requires employing the exocentric reference to retrieve the object-to-object relationship in spatial memory. In fact, JRD tests survey knowledge acquired in a built space. The accuracy of the direction judgment and the response time were compared in following three pairs of conditions: between the virtual buildings augmented with and without a 3D map, between the virtual buildings augmented with a 3D floor map and with a 3D building map, between the virtual and real buildings. As the degree of the building complexity was increased from Experiment 1 to Experiment 2, we combined both experiments to examine the interaction between the 3D map and the building complexity on building the mental representation of a multilevel building.

Three hypotheses were tested in the present study. First, the three spatial biases introduced above would be observed in the virtual building augmented without a map aid, while the three spatial biases would be not observed in the virtual building augmented with a 3D floor or building map. Second, compared with the 3D floor map, the 3D building map could better facilitate building the mental representation of a multilevel building as the latter illustrated more global structural information of the building (Fontaine, 2001; Ruddle, Payne and Jones, 1999). Finally, the three spatial biases introduced above would be attenuated as the degree of the building complexity is increased.

2. EXPERIMENT 1

2.1. Participants

Thirty undergraduate and graduate students (15 males and 15 females, all age between 20 and 30 years, M =21.7, SD =2.5) from Nanyang Technological University participated in this experiment for the monetary payment. They had normal or corrected-to-normal vision.

2.2. Materials

A HP xw4300 workstation with a 19-in LCD monitor was used to display virtual environments (VEs) which were created by using EON software (Eon Reality Company, 2004). Movement through the VE was effected by pressing the arrow keys on the keyboard: the up and down arrows effected forward and backward movements, whereas the left and right arrows effected left and right rotations. Participants could hold down the keys to obtain the continuous translation with 1 meter per second and rotation with 60^0 per second.

The virtual building comprised three levels. The geometry and shape of the virtual building was the same as one subway station in downtown Singapore, which was replicated in the computer and introduced in the Experiment 2. Specifically, the lowest level was rectangular and measured 118 m × 10 m. The middle and upper levels were irregular in shape: the maximum length and width of the middle level was 125 and 37 meters, respectively, and the maximum length and width of the upper level was 54 and 66 meters, respectively. As shown in Figure 1, one elevator connected three levels, and two escalators connected upper and middle levels and middle and lowest levels, respectively. Nine common objects (e.g. chair, cabinet, etc) were included in the present virtual building, three positioned in each level. Among them, eight objects were also used in the building in our previous study (Luo, 2008). The main differences between the buildings in the present study and in our previous study were introduced in section 1.2.

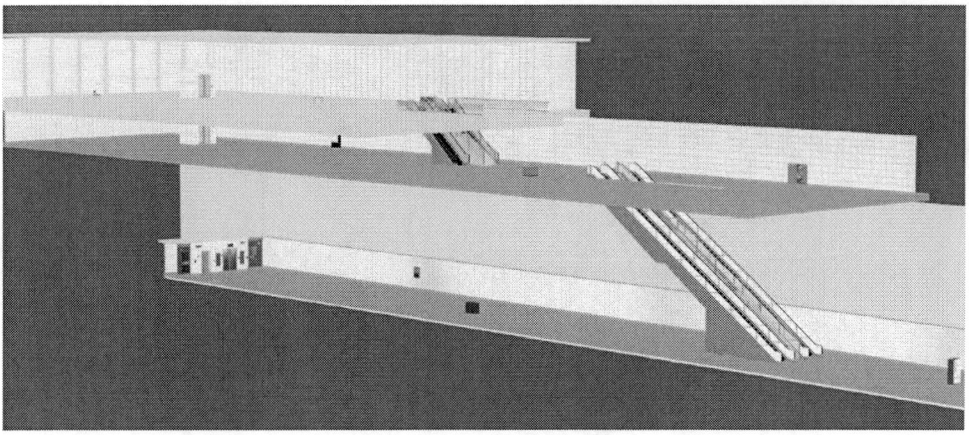

Figure 1. The design of large virtual three-level building in Experiment 1. There are three objects on each level, an elevator on the left side connects all three levels, and two escalators connect the upper level with the middle level, and the middle level with the lower level, respectively.

It should be noted that the present virtual building was only partially replicated the subway station. That is, only the geometry and shape of each level, the elevator and two escalators of this virtual building were similar with those in the subway station. The signage and other facilities of the subway station were not included in the present virtual building. Therefore, the virtual building did not look like a subway station at all.

The 3D floor map (Figure 2(a)) presented the layout of each level from the viewpoint 17 meters above the level depicted, looking from the elevator. The 3D building map (Figure 2(b)) presented the whole layout of building layout from the viewpoint 21 meters above the down level, looking from the elevator side. The geometric field of view (GFOV) of the exocentric map was the middle size with 74^0 on the horizontal axis and 59^0 on the vertical axis. This setting could help participants to make small errors when they judged the relative horizontal and vertical angles between objects in the exocentric map (McGreevy and Ellis, 1986), and could preserve enough objects' information to depict spatial layout clearly in the exocentric map.

2.3. Design

The design of the present experiment was similar with that of our previous study (Luo, 2008) except the building environment. The independent variables included one between-subjects variable and two within-subject variables. The between-subjects variable defined three kinds of navigation treatment: no map, 3D floor map, and 3D building map. Participants were randomly assigned to each of three experimental conditions. The no map group was the control group, in which participants explored the virtual building without any map aid. In the 3D floor map and 3D building map conditions, a small (10.2cm×8.1cm) map was embedded in the 3D immersive view and located in the top left of the computer screen (Olmos, Wickens and Chudy, 2000). Furthermore, when participants arrived on a new level by riding on the escalator, the content of the 3D floor map was automatically changed to show the new level layout. The view of the second level in the 3D floor-map condition is shown in Figure 2(a).

a)

b)

Figure 2. Virtual views in Experiment 1. (a) The view in 3D floor map condition of Experiment 1. The picture on the left up small window is the 3D floor map of the current floor, and the view in the big window is the forward view faced in the virtual multilevel building. The forward view in the big window will be updated as participants navigate in this multilevel building while the 3D floor map in the small window will be changed only when participants arrive at a new level. (b) The view in 3D building map condition of Experiment 1. The picture on the left up small window is the 3D building map of this building, and the view in the big window is the forward view faced in the virtual multilevel building. The forward view in the big window will be updated as participants navigate in this multilevel building and the 3D building map in the small window will not be changed during the whole navigation.

The 3D building map simultaneously rendered all spatial layouts across three levels. The content of the 3D building map was not changed during navigation. The sample view of the second level in the 3D building map condition is shown in Figure 2 (b).

The two within-subject variables defined the characteristics of probe questions to be asked in the judgment of relative direction task (JRD, "Imagine you are standing at object A and facing object B, point to object C") (Easton and Sholl, 1995): (1) the level difference between the target objects C and the reference objects A and B and (2) the imagined facing direction from object A to object B. The level difference along the vertical dimension could be two levels up, one level up, same level, one level down, two levels down, designed to reveal the vertical same level bias and downward bias in spatial memory. The imagined facing direction along the horizontal dimension could be forward (e.g. facing forward before walking down the escalator) or backward (e.g. facing backward when taking the escalator to the upper level), designed to reveal the preferred orientation in spatial memory. The orientation of the 3D floor or building map was consistent with the forward direction in the virtual building.

2.4. Procedure

Participants were tested individually in a quiet room. In order to screen out participants with the poor memory, all participants first took a memory test. They were required to scan nine objects printed on a piece paper for 30 seconds and then generate these objects at the corresponding positions on a piece of blank paper with the same size. These nine objects were not used in the virtual building. All participants could recall more than six objects in this test and were allowed to proceed to the next phase.

Participants were then seated approximately 0.42 meters from the computer screen. They first observed the nine experimental objects printed as 3D objects on a piece of paper. After they were familiar with the objects and could associate each with a unique name, participants were instructed to freely navigate the virtual multilevel building with nine objects. They were told that the purpose of this exploration was to remember the locations of the nine objects and that they would later be asked to point out these locations. The experimenters would supervise that participants should go close to each landmark at least twice. Because the objects on each level were not close to each other, participants needed to go across the level to observe the exact locations of objects. Participants were asked to arrive on each level at least twice during the 20 minutes of free navigation.

After exploring the virtual building, participants were asked to perform the JRD task. When performing the task, participants stood at the mark which was 1 meter in front of a vertically mounted board. A coordinate system was set up in this test environment. The original point of this coordinate system was the mark on the ground, the Z axis was defined to be vertical to the ground, the Y axis paralleled the front board, and the X axis was orthogonal to the front board. Therefore, each position in the test environment could be represented by a coordinate of this system (x, y, z). Moreover, the target object C in the JRD task were all in front of participants as they imagined facing the reference object B, so participants would not need to point to objects behind them. The instruction of each trial was displayed on the computer. Participants were required to use a laser pointer to project a point on the board, through which they could imagine seeing the top of the target assigned in the instruction. The experimenter recorded the coordinates of the eye and the point on the board. From this, the horizontal and vertical angles between the eye and the point in the coordinate system could be computed (Luo and Duh, 2009).

In this test, the dependent variables were the angular error and the response time. The angular error was measured as the absolute angular difference between the pointing direction and the actual direction where the target would have been. There were two angular errors: the error of horizontal angle and the error of vertical angle. The response time was measured as the time from the presentation of instruction to the end of the subject's response, which was recorded by a stop watch. The total time of this experiment was approximately 60 minutes.

2.4. Results

All dependent measures were subjected to an analysis of variance (ANOVA) with terms for navigation treatment, level difference and imagined facing direction.

2.4.1. The Judgment Accuracy of Horizontal Direction

The main effect of navigation treatment on the judgment of horizontal direction was not significant, $F(2, 27) = .065, p = .937$. The main effect of level difference was significant, $F(4, 108) = 23.217, p < .01$, and as shown in Figure 3(a), the performance under the one level down and the same level were best while the performance under the two levels down and two levels up were worst. The interaction between navigation treatment and level difference was not significant.

The main effect of imagined facing direction was significant, $F(1,27) = 7.844, p < .01$, and as shown in Figure 4(a), participants estimated horizontal direction more accurately when imagining facing the forward direction than when imagining facing the backward direction. The interaction between navigation treatment and imagined facing direction was not significant.

2.4.2. The Judgment Accuracy of Vertical Direction

The main effect of navigation treatment on the judgment of vertical direction was not significant, $F(2,27) = 3.181, p = .057$. The main effect of level difference was significant, $F(4,108) = 16.994, p < .01$, and as shown in Figure 3(b), the performance under the same level was best, followed by the performance under the two downward levels, and was poorest with the two upward levels. The interaction between navigation treatment and level difference was not significant.

The main effect of imagined facing direction was again significant, $F(1,27) = 14.528, p <.01$, and as shown in Figure 4(b), participants estimated the vertical direction more accurately when imagining facing the forward direction than when imagining facing the backward direction. The interaction between navigation treatment and imagined facing direction was not significant.

2.4.3. Response Time

As depicted in Figure 3(c), the main effect of navigation treatment was significant, $F(2,27) = 5.875, p <.01$. Multiple comparisons showed that the response time was significantly longer in the no map condition than in the two conditions with maps, while there was no significant time difference between the two conditions with maps ($F(1,18) = 1.318, p = .266$). Further analysis showed that response time was only significantly different when subject pointed to objects at the same level and at one upward level. When the target object was at the same level, participants responded fastest with the 3D floor map, followed by the 3D building map, and slowest with no map aid. When the target object was at one upward level, participants with the 3D floor and building maps responded faster than their counterparts with no map aid; while there was no significant difference between participants with 3D floor and building maps. The main effect of level difference was significant, $F(4,108) = 5.071, p < .01$, and responses were significantly faster in the conditions of the same level than in the other four conditions. The interaction between navigation treatment and level difference was not significant.

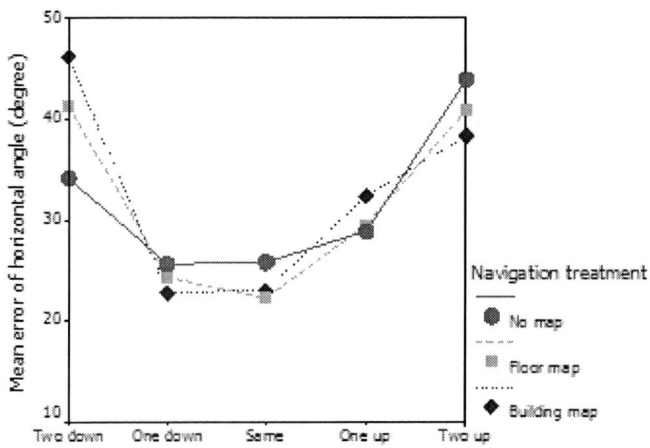

a)

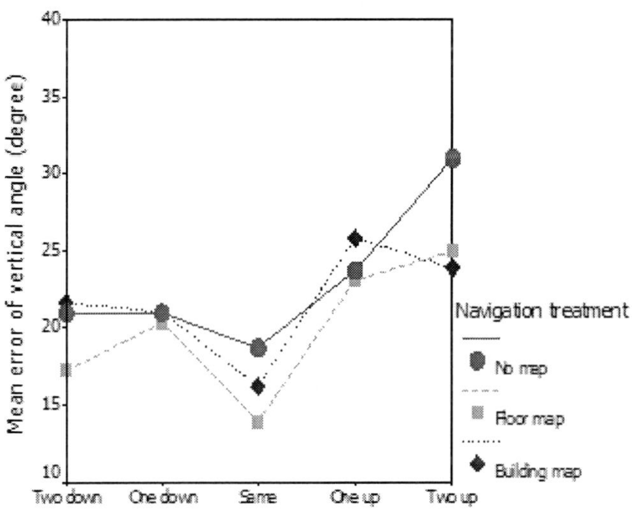

b)

Figure 3. (continued).

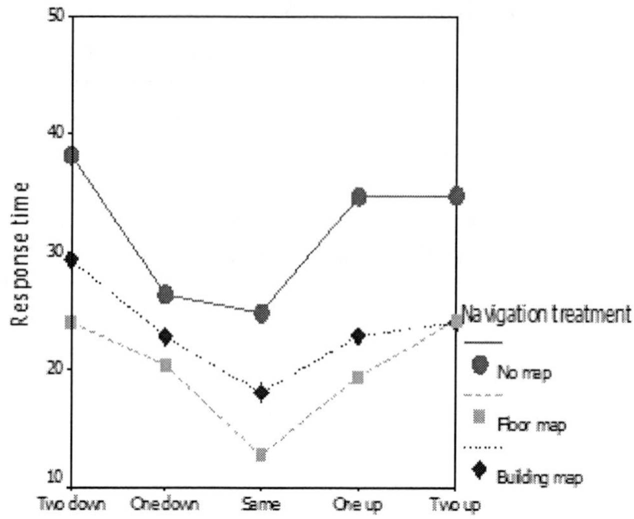

c)

[a]Mean horizontal direction errors.
[b]Mean vertical direction errors.
[c]Response time.

Figure 3. Mean angular errors and response time as a function of level difference and navigation treatment in Experiment 1.

The main effect of imagined facing direction was also significant, $F(1,27) = 7.164$, p =.012, as depicted in Figure 4(c), participants responded faster when imagining facing the backward direction than when imagining facing the forward direction. The interaction between navigation treatment and imagined facing direction was not significant.

2.5. Discussion

The results of Experiment 1 showed that the three spatial biases were observed after participants navigated in this virtual three-level building augmented with or without a 3D map, which did not support the first hypothesis. First, the vertical same-level bias was observed in the mental representation of the virtual three-level building. Participants estimated both the horizontal and vertical relations of objects on the same level at least as accurately as they estimated the directions of objects on different levels, and usually more so (see Figures 3(a) and 3(b)). This result indicated that the vertical same-level bias is a strong attribute of the mental representation of a multilevel building, regardless of the use of a 3D map.

Second, as indicated by the angular error of vertical direction (see Figure 3(b)), participants generally made the downward pointing more accurately than the upward pointing, which supported the downward bias. The result, however, did not totally replicate the finding observed in the previous study (e.g. Luo, 2008; Wilson, Foreman, Stanton, and Duffy, 2004a). The judgment accuracy of vertical direction was not worst when the objects on the farther level than when the object on the nearer level. For example, the directional judgments of objects under two levels were even slightly more accurate than the direction judgment of objects under one level. As the main difference between the present experiment and our previous study was the building environment, the different result of the vertical direction judgment suggested that the downward bias of spatial representation be attenuated as the degree of building complexity is increased. To further test the suggestion, the next experiment would be conducted in the subway station which was more complex than the three-level building in the present experiment.

Last, participants estimated both horizontal and vertical directions more accurately when imagining facing the forward direction than when imagining facing the backward direction (as depicted in Figures 4(a) and 4(b)), which replicated the finding of previous studies (e.g. Shelton and McNamara, 1997; 2004; Sholl, 1999). The results indicated that the bias of preferred orientation is also a strong attribute in the mental representation of a multilevel building, despite the use of a 3D map.

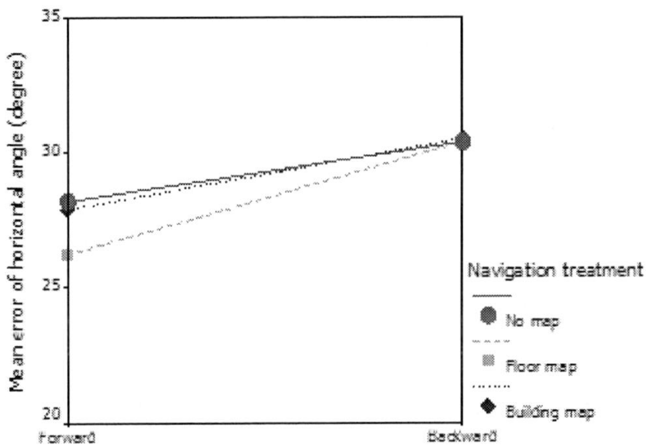

a)

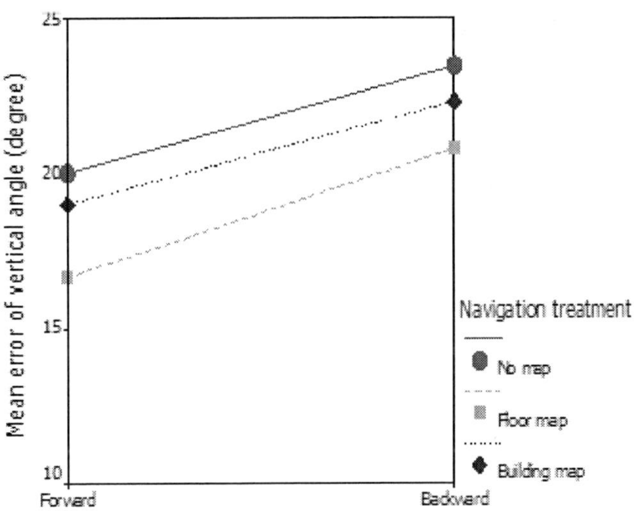

b)

Figure 4. (Continued).

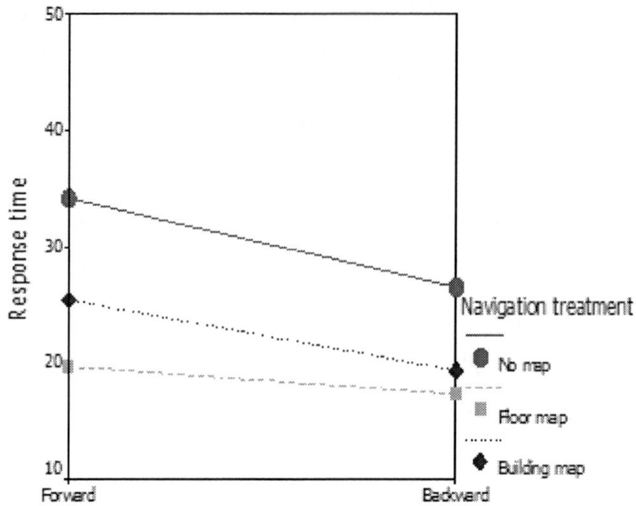

c)

[a]Mean horizontal direction errors.
[b]Mean vertical direction errors.
[c]Response time.

Figure 4. Mean angular errors and response time as a function of imagined facing direction and navigation treatment in Experiment 1.

Comparing the performance across three conditions showed that participants with a map aid responded faster than their counterparts without a map aid (Figure 3(c) and 4(c)). The results suggested that although the 3D map could not significantly affect spatial biases, the 3D map did facilitate building the mental representation of the three-level building. Furthermore, the performances were generally better in the 3D floor map condition than in the 3D building map condition. The results did not support our second hypothesis. Further analysis suggested that the 3D floor map played a more important role than the 3D building map when participants remembered objects at the same level in this three-level building.

One remaining question was that participants spent less time in the direction judgment when imagining facing the backward direction than when imagining facing the forward direction. Two possible explanations were suggested. First, the nine objects were mainly distributed at the back side of the building, for example six of nine objects were lying behind two escalators (see Figure 1). When participants performed the JRD task, most objects lied in the imagined backward direction while few objects were in the imagined forward direction. The workload for mental transformations, such as the mental rotation (Aretz and Wickens, 1992; Sholl, 1999; Wickens, Vincow and Yeh, 2005), should be less in the backward direction rather than in the forward direction when participants made the direction judgment. Therefore, the response was faster when participants imagined facing backward direction than when they imagined facing forward direction. But the less mental transformation might cause the lower accuracy of direction judgment in the backward direction than in the forward direction.

Second, participants might employ the landmarks strategy to build the mental representation of this relatively complex building (Hölscher, Meilinger, Vrachliotis, Brösamle and Knauff, 2006). Landmark strategy suggests that people employ the landmarks to refer and encode spatial relationships among spatial layout in environment, especially in the large-scale environment (Sovrano and Vallorigara, 2006). The routes to connect landmarks and the environment boundaries form the skeleton of survey cognitive map in mind (Kuipers, Tecuci and Stankiewicz, 2003). Foo, et al. (2007) found that their participants depended on the landmarks to find novel shortcuts that were not travelled in a new environment. The two escalators and the elevator might be the most salient landmarks in this three-level building because of their salient functions and features. When making the direction judgments, participants might mentally estimate the relative direction and distance between the objects and the landmarks and then point out the objects' directions. The mental process to estimate spatial relationship between the objects and the landmarks was time consuming but improved the accuracy of the direction judgment. Therefore, the response was faster (while the accuracy of direction judgment was lower) when participants imagined facing the backward direction rather than the forward direction.

3. EXPERIMENT 2

To further examine the function of a 3D map on building the mental representation of a complex multilevel building, the performances in both the real and virtual subway station were compared in the present experiment. Partly due to the difference of the building complexity, no consensus has been reached in the previous study in terms of the spatial representation in real versus virtual environments. When the built space was relatively simple, like only one floor layout, no significant difference was found between the spatial representations acquired from the real and virtual environments (e.g. Koh, Wiegand, Garnett, Durlach, and Shinn-Cunningham, 1999); however, when the built space was relatively complex, like the two-level layout, spatial representation tended to be better in the real environment than in the virtual environment (e.g. Richardsonk, Montello, and Hegarty, 1999).

In the present experiment, it was assumed that participants in the real subway station would build mental representation of the subway station better than their counterparts in the virtual subway station augmented without a map aid, but they would acquire the same mental representations of the subway station as their counterparts in the virtual subway station augmented with the 3D floor or building map.

3.1. Participants

Forty undergraduate and graduate students (20 males and 20 females, all age between 20 and 30 years, M =24, SD = 2.7) from Nanyang Technological University participated in this experiment. Among them, thirty participants volunteered to navigate in the virtual station whereas ten participants navigated the real station for the monetary payment. They had normal or corrected-to-normal vision. Although some participants passed this subway station a few times, since the station is very large and busy and they just followed the passenger flow to find their way. As they stated, they seldom paid attention to the layout of the station. These participants were randomly assigned into each group.

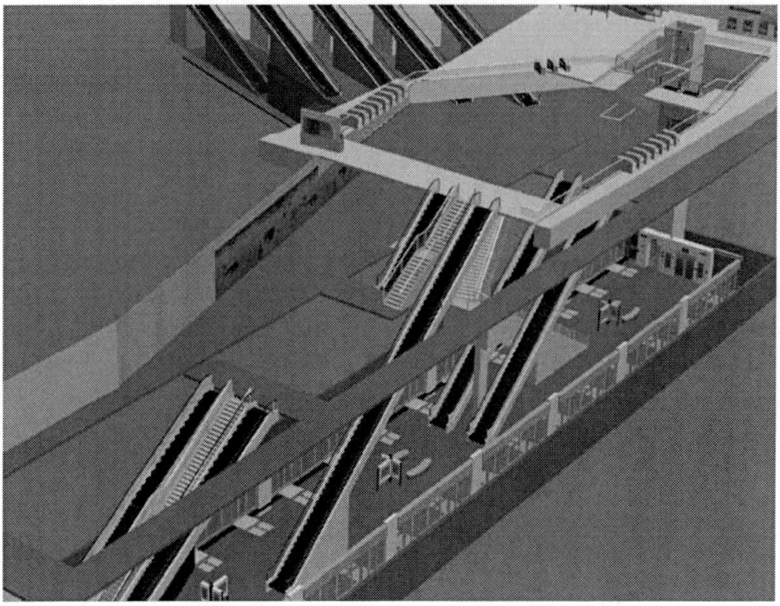

Figure 5. The 3D building map of subway station in Experiment 2. Some walls and floor components were not rendered on the map so that participants could watch facilities inside the station. To differentiate each level, the three levels are rendered in different colors. Passengers in the real station enter the station from the top level and walk through staircase, take elevator, or take elevator to go to the platform at the bottom level.

3.2. Materials

The hardware and operation in the virtual environment were the same as those in Experiment 1, but the building layout was much complex. Nine facilities were chosen as spatial targets in this station comprising three levels: the platform (B4), the middle level (B3) and the upper level (B2). The nine facilities included one entrance gate and the ticket office on B2, the long escalator connecting B2 and B4, one staircase connecting B2 and B3, one escalator connecting B3 and the corridor, one escalator connecting B3 and B4, the elevator door, onc information booth and one emergency board on B4, as shown in Figure 5.

3.3. Design and Procedure

The design and procedure were similar to those in Experiment 1, with four notable changes. First, the real environment condition was introduced, and thus there were four navigation treatments including the no map, 3D floor map, and 3D building map conditions in the virtual environment and the real environment condition. Second, subject's navigation behavior would be different as the spatial configuration was different. Since there were many escalators and staircases vertically connecting levels in the subway station, participants had more choices of changing elevation between levels, which was not restricted to the two escalators in Experiment 1. Third, the spatial layout on each level distributed among these escalators and stairs was not mainly distributed at the back side of the multilevel building, which was different from the distribution of spatial layout in Experiment 1 too. Last, the orientations of the 3D floor and building maps were opposite to the forward direction in which passengers enter the station, as shown in Figure 5. The opposite direction was chosen to examine whether or not the orientation of a 3D floor or building map can affect the preferred orientation bias.

It should be noted that participants in the real environment were treated the same as their counterparts in the virtual environment. Experimenters supervised participants to arrive at each landmark and each level at least twice during the whole process of navigation. After that, participants performed the JRD task at one place near the real station. The total time of the experiment in the virtual and real stations was 60 minutes.

3.4. Results

All dependent measures were subjected to an analysis of variance (ANOVA) with terms for navigation treatment, level difference and imagined facing direction.

3.4.1. The Judgment Accuracy of Horizontal Direction

The main effect of navigation treatment on the judgment of horizontal direction was not significant. The main effect of level difference was significant, $F(4, 144) = 9.40$, $p < .01$, and as shown in Figure 6(a), the performance under the two levels down and the same level were better than those under the one level down, one level up, and two levels up. The interaction between navigation treatment and level difference was not significant.

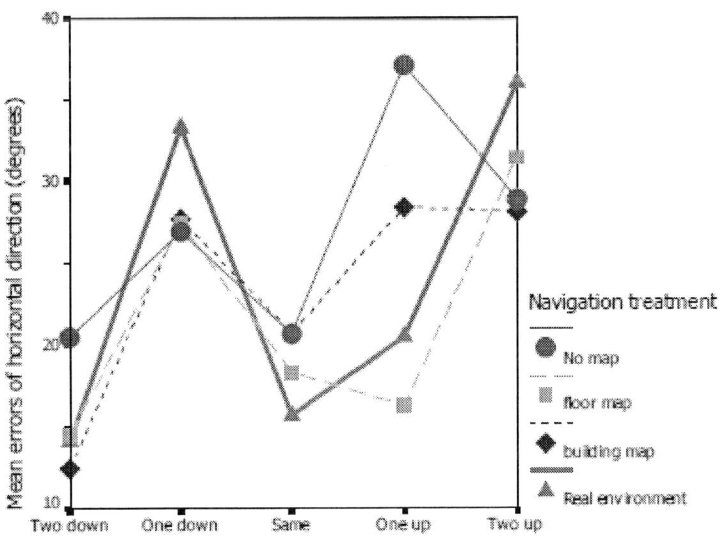

a)

Figure 6. (Continued).

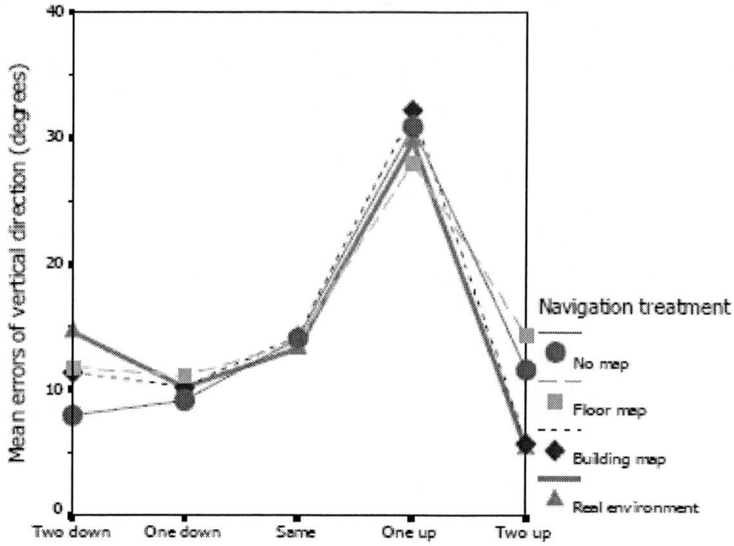

b)

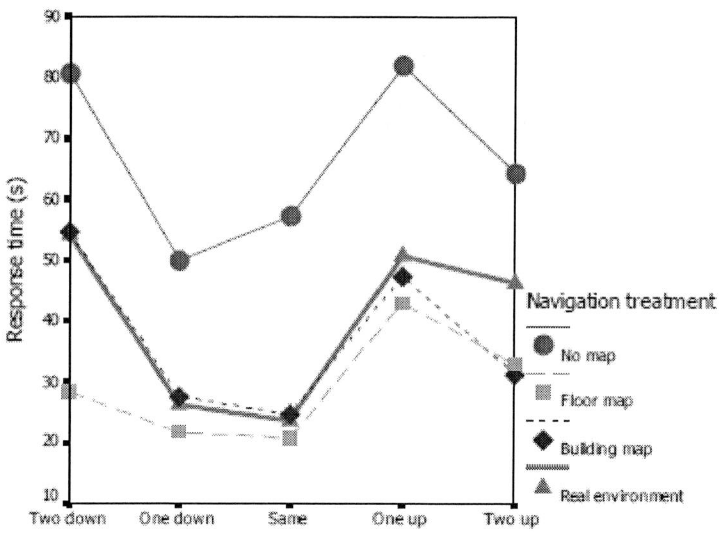

c)

[a]Mean horizontal direction errors.
[b]Mean vertical direction errors.
[c]Mean response time.

Figure 6. Mean angular errors and response time as a function of level difference and navigation treatment in Experiment 2.

The main effect of imagined facing direction was significant, $F(1, 36) = 7.63$, $p < .01$, and as shown in Figure 7(a), participants estimated horizontal direction more accurately when imagining facing the forward direction than when imagining facing the backward direction.

The interaction between navigation treatment and imagined facing direction was not significant.

3.4.2. The Judgment Accuracy of Vertical Direction

The main effect of navigation treatment on the judgment of vertical direction was not significant. The main effect of level difference was significant, $F(4, 144) = 43.31$, $p < .01$, and as shown in Figure 6(b), the performance under the one level up was worse than performance under other four level differences. The interaction between navigation treatment and level difference was not significant.

The main effect of imagined facing direction was again significant, $F(1, 36) = 214.62$, $p < .01$, and as shown in Figure 7(b), participants estimated the vertical direction more accurately when imagining facing the forward direction than when imagining facing the backward direction. The interaction between navigation treatment and imagined facing direction was not significant.

3.4.3. Response Time

As depicted in Figure 6(c), the main effect of navigation treatment was significant, $F(3, 36) = 6.90$, $p < .01$. Multiple comparisons showed that the response time was significantly longer in the no map condition than in other three conditions. The main effect of level difference was significant, $F(4, 144) = 8.82$, $p < .01$, and responses were significantly faster in the conditions of one level down and the same level than in the conditions of two levels down and one level up. The interaction between navigation treatment and level difference was not significant.

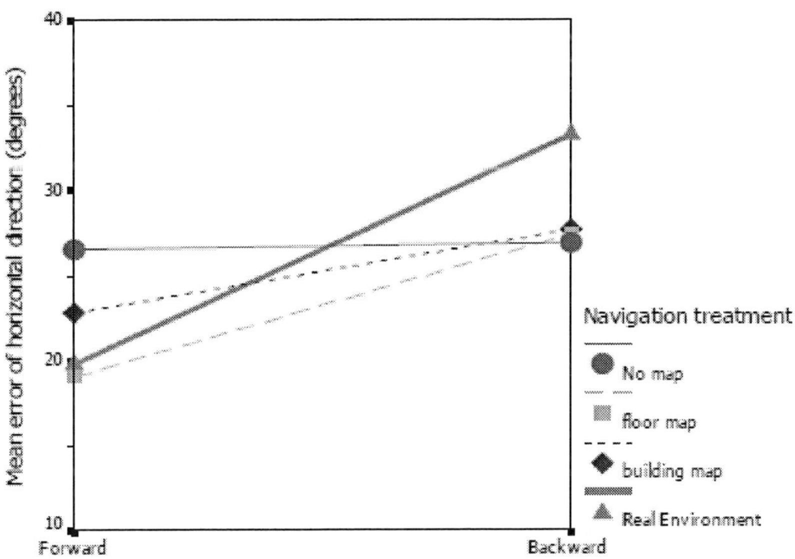

a)

Figure 7. (Continued).

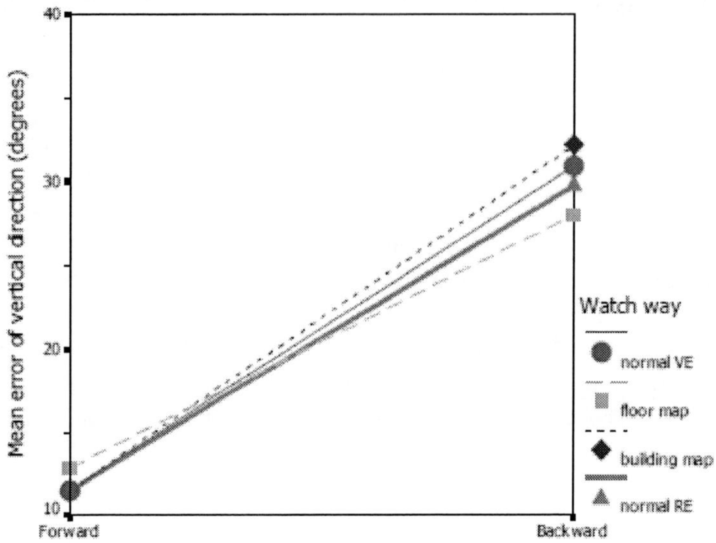

b)

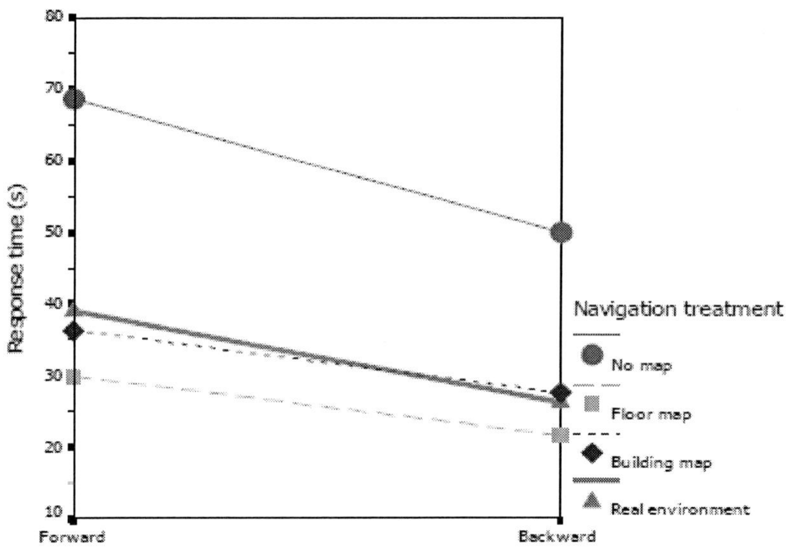

c)

[a]Mean horizontal direction errors.
[b]Mean vertical direction errors.
[c]Mean response time.

Figure 7. Mean angular errors and response time as a function of imagined facing direction and navigation treatment in Experiment 2.

The main effect of imagined facing direction was also significant, $F(1, 36) = 13.94$, $p< .01$, as depicted in Figure 7(c), participants responded faster when imagining facing the backward direction than when imagining facing the forward direction. The interaction between navigation treatment and imagined facing direction was not significant.

3.5. Discussion

The present results suggested the three spatial biases (see section 1.1) were observed in the virtual subway station augmented with or without a 3D map, which did not support our first hypothesis again. Participants estimated both the horizontal and vertical relations of objects on the same level at least as accurately as they estimated the directions of objects on different levels (see Figure 6(a) and 6(b)), which revealed the vertical same-level bias. As indicated by the angular error of vertical direction as the function of level difference (see Figure 6(b)), participants generally made the downward pointing more accurately rather than the upward pointing, which revealed the downward bias. Similar with the findings in Experiment 1, the judgment accuracy of vertical direction was not worse when the objects on the farther level than when the object on the nearer level. The results supported again that the downward bias of spatial memory was attenuated as the degree of building complexity was increased. As indicated by the judgment accuracy of both horizontal and vertical directions as the function of imagined facing direction (see Figures 7(a) and 7(b)), the forward direction was again observed as the preferred orientation.

Comparing the performance across three conditions in the virtual subway station, participants with a 3D map aid responded faster than their counterparts without a map aid (Figure 6(c) and 7(c)). The results replicated the finding in Experiment 1, suggesting that the 3D map can facilitate building the mental representation of a complex multilevel building. The performances in the 3D floor map condition were again better than those in the 3D building map condition in the present experiment, which did not support the second hypothesis.

In this experiment, participants again spent less time in the direction judgment when imagining facing the backward direction than when imagining facing the forward direction (see Figures 7(c)). Since the spatial layout in the present subway station was not mainly distributed at the back side of building, the same finding observed in both experiments supported our second explanation proposed in Experiment 1 (see section 2.5): participants employed the landmarks strategy to build mental representation of a complex multilevel building (Hölscher, Meilinger, Vrachliotis, Brösamle and Knauff, 2006; Kuiper, Tecuci and Stankiewicz, 2003). The more detailed explanation about the effect of landmarks on the mental representation of a complex multilevel building will be introduced in section 4.2.

Last, compared with the response time in the virtual subway station without a map aid, the response time was much less in the real subway station (Figure 7(c)). The result indicated the advantage of spatial learning in the real environment over in the virtual environment, which was consistent with previous studies (e.g. Richardsonk, Montello, and Hegarty, 1999). Participants in the real subway station, however, had the same performance on the judgment accuracy and response time as their counterparts in the virtual subway station augmented with a 3D floor or building map. The results indicated that participants with the aid of a 3D floor or building map in the virtual subway station acquired the same mental representation of the subway station as their counterparts in the real subway station. The finding supported our hypothesis proposed at the beginning of section 3.

4. The Interaction between the 3D Map and the Building Complexity

In order to reveal the function of the 3D floor and building maps on building mental representations of the two multilevel buildings with different degree of building complexity, the data under the no map, 3D floor map, and 3D building map conditions in virtual buildings of both experiments were subjected to ANOVA with terms for building type (the "simple" virtual building in Experiment 1 and the "complex" virtual building, the virtual subway station in Experiment 2), navigation treatment (no map, 3D floor map, 3D building map), and level difference. Only the results related with the building type and the navigation treatment are reported. Relevant means are shown in Table 1.

4.1. Results

4.1.1. The Judgment Accuracy of Horizontal Direction

The main effect of the building type on the judgment accuracy of horizontal direction was significant, $F(1, 54) = 27.143$, $p < .01$, and the performance in the "complex" virtual building was better than that in the "simple" virtual building. The main effect of navigation treatment was not significant, $F(2, 54) = .958$, $p = .390$. The interaction between the building type and the navigation treatment was also not significant, $F(2,54)=1.073$, $p = .349$.

4.1.2. The Judgment Accuracy of Vertical Direction

The main effect of the building type on the judgment accuracy of vertical direction was significant, $F(1, 54) = 62.451$, $p < .01$, and the performance in the "complex" virtual building was better than that in the "simple" virtual building. The main effect of navigation treatment was not significant, $F(2, 54) = .556$, $p = .577$. The interaction between the building type and the navigation treatment was also not significant, $F(2,54)=2.328$, $p = .107$.

4.1.3. Response Time

The main effect of the building type on the response time was significant, $F(1, 54) = 21.764$, $p < .01$, and the speed in the "simple" virtual building was faster than that in the "complex" virtual building. The main effect of navigation treatment was significant, $F(2, 54) = 13.010$, $p <.01$, and participants with either the 3D floor or building map responded faster than their counterparts without a map aid.

The interaction between the building type and the navigation treatment was significant, $F(2,54)=3.724$, $p = .031$. In the "simple" virtual building, participants with the map aid responded faster than their counterparts without the map aid when estimating the objects at the same level and one-up level. In the "complex" virtual building, participants with the map aid responded faster than their counterparts without the map aid when estimating objects at different levels (see Table 1). Further analysis showed that when the degree of building complexity was increased, the response time was increased much less (1) when the building was augmented with rather than without a 3D floor or building map; (2) when the building was augmented with the 3D floor map rather than the 3D building map.

Table 1. Mean accuracy (degree) and response time (second) of direction judgment in the virtual multilevel building in Experiment 1 and 2

Experiment 1	Error of horizontal angle	No map	34.15	25.67	25.82	28.86	43.86	31.68	*
		3D floor map	41.46	24.35	22.28	29.5	40.91	31.67	*
		3D building map	46.16	22.83	23.02	32.36	38.37	32.55	*
		Total	40.55	24.28	23.7	30.24	41.04		
		Sig	n.s.	n.s.	n.s.	n.s.	n.s.		
	Error of vertical angle	No map	20.95	20.98	18.72	23.71	31.03	23.08	*
		3D floor map	17.25	20.35	13.88	23.08	24.96	19.9	*
		3D building map	21.63	21.03	16.18	25.8	23.85	21.7	*
		Total	19.94	20.78	16.26	24.2	26.61		
		Sig	n.s.	n.s.	n.s.	n.s.	n.s.		
	Response time	No map	38.2	26.39	24.81	34.75	34.8	31.79	n.s.
		3D floor map	24	20.4	12.68	19.39	24.2	20.13	*
		3D building map	29.3	22.81	18.03	22.88	24	23.31	*
		Total	30.5	23.2	18.51	25.67	27.67		
		Sig	n.s.	n.s.	*	*	n.s.		
	Measure	Navigation treatment	Level difference						
			Two down	One down	Same	One up	Two up	Total	Sig
	Error of horizontal angle	No map	20.47	26.94	20.64	37.03	28.83	26.78	n.s.
		3D floor map	14.46	27.4	18.3	16.24	31.44	21.57	*
		3D building map	12.48	27.67	20.69	28.38	28.12	23.47	n.s.
		Total	15.8	27.34	19.88	27.22	29.46	23.94	
		Sig	n.s	n.s.	n.s.	n.s.	n.s.		
	Error of vertical angle	No map	7.91	9.09	14.11	30.87	11.53	14.7	*
		3D floor map	11.79	11.04	13.8	27.99	14.3	15.78	*
		3D building map	11.32	10.2	14.24	32.14	5.79	14.74	*
		Total	10.34	10.11	14.05	30.33	10.54	15.07	
		Sig	n.s	n.s.	n.s.	n.s.	n.s.		
	Response time	No map	80.5	49.85	57.13	82.05	64.2	66.75	n.s.
		3D floor map	28.3	21.65	20.61	42.95	32.9	29.28	*
		3D building map	54.5	27.55	24.57	47.38	31.2	37.04	*
		Total	54.43	33.02	34.10	57.46	42.77	44.36	
		Sig	n.s.	*	*	*	*		

Note: *indicates significant (<.05); n.s. indicates not significant.

4.2. Discussion

The results provided insights on the interaction of the 3D map and building complexity on building the mental representation of a multilevel building. First, the increased degree of building complexity improved the accuracy of mental representation of a multilevel building, as indicated by the improved accuracy of direction judgment in the "complex" virtual building. On first sight, this finding was at odds with previous studies (e.g. Weisman, 1981). But in fact, this finding was reasonable in the situation when participants employed the landmark strategy (see section 2.5) to build mental representation of a complex multilevel building; that is, the landmarks play the vital role in acquiring spatial knowledge in a complex building. Mental representation of a complex multilevel building is supposed with a topological map structure, which preserves salient places and their connections (Haq and Zimring, 2003; Moeser, 1988). Wayfinding performance in the complex environment will be improved when the target places and routes are associated with landmarks or distinctive environmental structure (Kuipers, Tecuci and Stankiewicz, 2003). As discussed in Experiment 1, however, the mental process to estimate the spatial relationship between the spatial objects and the landmarks is time consuming but improves the accuracy of direction judgment. The conclusion can also be applied here to explain the improved accuracy of direction judgment and the increased response time as the degree of building complexity is increased.

The mental process is suspected to mainly include the mental computation (Foo, Duchon, Warren and Tarr, 2007). Participants mentally computed the relative directions and locations between the spatial targets and the landmarks. As the degree of building complexity was increased (specifically, the number of spatial objects in the building was increased from Experiment 1 to Experiment 2), the number of available landmarks would be increased. Thus the accuracy of the direction judgment should be improved because participants built the relatively accurate mental representation of the building based on the increased number of landmarks. However, the response time would be increased in order to mentally find the optimum landmarks from amount of available landmarks to make direction judgments.

Second, the 3D map also plays a significant role in building the mental representation of a complex multilevel building. Compared with participants without a map aid, participants with the 3D floor or building map responded faster to estimate the spatial direction of objects at various levels and directions. The result indicates that the 3D map can facilitate building the mental representation of a complex multilevel building. The reasons are that the 3D map facilitates the integration of landmark and route information into survey knowledge (Moeser, 1988; Montello, 1998) and explicitly provides the survey spatial information in a complex multilevel building (Thorndyke and Hayes-Roth, 1982). Therefore, a 3D map can help user overcome the navigation problems brought by the building complexity.

In particular, the present study finds that participants with the 3D floor map responded faster than their counterparts with the 3D building map. The 3D floor map provides more spatial information on each level than the 3D building map, such as the relatively accurate locations of escalators, staircase, and elevator on each level. The finding indicates the advantage of a 3D floor map over a 3D building map to facilitate the development of the topological survey knowledge in a complex multilevel building.

5. General Discussion and Implications

The present study was conducted to explore mental representations of two multilevel buildings where two multilevel buildings had different degrees of complexity and each multilevel building was augmented with either a 3D map or none. The accurate mental representation of a built space is quite useful for navigation in a complex multilevel building, for example the public building (e.g. the subway station studied in Experiment 2) in city. People may use the sign system and follow a few well-traversed (familiar) routes to navigation in that building. However, the use of sign system and familiar routes is not as efficient as the use of mental representation of that building in navigation (Moeser, 1988). One example is that people can become disoriented when accidently altering their familiar routes (Weisman, 1981). If in emergency, people may not find the previously available signs and routes and have to find a new route by their own. Meanwhile, to solve the problems encountered by the building complexity, people need the navigational aid to effectively acquire spatial knowledge in a complex building. The present study demonstrates that a 3D map is an effective navigational aid for people in the complex multilevel building.

The implications of the present study on designing a 3D map of a multilevel building are twofold. First, a 3D map should preserve enough environmental fidelity (Waller, Hunt, and Knapp, 1998). The present study found that a 3D floor map can better facilitate building the mental representation of a multilevel building than a 3D building map. Compared with a 3D building map, a 3D floor map can preserve more fidelity of building layout, for example illustrating the landmarks with greater details. The present study also found the significant effect of the landmark on facilitating building the accurate mental representation of a multilevel building. Thus, it is expected that preserving the fidelity in a 3D map can facilitate building the mental representation of a complex multilevel building.

Second, when choosing the scale (Roscoe, 1968; Stelzer and Wickens, 2006) of a 3D map of a complex multilevel building, the scale of a 3D floor map is preferred. The 3D floor map can best illustrate the structure information as well as the fidelity of spatial layout in the present study. Participants with the 3D floor map were found to perform best in the present study. This implication suggests that architectural designers must be cautious of choosing a building map which illustrates spatial layout across different levels.

In closing, it should be noted that the present study was not free of limitations. The results of this study may lack full generalization to other multilevel buildings because of the different spatial layout and its complexity. In addition, in Experiment 2 participants in the real environment condition (in a real subway station) were paid while participants in the three virtual environment conditions were not, and thus, participants in the real environment might be more motivated. The degree of familiarity to the subway station may confound the findings in this experiment although participants with various familiarity were random assigned to each experiment condition. However, despite these constraints, the results of Experiment 2 indicated that the training in the virtual environment with a 3D map can be as good as the training in the real environment.

REFERENCES

Aretz, A. J. and Wickens, C. D. (1992). The mental rotation of map displays. *Human Performance,* 5, 303-328.

Bryant, D. J. and Tversky, B. (1999). Mental representations of perspective and spatial relations from diagrams and models. *Journal of Experimental Psychology: Learning, Memory, and Cognition,* 25, 137-156.

Burgess, N. (2006). Spatial memory: how egocentric and allocentric combine. *Trends in Cognitive Sciences,* 10(12), 551-557.

Easton, R. D. and Sholl, M. J. (1995). Object-array structure, frames of reference, and retrieval of spatial knowledge. *Journal of Experimental Psychology: Learning, Memory, and Cognition,* 21(3), 483-500.

Foo, P., Duchon, A., Warren, W. H. J., and Tarr, M. J. (2007). Humans do not switch between path knowledge and landmarks when learning a new environment. *Psychological Research,* 71, 240-251.

Fontaine, S. (2001). *Spatial cognition and the processing of verticality in underground environments.* Paper presented at the Proceedings of the international conference on spatial information theory: Foundations of geographic information science (COSIT' 2001).

Haq, S. and Zimring, C. (2003). Just down the road a piece: The development of topological knowledge of building layouts. *Environment and Behavior,* 35(1), 132-160.

Hickox, J. C. and Wickens, C. D. (1999). Effects of elevation angle display, complexity, and feature type on relating out-of-cockpit field of view to an electronic cartographic map. *Journal of Experimental Psychology: Applied,* 5(3), 284-301.

Hölscher, C., Meilinger, T., Vrachliotis, G., Brösamle, M., Knauff, M. (2006). Up the down staircase: Wayfinding strategies in multi-level buildings. *Journal of Environmental Psychology,* 26, 284-199.

Hölscher, C., Büchner, S. J., Meilinger, T., and Strube, G. (2007). *Map use and wayfinding strategies in a multi-building ensemble.* Paper presented at the Spatial Cognition V: Reasoning, Action, Interaction. Heidelberg: Springer.

Koh, G., Wiegand, T. E. v., Garnett, R. L., Durlach, M. I., and Shinn-Cunningham, B. (1999). Use of virtual environments for acquiring configurational knowledge about specific real-world spaces: 1. Preliminary experiment. *Presence: Teleoperators and Virtual Environments,* 8(6), 632-656.

Kuiper, B.,Tecuci, D., Stankiewicz, B. J. (2003). The skeleton in the cognitive map: A computational and empirical exploration. *Environment and Behavior,* 35(1), 81-106.

Levine, M. (1982). Your-Are-IIere maps: psychological considerations. *Environment and Behavior,* 14(2), 221-237.

Luo, Z. Q. (2008). *Spatial representation of real and virtual environments.* Unpublished doctorial thesis. Nanyang Technological University, Singapore.

Luo, Z. Q. and Duh, H. B. L. (2009). Effects of Perspective Elevation and Environmental Geometry on Representation of a Virtual Room. *Virtual Reality.* 13(1), pp. 27-35.

McGreevy, M. W. and Ellis, S. R. (1986). The effect of perspective geometry on judged direction in spatial information instruments. *Human factors*, 28(4), 439-456.

Moeser, S. D. (1988). Cognitive mapping in a complex building. *Environment and Behavior,* 20, 21-49.

Montello, D. R. (1998). A new frame work for understanding the acquisition of spatial knowledge in large-scale environments. In: M. J. Egenhofer and R. G. Golledge (Eds.), *Spatial and temporal reasoning in geographic information systems* (pp. 143-154). New York: Oxford University Press.

Montello, D. R., Hegarty, M., Richardson, A. E., and Waller, D. (2004). Spatial memory of real environments, virtual environments, and maps. In: G. L. Allen (Ed.), *Human Spatial Memory: Remembering Where* (pp. 251-285). Mahwah, New Jersey: Lawrence Erlbaum Associates, Inc., Publishers.

Montello, D. R. and Pick, H. L. J. (1993). Integrating knowledge of vertically aligned large-scale spaces. *Environment and Behavior,* 25, 457-484.

Olmos, O., Wickens, C. D. and Chudy, A. (2000). Tactical displays for combat awareness: An examination of dimensionality and frame of reference concepts and the application of cognitive engineering. *The International Journal of Aviation Psychology,* 10(3), 247-271.

Passini, R. (1984). *Wayfinding in architecture.* Van Nostrand Reinhold, New York.

Richardson, A. E., Montello, D. R. and Hegarty, M. (1999). Spatial knowledge acquisition from maps and from navigation in real and virtual environments. *Memory and Cognition,* 27(4), 741-750.

Roscoe, S. N. (1968). Airborne displays for flight navigation. *Human Factors*, 10, 321-332.

Ruddle, R., Payne, S. and Jones, D. (1999). The effects of maps on navigation and search strategies in very-large-scale virtual environments, *Journal of Experimental Psychology: Applied* 5 (1), 54–75.

Shelton, A. L. and McNamara, T. P. (1997). Multiple views of spatial memory. *Psychonomic Bulletin and Review,* 4, 102-106.

Shelton, A. L. and McNamara, T. P. (2004). Orientation and perspective dependence in route and survey learning. *Journal of Experimental Psychology: Learning, Memory, and Cognition,* 30(1), 158-170.

Sholl, M. J. (1999). Egocentric frames of reference used for the retrieval of survey knowledge learned by map and navigation. *Spatial Cognition and Computation,* 1, 475-494.

Siegel, A. W. and White, S. H. (1975). The development of spatial representations of large-scale environments. In: H. W. Reese (Ed.), *Advances in child development and behavior.* New York: Academic.

Sovrano, V. A. and Vallortigara, G. (2006). Dissecting the geometric module: A sense linkage for metric and landmark information in animals' spatial reorientation. *Psychological Science* 17, 616-621.

St. John, M., Cowen, M. B., Smallman, H. S., and Oonk, H. M. (2001). The use of 2D and 3D displays for shape-understanding versus relative-position tasks. *Human Factors,* 43(1), 79-98.

Stelzer, E. M. and Wickens, C. D. (2006). Pilots strategically compensate for display enlargements in surveillance and flight control tasks. *Human Factors,* 48(1), 166-181.

Thorndyke, P. W. and Hayes-Roth, B. (1982). Differences in spatial knowledge acquired from maps and navigation. *Cognitive Psychology,* 14, 560-589.

Waller, D., Hunt, E. and Knapp, D. (1998). The transfer of spatial knowledge in virtual environment training. *Presence: Teleoperators and Virtual Environments,* 7, 129-143.

Waller, D., Knapp, D. and Hunt, E. (2001). Spatial representations of virtual mazes: The role of visual fidelity and individual difference. *Human Factors,* 43(1), 147-158.

Weisman, J. (1981). Evaluating architectural legibility: Way-Finding in the Built Environment. *Environment and Behavior,* 13, 189-204.

Werner, S. and Long, P. (2003). Cognition meets Le Corbusier - Cognitive priciples of architectural design. In: C. Freksa, W. Brauer, C. Habel and K. F. Wender (Eds.), *Spatial cognitive III -Routes and navigation, human memory and learning, spatial representation and spatial learning*. Heidelberg: Springer Verlag.

Wickens, C. D., Vincow, M. and Yeh, M. (2005). Design application of visual spatial thinking: The importance of frame of reference. In: P. Shah and A. Miyake (Eds.), *The Cambridge handbook of visuospatial thinking* (pp. 383-425): Cambridge University Press.

Wilson, P. N., Foreman, N., Stanton, D., and Duffy, H. (2004a). Memory for targets in a multilevel simulated environment: Evidence for vertical asymmetry in spatial memory. *Memory and Cognition,* 32(2), 283-297.

Wilson, P. N., Foreman, N., Stanton, D., and Duffy, H. (2004b). Memory for targets in a multi-level simulated-environment: A comparison between able-bodied and physically disabled children. *British Journal of Psychology*, 95(3), 325-338.

In: Virtual Environments
Editors: Stephanie Trautman and Franchesca Julien
ISBN: 978-1-62618-090-1
© 2013 Nova Science Publishers, Inc.

Chapter 3

THE EFFECTS OF PERSPECTIVE AND PRESENTATION: USER EXPERIENCE IN A VIRTUAL ART GALLERY

Daniel Ivancic,[1] Damian Schofield[2] and Lisa Dethridge[3]

[1]Masters Student, Human Computer Interaction Program, SUNY Oswego, US
[2]Director of the Human Computer Interaction Program, SUNY Oswego, US and Adjunct Professor of Forensic Computing, Edith Cowan University, Australia
[3]Senior Lecturer, School of Media and Communication, RMIT University, Melbourne, Australia

ABSTRACT

One recent application of virtual reality technology is the creation of virtual art galleries. These allow artists and enthusiasts to showcase works in an accessible, online environment and are usually free to access. The aim of this research project is to analyze virtual art representations in an online, three-dimensional graphic environment. Specifically the research aims to discern how viewing art through these environments relates to the user experience. The representation of art in virtual environments is also examined to increase our understanding of the spectrum of reality/virtuality in media presentations.

This chapter describes a series of experiments involving 24 participants who experienced virtual artworks in multiple gallery environments and utilizing different viewing perspectives. Key terms are initially defined and introduced during a discussion of virtual worlds. The chapter then provides and analysis of the data recorded and gathered during user-testing and experimentation within a specific virtual art gallery in the online virtual world *Second Life*. Demographic data is linked to the user experience focusing on the use of first person (egocentric) and third person (exocentric) screen perspectives. An examination of the user's perception of both two-dimensional and three-dimensional virtual artifacts is also provided. The chapter concludes with an insight into the usability and effectiveness of designing, presenting and experiencing art in a three-dimensional virtual environment.

INTRODUCTION

Virtual Reality systems have been in existence for many years and their technical advances follow the developmental curve of computing technology. Increasingly, within the last decade, realistic looking environments and images have begun to appear in the displays of many mainstream applications. Various conceptions of virtual reality involve specialized immersive setups such as Head Mounted Displays (HMDs), three-dimensional displays, movement capture and haptic feedback. Accepted definitions of virtual reality however often refer to a broad spectrum of implementations including everything from text-based adventure games to the simulated, immersive world of the Matrix movie (Silver et al, 1999).

The image on the screen represents the user's view of the world and may be presented from the viewpoint of the avatar (first person or egocentric) or from a viewpoint somewhere outside the avatar's position in the action. This latter viewpoint is known as third person or exocentric view and depicts the onscreen action as if from an over-the-shoulder or behind and slightly above the imaginary viewpoint of the user or player. In a standard setup, a user/player controls an avatar in a virtual three-dimensional graphic environment. The avatar is a graphic depiction or image of a character which represents the user within the "world" of the screen. The user or player then observes this imaginary version of their online character participating in onscreen action that is facilitated by keyboard and mouse or by a joy-stick or game-pad game controller. One of the many possible applications for such interactive, real-time technology is in the development of virtual art galleries which allow artists and enthusiasts to showcase art works in an accessible online environment. Using computer-graphics hardware, artworks can be sampled, reproduced or rendered in high quality photo-realistic detail using digital photography and three-dimensional modeling tools. This makes virtual exhibition an affordable way for artists to showcase their work online. The nature of virtual environments allows for many possibilities that could not be achieved in the real world - such as gravity defying sculptures, living paintings, epic scales and improved interactivity with the works - allowing online visitors to view and interact with the artwork. As general examples, both the official site for the Louvre (http://www. louvre.fr/en) and Washington's National Gallery of Art (http://www.nga.gov) have virtual tours for some sections of their collections. In both of these online galleries, an exhibit can be viewed virtually via a system of connected panoramic views of each room. Virtual galleries could theoretically be built inside any existing virtual environment and can either recreate a real museum or gallery location (such as the Louvre's "Explore in 3D" section of their online gallery) or stand alone, abstracted, with no real-world counterpart.

SECOND LIFE - A SHARED MULTIPLAYER SPACE

Second Life is a shared online space where users construct virtual characters, objects and scenarios using graphic modeling tools, these are analogous to virtual sculpting or object construction tools (www.secondlife. com). Launched in 2003 Second Life is a shared, multiplayer online virtual world which allows users to interact with each other and with the environment. Users construct models and simulations of real world environments including buildings, landscapes and objects. Multimedia (images, audio, movies and photographic images) can also be attached to these virtual objects and viewed by those exploring the virtual space. The Second Life software allows users to create, to purchase and to sell their virtual property. Many virtual counterparts to real life locations including corporations, universities, institutions and organizations can be visited by users who may interact with uploaded information taking the form of text, audio, picture, video and webpages.

Such shared online spaces are known as "persistent" as they exist online twenty four hours a day and are not switched off or on the way a TV set is. This means virtual locations can be visited or accessed by users online at any time. Second Life has many communication functions and users can communicate with others in their avatar form using messaging, chat and real time spoken audio functions. This makes Second Life a versatile social networking environment as users can form groups and exchange files.

Testing the User Experience of Virtual Art

The aim of this research is to examine the way virtual art is represented and viewed in a three-dimensional environment. How may an examination of the user experience help us understand the spectrum of reality and virtuality as it relates to media representations in a virtual gallery context? To answer this, the researchers identified and accounted for a number of possible factors which may influence the quality of the user experience.

A series of experiments was undertaken to examine aspects of the user experience relating to environment usability. Users were surveyed and data was collected regarding the factors that contributed to a successful user experience. These factors relate to the user and include gender, age, assertiveness, computer use, and their interest level in art. These factors were then correlated with variables in the virtual environment, where the perspective of the user and the mode of presentation of the artworks were assessed. During the experimental sessions, the user experiences were recorded and the users were surveyed. This allowed for the acquisition of quantitative data. Affective data was also collected from the users after each trial. Video recording of the user's behavior was used to discern time spent viewing specific works and the actual behavior within the virtual world. This chapter reports on the results of this experimental work and discusses the correlations linking demographic data to user experience gathered from the multiple methods of data acquisition that were applied.

Reality, Mixed Reality and Virtual Reality

The idea for the spectrum of real and virtual was first developed in the seminal paper "A Taxonomy of Mixed Reality Visual Displays" by Milgram and Kishino (1994). According to Milram and Kishino, we may understand virtual reality by observing a "virtuality continuum" which encompasses both "real" and technologically augmented forms of visual representation. This scheme is simply laid out as a linear path between the quintessential "real" and the quintessential "virtual". At one end is the real world of physical objects and at the other is a purely virtual computer generated world. The authors examine how various media of representation, including video and photographs may contrast with "real" objects (Figure 1).

The taxonomy of Milgram and Kishino (1994) classifies objects as either real or virtual depending upon two factors. On one hand, reality is defined by objects which have an actual physical existence.

On the other hand, reality is also defined by the authors according to the means by which an object is displayed in a media context. In this context, direct viewing is defined as seeing the actual object itself while non-direct viewing is seeing it recreated by some type of display. Direct viewing of real objects can be considered to be technically at the maximum possible resolution, as real objects may be observed down to the level of atomic particles and beyond. Therefore, theoretically, resynthesizing these objects loses content no matter what digital resolution is used.

However, this does not necessarily affect the perceived quality of the experience, as the viewer's sensory faculties only permit a certain level of detail. Using currently available technologies, it is possible for purely virtual objects to be presented at qualities (or resolutions) which match our human perception of directly viewed real objects.

According to Milgram and Kishino (1994) the image quality may impact the viewer's perception of that object. This suggests that "realness" is a function of perception, since the synthesized object may no longer accurately represent the real object.

Any attempt to define a synthesized object as being either real or virtual is difficult because the classification is absolute while the qualities and characteristics of the representation are not. There may therefore be a point at which the synthesized object will completely disconnect from what it is intended to represent.

In figure 2, is it practical to consider the representation of the landscape in the fourth frame as a real object? If we keep lowering the quality of the image, the environment will eventually cease to be recognizable as anything at all. Any virtual taxonomy perhaps needs a gradating classification in order to describe the resolution of synthesized objects.

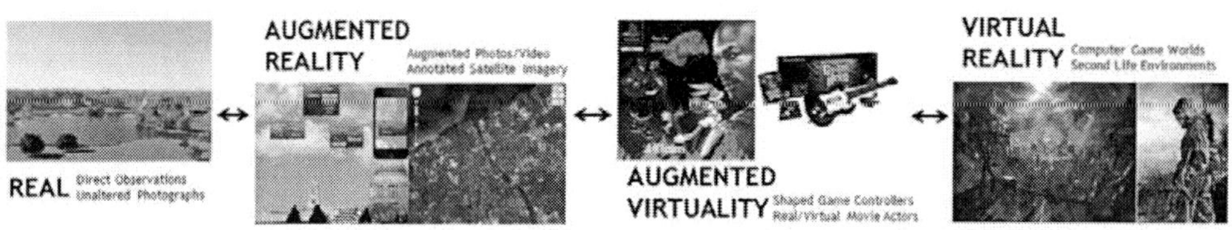

Figure 1. The Reality-Virtuality Continuum.

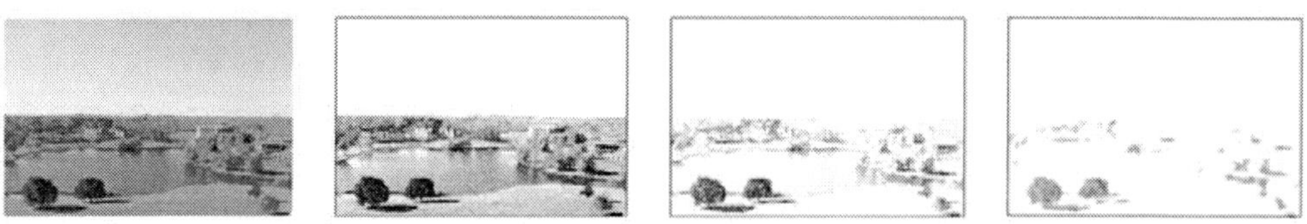

Figure 2. Demonstrating the Progressive Degradation of an Image.

The image usage context may also determine whether a representation is effective or not. For example, a newspaper cartoon of the Mona Lisa is still a recognizable representation of the Mona Lisa. A simplified or abstract on-screen symbol or metaphor may be sufficient in situations where a real object is previously known or available directly. However, when the synthesized object is responsible for supplying the user with all their knowledge and perceptions about the object, any perceptual discrepancies with the real object will become important and may be open to potential misinterpretation.

AUGMENTED AND MIXED REALITY

Towards the "real" end of the Milgram/Kishino spectrum is the realm of "Augmented Reality" which describes the use of virtual information which is projected by computer of photographic media into a primarily real experience. Augmented reality displays may include Head Up Displays (HUDs) which provide the user with a transparent screen that enhances augments their view of the world with additional digital information. Specific examples include computer software devices like Global Positioning Systems (GPS) or Google Maps which superimpose road lines and labels onto real world satellite images. GPS systems usually display synthesized abstractions of real objects such as landscapes and buildings. These abstract symbols may register at the "virtual" end of the spectrum. In contrast, direct images of "reality" such as photographs or landscapes or satellite images used on Google maps would belong at the "real" end of the spectrum (Ratliff, 2007).

Other examples include augmented reality navigation systems on mobile phones where the user can see the location of nearby locations of interest, such as the Tube/Subway stations shown in the application in Figure 3.

Figure 3. Augmented Reality Mobile Phone Application to Locate Tube Stations in London (Acrossair©).

These systems use a mix of photographic and abstract symbols to convey information to the user and may be seen in Milgram and Kishino's terms as "mixed reality systems." Alongside Augmented Reality (AR) sits the less mainstream Augmented Virtuality (AV) which describes a synthetic or virtual world mediated or shared by real objects or elements. These include tangible game controllers such as a guitar, sword or gun. The tangible interface allows a user to control a similar virtual object (guitar, sword or gun) as part of the action on-screen. In this way, virtual objects imitate "real" objects to increase the immersion felt by the game players. The tangible or haptic qualities of the controller may give players the feeling they are really holding a virtual object and are therefore connected to the world in a more intimate way.

In an example of augmented virtuality, images of real actors may be inserted into a computer-generated screen scenario. For instance, images of Michael Jordan playing basketball are mixed in with animated Looney Tunes characters in the movie Space Jam (Goldberg, 1996). Another example from the videogame Metal Gear Solid (1998) requires players to refer to the actual box used to package the game in order to read a required piece of information for use within the game. This Metal Gear Solid example urges players to think outside the virtual box, challenging their usual expectation of getting lost within the game's story world by reconnecting unexpectedly with the real world (Figure 1).

Milgram and Kishino (1994) discuss the dimensions applicable to "merging real and virtual worlds". These three dimensions can be used to create a map that describes for the user an experience of how realistic or immersive an environment is. Theytake into account three key metaphors which express how realistic or immersive an environment may appear. These metaphors describe Extent of World Knowledge, Reproduction Fidelity and Extent of Presence.

Extent of World Knowledge (EWK) describes "how much information exists in the world". This is often useful when assessing whether a design is logical and structured. It refers to the number and breadth of objects and information which exists in the world. For example, this metaphor allows us to compare a gameworld in which there is a maze of identical hallways with one which has a richer environment with a greater variation of interiors and landscapes.

Reproduction Fidelity (RF) refers to the level of detail that is displayed onscreen. This takes into account resolution and the graphical detail of the world. It also deals with dimensions of display such as two-dimensional sprites, three-dimensional models rendered for a two-dimensional display or three-dimensional models displayed in three-dimensions. Reproduction fidelity relates to the whole quality of the visual presentation and would logically extend to include all sensory information of the virtual world.

Extent of Presence Metaphor (EPM) also refers to how the world is visually presented. It accounts for viewing modes such as in a panoramic display or a head-mounted display unit. It also considers interactive features such as head-tracking and feedback. This metaphor accounts for interactivity features which allow the user to control their impact on the virtual world, from buttons and text input to full body suits and head-tracking.

Described in more simple terms, these three attributes look at the content of the world (EWK), the presentation quality of the world (RF), and the quality of interaction (EPM). Another early taxonomy used to describe "all varieties of technologically-mediated experience" or "synthetic experience" was created by Warren Robinett (1992). Rather than focus directly on distinctions between real and virtual, Robinett uses categories which define how the human user's interactions with the world are enabled by the 'mediating' technology. These categories are Causality, Model Source, Time, Space, Superposition, Display Type, Sensor Type, Action Measurement Type and Actuator Type. Table 1 provides a clear picture of the content of each of these categories (Robinett, 1992).

These categories allow designers to consider the perspective, the dimensions, feelings and tools that the user experiences within the virtual world. They also focus on the sensory feedback a user may receive from the virtual program. The first person perspective does not include an onscreen image of the user's avatar. In this way, the first person perspective is, by its very nature, a more disembodied design aesthetic. In a first-person perspective (egocentric) the expectations for realistic sensation may diverge from what is expected in a third person user perspective (exocentric.)

For example, a viewer controlling a virtual avatar with a third person viewpoint may receive haptic, feeling or sensory feedback as if the events in the world are happening to them. This extra feedback may enhance their visual field.

This brings us to another way of classifying the virtual experience which considers the level of sensory stimulation and reproduction. We may classify virtual reality systems according to what perceptual systems they stimulate and to what effect.

Table 1. A Classification System for Types of Synthetic Experience (Robinett, 1992)

Dimension	Possibilities	Contrasting examples
causality	simulated recorded transmitted	flight simulator film teleoperation
model source	scanned constructed computed edited	night vision goggles video game computational fluid dynamics film
time	1-to-1 accelerated (or retarded) frozen distorted	film time-lapse photography photograph edited video recording of event
space	registered remote miniaturized (or enlarged) distorted	night vision goggles teleoperation micro-teleoperation (STM) STM with heights exaggerated
superposition	merged isolated	augmented reality virtual reality
display type	HMD screen speaker (many more -- see Table 3)	virtual reality video game recorded music
sensor type	photomultiplier STM ultrasound scanner (many more -- see Table 4)	night vision goggles micro-teleoperation medical "X-ray vision"
action measurement type	tracker & glove joystick force feedback arm (many more -- see Table 5)	virtual reality video game teleoperation
actuator type	robot arm STM tip aircraft flaps (many more -- see Table 6)	teleoperation micro-teleoperation remote piloted aircraft

Some example categories of this method are (Latta and Oberg, 1994):

- Haptics/orienting (encompassing gravity and acceleration, movement, temperature, contact with solid and deformative compounds both passive and active);
- Auditory (sound quality);
- Location (surrounding environment);
- Vision quality (resolution) and dimension (two or three dimensional viewing);
- Other senses (such as taste and smell).

Some of these categories are not suitable as display mechanisms using our current technologies. However there are expensive (and often impractical) devices such as multi-directional treadmills, motion capture and feedback suits which can potentially begin to bridge some of these gaps between the real and virtual.

THE DIGITIZATION OF ART

Before high-quality images and photographs were available, museums and art galleries were the best option for observing many culturally important objects in significant detail. Even in today's age of high-quality reproductions and prints, the general public still visits art galleries. This social activity reinforces the desirability of seeing real art objects in a real context as opposed to looking at reproductions in a book or onscreen. People enjoy the experience of physically visiting a location which is demonstrated by the attendance spikes which occur during periods of economic downturn. This suggests that people visit these locations in lieu of more expensive vacations. It is likely that people value the social and active components of visiting the museums or gallery as much as they like to observe the art works and learn about the exhibits (Goldstein, 2009).

Painting and photo exhibits continue to attract attendance despite the prevalence of high-quality physical and digital reproduction. Some of this may be due to attendance factors including sociability, scale, professional arrangement and organization. The viewer may perceive a sense of authenticity while viewing real works. Three-dimensional or sculptural artworks and artifacts are more expensive to reproduce and generally not easily available for viewing in a representative three-dimensional digital form. While it is not hard to find online images of sculpture, these are often reported to be less gratifying to the viewer when compared to seeing the objects firsthand (Miller et al, 2006). Finding images online is often a simple process of 'search' while finding and viewing three-dimensional objects online can be a complicated process. It is far easier to imagine someone foregoing a visit to a Van Gogh exhibit due to finding similar content online than it is to imagine the same for a classical or modern sculpture exhibit.

One may visit the world's great museums online or wait in a line of people to see them in a real gallery.

The online viewer has the advantage of accessing the work at all hours, spending as much time with the work as they wish. In some cases, users may even download and save their favorite images. Julian Stallabrass (2010) observes that the status of owning or viewing an 'original' digital artwork may be lost in the digitizing process : *"There are some examples of artists selling versions of online work in limited editions with certificates of authenticity (along the lines of video art), but the gesture appears even more absurd than with video, since the work also appears in its original form for access by anyone with an Internet connection."*

Artists are perhaps able to avoid this issue by using low-resolution images and/or watermarks until payment is received. In the contemporary online environment perhaps artists may embrace methods such as product merchandising, mail order or retail sale of physical reproductions in order to make a profit from their online art.

Digital image reproduction has not only opened artwork and proprietary content to reinterpretation, cultural hacking and subversion but allowed novel forms of art to develop (Stallabrass, 2010). Reworking and "mash-ups" of logos, movie trailers and popular songs are commonplace online and can almost be considered as a new art form. Another example of a new art form arising from digitization is photo manipulation art which involves using Photoshop (2012) or a similar program to alter photographs often in a surrealistic manner (Outlaw, 2011).

The most common scenario for experiencing digital content is of "unmediated presence" where the user can view objects and images directly onscreen, usually through a web-browser. As three-dimensional virtual worlds become more engaging, we may expect broader content and a wider variety of purposing, as the technologies used for the experience mature. The virtual environments of today were unthinkable just one or two decades ago. The results of technological evolution permeate most of contemporary life (Schofield, 2012).

Virtual worlds will continue to grow ever more immersive and to become capable of producing the types and qualities of experience similar to those the viewer enjoys in the real world.

STEPING INTO THREE DIMENSIONS

Three-dimensional environments exist for the purposes of gaming, networking and training and their qualities and attributes vary greatly. They can be very graphically detailed in both realistic and imaginative ways, content-rich by design and as a function of multiuser interaction. Virtual environments can incorporate complex methods of control. The controls of simulation and training programs may carefully mimic their real-world equivalents or even use identical hardware perhaps even with haptic feedback (physical pressure, resistance, jostling or tilting). Complex simulators are used by the Air Force, Army, and Navy as well as many business and industrial applications (Strickland, 2007; Schofield, 2011a). For example, NASA uses sophisticated simulators to recreate experiences in space to train for standard operation and crisis situations (Wheelan, 2008).

Networked simulated three-dimensional worlds are a fast-growing area, as is evidenced by the popularity of Massively Multiplayer Online Role-Playing Games (MMORPGs) such as World of Warcraft (2004). Online, multi-person simulated environments, such as Second Life, are potentially more useful to users because their content is mostly real-world information about individuals, businesses, products and locations. (Dethridge, 2009)

These virtual worlds embody realities created by the mind allowing them realization as palpable entities. By entering a virtual world we allow its creators greater freedom to influence us, as at best they are controlling not just an object of our attention but the entirety of the world we are inhabiting (Ryan, 1999). Using a virtual three-dimensional environment to display art may not only help recreate the experience of seeing it in person but give willing artists greater dimension within to work and all while making it more accessible and far less expensive to operate than a physical location.

One such world that would be well suited for this is Second Life (www.secondlife.com). It is an open and persistent world which means it has locational geography and that it continues to exist when the user logs off. While connected, users are able to communicate with other players they encounter through both natural speech and typed messages. Second Life is currently the most prevalent of the 'social' three-dimensional environments, but there have been similar attempts at creating other, similar, multi-user, interactive experiences. These include Sony's PlayStation Home environment (http://us.playstation.com/psn/playstation-home/) allowing PlayStation 3 owners access to a range of shopping, games and social media and Habbo Hotel (www.habbo.com) which is predominantly used as a social network for younger users.

As far as its utility in education, Second Life currently has a balance of advantages and disadvantages. Its substantial learning curve and usability issues, difficulty of creating quality and novel content, and its fairly substantial computational and bandwidth requirements are its major impediments to finding wider and more general use.

Also it is still much less compelling than an analogous real-world experience. Looking on the positive side, Second Life offers the ability to access content with no physical travel, drastically reduced expense of 'field trips' and the lifted restrictions of reality. Transitions to digital content are also made very easy as links and files can be placed appropriately in the environment and accessed instantly (Dethridge, 2009; Boulos et al, 2007; Berge, 2008; Warburton, 2009)

If there is ever going to be widespread acceptance of the use of virtual worlds as alternatives or supplements to real world experiences then there is a need to understand how they differ from real-world interactions and what aspects influence the user experience in what ways. As a species we have devoted much research to understanding our natural behavior and it is practical to understand how these behavioral principles translate into the usability of virtual environments.

One important principle is that "immersion" to describe how a user behaves in a virtual world. This quality helps us describe the value and quality of the user's virtual experience. The more "immersed" they are in the virtual world, the more the actual world recedes into the background. Further, the more "immersed" they are in the virtual world, the more willing and able the user is to embrace the virtual world and the content within. Paradoxically, the virtual user experience still feels like "reality" even though it may have some "magical" aspects. In Second Life, the user's avatar can fly, transform in appearance or teleport through time and space. In this way, the virtual world shares aspects of the fictitious imaginary spaces provided by authors of fantasy or magic realist fiction (Dethridge, 2009)

Therefore, for reasons of productivity and efficiency, the attributes of presence and immersion may work well when pushed to the high levels of realism (Montaya and Massey, 2008; Wheelan, 2008). One study analyzed group behavior both inside and outside of virtual worlds and found strong correlations between immersion and behavior. The experiment also showed that users can experience social factors such as embarrassment and co-presence in the virtual world and that these increase with immersion, or presence (Slater et al, 2006).

In another study, a comparison between two-dimensional and three-dimensional videoconferencing showed that three-dimensional environments foster much higher levels of social presence (Hauber et al, 2005). A further study suggests that information observing and 'lurking' is likely to foster future active participation in virtual environments. Creating an open atmosphere and availability of information should be expected to encourage a willingness to engage and participate. (Li and Lee, 2010). Realistic avatars tend to increase feelings of presence with the exception of cases in which the gap between appearance and behavior is large. Users with lifelike avatars may experience greater feelings of presence compared to low-realism avatars. This is perhaps related to the 'uncanny valley' phenomenon (Bailenson et al, 2005; MacDormand, 2006). Another study revealed that avatars in male groups tended to keep larger distances between them than female groups. This all reflects trends in the real world and suggests that feelings of identity in avatars are strongly at work. (Yee et al, 2007; Eastwick and Gardner, 2008) One constant theme that can be drawn from these experiments is that the salience and meaningfulness of virtual experiences increases with immersion. Immersion is created by several factors well outlined by the framework incorporating world content (EWK); production quality (RF) and interactivity (EPM) (Milgram and Kishino, 1994). These dimensions are high-level and in order to fully specify all contingencies of virtual environments we must examine each one further. Of primary concern to us is which aspects of virtual worlds that connect the users to reality and how may these influence the user's behavior, experience and utility within the environment? Consider the outside world in connection with the attributes of virtual worlds. Virtual worlds such as Second Life or games like World of Warcraft allow a user to engage with other users in a social environment using standard social media tools. These tools are used in a similar manner to the way two-dimensional, social networking, graphical user interfaces (such as Facebook) perform. The three-dimensional environments, however, provide large amounts of virtual visual content as well as the ability for the user to create or to link to story or narrative elements. In this way, virtual experiences add new dimensions to the online interactions. In analyzing the behavior of users it is important to consider the information added to the world by virtue of this "World Content" dimension and to compare this to the increased complexity within the "Interaction" dimension. Considering social media within these dimensions one can see that Facebook is content rich and diegetically interactive and that it renders only an abstract or non-visual world. This is engaging to the users by virtue of its content despite its lack of realism as a world or environment.

This research work concerns itself with user's engagement with virtual art exhibits, which is dependent on immersion. We examine how engagement of the user can be achieved through graphics, interaction and content. Analyzing the effects and mediated effects between these dimensions and attributes may provide greater insight into the components that make up an engaging and productive virtual art experience for the user. It may also provide insight for the designer of such virtual worlds.

Experimental Methodology

This study utilized 24 participants who were recruited around the State University of New York, Oswego campus through social networks, bulletin board postings, and academic incentives for select courses. The participant group was composed of various demographics, although heavily weighted towards 20-25 year olds. A Human-Computer Interaction (HCI) laboratory on the SUNY Oswego campus was used for this experiment. Laptops running the Windows 7 operating system were used as the platform on which Second Life and Affect Map software (to assess the emotional state of participants) was run for the trials. Graphic settings were balanced to achieve the highest level of visual quality while retaining consistently responsive play, this equated to a 'mid' quality setting in the Second Life preferences.

A number of questionnaires were used to collect data from the participants:

- A *pre-experimental* questionnaire was used to collect information regarding basic demographics, computer usage, virtual world experience/video game usage, assertiveness, interest in visual art and prior second life experience.
- After each trial (a visit to one of the two Second Life locations) the participant was given a *post-trial questionnaire*. This collected data on their engagement, recollection of the art work, experience of the work, interest in the work and opinion of the control scheme.
- After both Second Life sessions were completed a final *post-experimental questionnaire* was used to gather information about the overall engagement and enjoyment of the virtual experience, opinion of virtual worlds and enjoyment of the experienced art.

Before beginning Second Life and after each trial participants were instructed to select a value from the Affect Map software, a java-based program designed to measure affect and activation (Ivancic and Taylor, 2010). This was used to provide information about whether the user's affective state had changed after each trial. Video recordings of the onscreen-events occurring during each of the trials were also recorded by a high-definition video camera. This was analyzed to determine the time spent in each area and specific behaviors such as types of interactions, time, and control efficiency.

Figure 4. The Wall Gallery and Dark Luminance Virtual Worlds used in the Experiment.

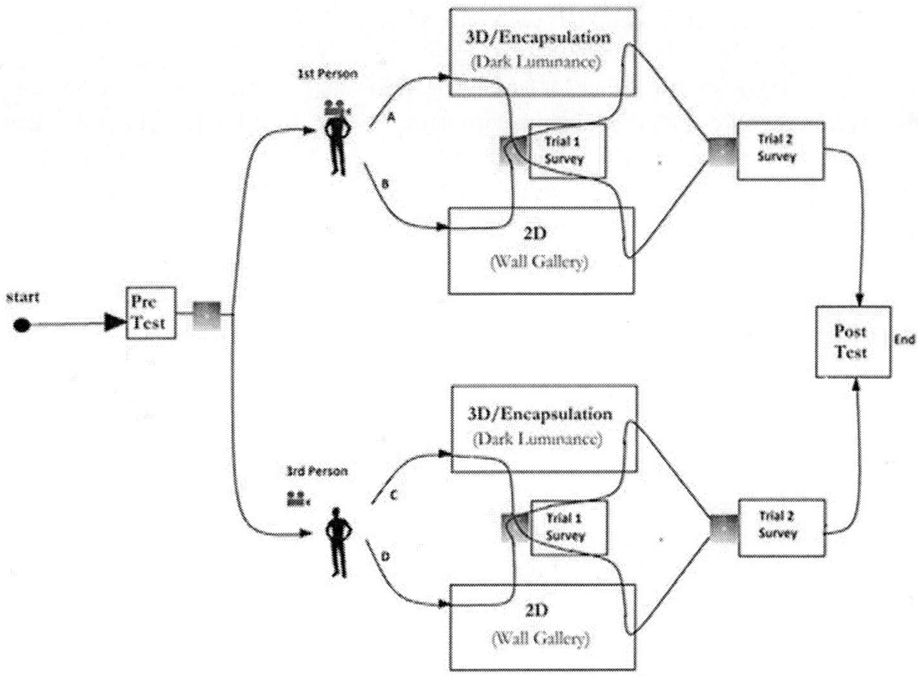

Figure 5. A Flowchart Showing the Experimental Procedure.

The design was a 2x2 mixed groups design, 50% of the participants used a 1st person perspective and the remaining 50% used a 3rd person perspective throughout the entire duration of their participation. These groups viewed two areas of Second Life in which identical works were displayed through different means.

One area, Dark Luminance (Dethridge, 2011), contained works in a three-dimensional rendered form that enclosed the user within the work by mapping it onto the walls and ceiling of a room as well as incorporating a number of interactive elements. The other, the Wall Gallery, presented the works as a traditional gallery with each work framed, hanging on the wall. Within these split groups the order of presentation was split 50/50 to avoid a confounding variable related to presentation order. The experimental environments are shown in Figure 4 and the experimental procedure is shown graphically in the flowchart in Figure 5.

The scheduled timeline of each experimental test was as follows:

- Completion of informed consent forms
- Completion of pre-experimental questionnaire
- Collection of 'Affect Map' Response
- Experimental Trial 1
- Collection of 'Affect Map' Response
- Completion of post-trial questionnaire
- Experimental Trial 2
- Collection of 'Affect Map' Response
- Completion of post-trial questionnaire
- Completion of post-experimental questionnaire

RESULTS AND ANALYSIS

After collecting data from the 24 participant trials and analyzing it in SPSS several significant results were found. Notable correlations were found based on the viewing perspective used, the order in which the locations were visited, the participants gender, the number of hours spent per week in a virtual world and the combined score from the various questions designed to gather interest level of the users in visual art.

Viewing Perspective (T-Test)

When analyzing the effects of viewing perspective on the user, multiple observations can be made. The 1st person perspective was positively correlated to increased ratings of engagement and immersion in the first trial regardless of location ($p = 0.003$ and 0.017 respectively).

In the Dark Luminance location 1st person perspective showed a similar effect however it did not reach a $p < 0.05$ or a less than 1/20 chance of being a type 1 error (significance was $p = 0.067$ for engagement and $p = 0.054$ for immersion). No statistically significant differences were found in the 3rd person perspective.

These results are summarized in Table 2 and Table 3. The difference in ratings of engagement and immersion between viewings of the Dark Luminance and those of the Wall Gallery may be due to one key factor. The Wall Gallery does not require as much interaction and viewing 'dexterity' as the Dark Luminance area. The art in the Wall Gallery is centralized and positioned at a consistent height which allows the user to keep a fixed camera angle. This simplicity could lessen the advantages of having a 1st person perspective.

An alternative hypothesis is that the difference is related to how the user experiences the nature of the two locations. The Wall Gallery, consisting of framed static pictures, has already removed the user from the 'actual' active experience of exploring the objects first hand. Since the user is in a more passive viewing state rather than an active exploratory state, as they are in the Dark Luminance environment, the shift of perspective from a more realistic view (1st person) to an abstract view (3rd person) may detract less from the experience.

It is interesting to note that the measured means for both engagement and immersion were higher across all trials using a 1st person perspective. This correlates well with previous research (Bryce and Rutter, 2002; Schofield, 2011b) and gives a good indication that this perspective is superior for creating immersion and engagement in a virtual art gallery setting.

Location and Order (T-Test)

There was a clear effect for the location itself on engagement and Immersion. Effects relating to the order in which the participants visited the two locations were also found to be significant (Table 4 and Table 5).

We note a difference between the participants who saw the Wall Gallery prior to Dark Luminance and the other half who saw the Dark Luminance Area prior to the Wall Gallery.

Table 2. Measures of Engagement and Immersion for the Users Related to Viewing Perspective

	Perspective	N	Mean	Std. Deviation	Std. Error Mean
Engagement (Trial 1)	1st Person	11	7.27	1.191	.359
	3rd Person	12	5.25	1.603	.463
Immersion (Trial 1)	1st Person	11	7.27	1.104	.333
	3rd Person	12	5.17	2.480	.716
Engagement (Trial 2)	1st Person	12	6.83	2.443	.705
	3rd Person	12	6.50	2.316	.669
Immersion (Trial 2)	1st Person	12	6.17	2.552	.737
	3rd Person	12	5.75	2.832	.818
Engagement (3D)	1st Person	11	8.00	1.342	.405
	3rd Person	12	6.58	2.065	.596
Immersion (3D)	1st Person	11	7.55	1.572	.474
	3rd Person	12	5.75	2.491	.719
Engagement (wall)	1st Person	12	6.17	1.992	.575
	3rd Person	12	5.17	1.850	.534
Immersion (wall)	1st Person	12	5.92	2.151	.621
	3rd Person	12	5.17	2.823	.815

Table 3. Measures of Engagement and Immersion T-Test

Independent Samples Test

		Levene's Test for Equality of Variances		t-test for Equality of Means					95% Confidence Interval of the Difference	
		F	Sig.	t	df	Sig. (2-tailed)	Mean Difference	Std. Error Difference	Lower	Upper
Engagement (Trial 1)	Equal variances assumed	.790	.384	3.409	21	.003	2.023	.593	.789	3.257
	Equal variances not assumed			3.454	20.187	.002	2.023	.586	.802	3.244
Immersion (Trial 1)	Equal variances assumed	13.263	.002	2.587	21	.017	2.106	.814	.413	3.799
	Equal variances not assumed			2.667	15.472	.017	2.100	.760	.420	3.704
Engagement (Trial 2)	Equal variances assumed	.143	.709	.343	22	.735	.333	.972	-1.682	2.349
	Equal variances not assumed			.343	21.937	.735	.333	.972	-1.682	2.349
Immersion (Trial 2)	Equal variances assumed	.292	.595	.379	22	.709	.417	1.101	-1.866	2.699
	Equal variances not assumed			.379	21.766	.709	.417	1.101	-1.867	2.701
Engagement (3D)	Equal variances assumed	1.998	.172	1.930	21	.067	1.417	.734	-.110	2.943
	Equal variances not assumed			1.966	19.024	.064	1.417	.720	-.091	2.924
Immersion (3D)	Equal variances assumed	3.222	.087	2.044	21	.054	1.795	.878	-.031	3.622
	Equal variances not assumed			2.085	18.746	.051	1.795	.861	-.009	3.600
Engagement (wall)	Equal variances assumed	.118	.735	1.274	22	.216	1.000	.785	-.628	2.628
	Equal variances not assumed			1.274	21.981	.216	1.000	.785	-.628	2.628
Immersion (wall)	Equal variances assumed	2.684	.116	.732	22	.472	.750	1.025	-1.375	2.875
	Equal variances not assumed			.732	20.555	.472	.750	1.025	-1.384	2.884

The data illustrates that both groups rated the first area they saw almost equally. The mean rating for Dark Luminance when seen in Trial 1 is an engagement measure of 6.27 and an immersion measure of 5.91, while the mean rating for the Wall Gallery when seen in Trial 1 is an engagement measure of 6.17 and immersion measure of 6.42. These scores show no significant difference ($p = .887$ for engagement and $p = .590$ for immersion).

Significant differences were however found when the participants moved to Trial 2. Those who visited the Wall Gallery in Trial 2 gave it lower ratings of engagement (a measure of 5.17) and immersion (a measure of 4.67). Participants visiting Dark Luminance in Trial 2 gave it higher ratings of engagement (a measure of 8.17) and immersion (a measure of 7.25).

There is a high level of significance for the values measuring the differences between locations in Trial 2 ($p = .000$ for engagement and $p = .013$ for immersion).

When the differences in the location ratings of two groups who visited them in opposite order are compared the strongest effect is seen in the change in the engagement score for Dark Luminance which jumps from a measure of 6.27 in Trial 1 to 8.17 when measured in Trial 2. This effect is statistically significant ($p = .011$). None of the other analyses for location ratings between these two groups were significant (Table 5). Immersion in the Wall Gallery showed a small decreasing effect when viewed second (after the Dark Luminance environment). It is possible that more significant findings would appear with a larger sample size.

One explanation for the even ratings between the locations in the first trial is that perhaps the users have a predilection to remain neutral. This predilection may exist before a precedent for expectation has been set. The participants could be making judgments based on an abstract idea of engagement and immersion and once a precedent has been set, the scale may take on new meaning for them. It is possible that neither location offered a great 'thrill' to the users and simply rating the experience as slightly above neutral fulfilled the descriptive needs of most participants as both were somewhat enjoyable.

The higher and lower ratings in the second trial can be explained simply because the Dark Luminance area is aesthetically more engaging and immersive relative to the Wall Gallery. Dark Luminance provides an open interactive experience which could be perceived by the user as more 'fun' than a static gallery (Dethridge, 2011). However there could also be deeper causes at work. If the Wall Gallery puts the Dark Luminance images and artwork into the mind of the participant, this could then set expectations as to the content of the trials and what to expect from the art itself. When entering the Dark Luminance area the users encounter an unexpected transformation of the passive pictures into interactive models, buildings and displays. A similar thing happens when participants visit the Wall Gallery after seeing Dark Luminance. Instead of breathing life into static images, the Wall Gallery environment has removed life leaving only static images behind.

Further studies could pair two sets of locations which differ in the same respect as the Wall Gallery and Dark Luminance. One location may contain the same virtual artworks and one may contain different artworks. These experiments would then measure whether the two sets of users experienced a significant difference in how the ratings change between the equivalent Wall Gallery area and the equivalent Dark Luminance area in each.

Gender (T-Test)

No correlations to gender were found for either engagement or immersion. Gender was, however, found to have a significant relation to ratings of both control comfort and control naturalness (Table 6 and Table 7). The most powerful effects of this are seen in the ratings of control naturalness for Trial 2 which males rated at a mean of 7.90 while females rated it at

5.57 (p = .004) and control naturalness for the Dark Luminance environment which males rated at 8.22 while females rated it at 5.43 (p = .002).

A simple possible explanation for this difference is that demographically, males are more likely to spend greater amounts of time playing computer and videogames than females. Males are therefore perhaps more used to the interface and more capable of exercising control within a virtual world when using a standard computer mouse and keyboard setup (Shashaani, 1997). Data supporting this explanation is illustrated clearly within the experimental results collected which showed a mean of 28.3 computer use hours per week for males while females showed a mean of 13.14 computer use hours per week (p = .013).

A further possibility for the differences in ratings between control naturalness and control comfort is that 'comfort' may have had physical associations while 'naturalness' could be seen by the users to apply directly to the straight-forwardness and intuitiveness of the control. The control may have been deemed comfortable while still requiring a period of learning meaning it perhaps still felt 'unnatural' (Hall and Cooper, 1991). Hence, if the 'natural' rating is deemed to connote familiarity, propriety or proficiency it is likely a demographic used to similar styles of control (in this case the males in the user group) would rate the control interface higher.

Additionally, a likely reason the effect of natural control is stronger in the Dark Luminance environment than in the Wall Gallery environment is that it requires increased dexterity of movement and therefore exaggerates differences in control capability. The Wall Gallery requires users only to view a narrow band of the vertical axis and navigation is made simple by virtue of the confined area.

Table 4. Measures of Engagement and Immersion for the Users Related to Location and Order

Group Statistics

	Order	N	Mean	Std. Deviation	Std. Error Mean
Engagement (Trial 1)	DL/Wall	11	6.27	1.794	.541
	Wall/DL	12	6.17	1.749	.505
Immersion (Trial 1)	DL/Wall	11	5.91	2.468	.744
	Wall/DL	12	6.42	1.975	.570
Engagement (Trial 2)	DL/Wall	12	5.17	2.082	.601
	Wall/DL	12	8.17	1.467	.423
Immersion (Trial 2)	DL/Wall	12	4.67	2.708	.782
	Wall/DL	12	7.25	1.913	.552
Engagement (3D)	DL/Wall	11	6.27	1.794	.541
	Wall/DL	12	8.17	1.467	.423
Immersion (3D)	DL/Wall	11	5.91	2.468	.744
	Wall/DL	12	7.25	1.913	.552
Engagement (wall)	DL/Wall	12	5.17	2.082	.601
	Wall/DL	12	6.17	1.749	.505
Immersion (wall)	DL/Wall	12	4.67	2.708	.782
	Wall/DL	12	6.42	1.975	.570

Alternatively Dark Luminance allows for travel around and behind objects and requires the user to view much greater angular ranges both horizontally and vertically as well as allowing for interaction with some of the objects and images.

The difference between male and female ratings of comfort seems to increase between Trial 1 and Trial 2. Perhaps the best explanation is that this is simply due to chance. It could be that males gain competence with the control more quickly, as they demographically begin the experiment with a basic understanding of the controls and learn the specifics after a few minutes. Many of the females in the group could become frustrated as they may not have the existing knowledge and skill framework to easily pick up the control interface easily. The between Trials difference itself is small and not statistically significant, so this difference may be considered due to chance.

There was one other significant gender difference ($p = .022$) in the ratings given to Virtual World Potential (the user's view of the potential of the technology as a means of viewing artworks). We can hypothesize that perhaps this was also caused by the differences in experience or perhaps even partially related to frustrations caused by the difficulty of controlling the experience.

Hours in Virtual World (One Way ANOVA)

There were no significant effects of note regarding the hours the users used a computer. However, there is a non-significant correlation between this score and immersion both in Trial 1 and in Dark Luminance with significance factors of $p = .073$ and $p = .075$ respectively. This does not offer a reliable conclusion as to whether more frequent use and experience within virtual worlds make experiences in the virtual art galleries seem more immersive.

Table 5. Measures of Engagement and Immersion T-Test

Independent Samples Test

		Levene's Test for Equality of Variances		t-test for Equality of Means						
									95% Confidence Interval of the Difference	
		F	Sig.	t	df	Sig. (2-tailed)	Mean Difference	Std. Error Difference	Lower	Upper
Engagement (Trial 1)	Equal variances assumed	.004	.950	.143	21	.887	.106	.739	-1.431	1.643
	Equal variances not assumed			.143	20.720	.887	.106	.740	-1.434	1.646
Immersion (Trial 1)	Equal variances assumed	.767	.391	-.547	21	.590	-.508	.928	-2.438	1.423
	Equal variances not assumed			-.541	19.180	.594	-.508	.937	-2.468	1.453
Engagement (Trial 2)	Equal variances assumed	1.523	.230	-4.081	22	.000	-3.000	.735	-4.525	-1.475
	Equal variances not assumed			-4.081	19.763	.001	-3.000	.735	-4.535	-1.465
Immersion (Trial 2)	Equal variances assumed	2.675	.116	-2.699	22	.013	-2.583	.957	-4.568	-.598
	Equal variances not assumed			-2.699	19.789	.014	-2.583	.957	-4.581	-.585
Engagement (3D)	Equal variances assumed	.324	.575	-2.782	21	.011	-1.894	.681	-3.310	-.478
	Equal variances not assumed			-2.757	19.392	.012	-1.894	.687	-3.330	-.458
Immersion (3D)	Equal variances assumed	.790	.384	-1.464	21	.158	-1.341	.916	-3.246	.564
	Equal variances not assumed			-1.447	18.850	.164	-1.341	.927	-3.281	.600
Engagement (wall)	Equal variances assumed	.479	.496	-1.274	22	.216	-1.000	.785	-2.628	.628
	Equal variances not assumed			-1.274	21.387	.216	-1.000	.785	-2.631	.631
Immersion (wall)	Equal variances assumed	2.526	.126	-1.809	22	.084	-1.750	.968	-3.757	.257
	Equal variances not assumed			-1.809	20.122	.085	-1.750	.968	-3.768	.268

However it may indicate that this area could benefit from further study.

One could hypothesize that participants who used virtual worlds less often would potentially find this experiment more immersive.

However, the opposite is suggested by the data (although it is non-conclusive). The possible causes of this result could be:

1 That users who spend more time in virtual worlds do so because they have a disposition to find them more enjoyable.
2 That frequent use of virtual worlds causes higher ratings as an affinity already exists with the technology, or,
3 That feelings of immersion really do increase with more frequent use of similar technology.

Combined Art Score (One Way ANOVA)

The Combined Art Score was a combination of all of the data relating to the user's pre-existing appreciation, knowledge and interest in art from the pre-experimental questionnaire.

The categories comprised of Art Production, Artists Liked, Interest in Visual Art, Art Work Recognition, Exhibit/Gallery Attendance and Exhibit/Gallery Enjoyment. The combined art score was calculated by a direct summation as all were on the same scale and increasing values led to a greater appreciation of art in all cases.

Significant correlations were found to age and to academic year as well as to the user's perception of vividness and realism in the virtual galleries. No significant correlation existed with engagement or immersion, although there is evidence for a weak positive correlation to immersion in Trial 1 but stronger statistical power is needed to demonstrate this ($p = .087$).

Table 6. Measures of Comfort and Naturalness for the Users Related to Gender

Group Statistics

	Gender	N	Mean	Std. Deviation	Std. Error Mean
Control Comfort (Trial 1)	Male	9	7.44	1.944	.648
	Female	14	6.29	2.091	.559
Control Naturalness (Trial 1)	Male	9	7.78	2.224	.741
	Female	14	5.86	2.107	.563
Control Comfort (Trial 2)	Male	10	8.10	1.449	.458
	Female	14	6.50	2.175	.581
Control Naturalness (Trial 2)	Male	10	7.90	1.449	.458
	Female	14	5.57	1.950	.521
Control Comfort (wall)	Male	10	7.50	1.900	.601
	Female	14	6.21	2.225	.595
Control Naturalness (wall)	Male	10	7.50	1.900	.601
	Female	14	6.00	2.148	.574
Control Comfort (3D)	Male	9	8.11	1.453	.484
	Female	14	6.57	2.027	.542
Control Naturalness (3D)	Male	9	8.22	1.716	.572
	Female	14	5.43	1.869	.500

A positive relation seems to exist between the combined art score with age and academic year which no doubt share the same cause.

Table 7. Measures of Comfort and Naturalness T-Test

Independent Samples Test

		Levene's Test for Equality of Variances		t-test for Equality of Means						
									95% Confidence Interval of the Difference	
		F	Sig.	t	df	Sig. (2-tailed)	Mean Difference	Std. Error Difference	Lower	Upper
Control Comfort (Trial 1)	Equal variances assumed	.000	.995	1.332	21	.197	1.159	.870	-.651	2.968
	Equal variances not assumed			1.354	18.152	.192	1.159	.856	-.638	2.955
Control Naturalness (Trial 1)	Equal variances assumed	.004	.947	2.089	21	.049	1.921	.920	.008	3.833
	Equal variances not assumed			2.063	18.616	.055	1.921	.931	-.048	3.889
Control Comfort (Trial 2)	Equal variances assumed	1.239	.278	2.021	22	.056	1.600	.792	-.041	3.241
	Equal variances not assumed			2.162	21.940	.042	1.600	.740	.065	3.135
Control Naturalness (Trial 2)	Equal variances assumed	1.826	.190	3.191	22	.004	2.329	.730	.815	3.842
	Equal variances not assumed			3.356	21.934	.003	2.329	.694	.889	3.768
Control Comfort (wall)	Equal variances assumed	.110	.744	1.480	22	.153	1.286	.869	-.518	3.087
	Equal variances not assumed			1.521	21.190	.143	1.286	.845	-.471	3.043
Control Naturalness (wall)	Equal variances assumed	.456	.507	1.767	22	.091	1.500	.849	-.261	3.261
	Equal variances not assumed			1.805	20.684	.086	1.500	.831	-.229	3.228
Control Comfort (3D)	Equal variances assumed	.773	.388	1.989	21	.062	1.540	.762	-.086	3.166
	Equal variances not assumed			2.119	20.650	.046	1.540	.727	.027	3.053
Control Naturalness (3D)	Equal variances assumed	.294	.593	3.606	21	.002	2.794	.774	1.183	4.404
	Equal variances not assumed			3.679	19.306	.002	2.794	.759	1.200	4.387

Table 8. Measures of Engagement and Immersion ANOVA

ANOVA

		Sum of Squares	df	Mean Square	F	Sig.
Engagement (Trial 1)	Between Groups	24.691	7	3.527	1.284	.322
	Within Groups	41.222	15	2.748		
	Total	65.913	22			
Immersion (Trial 1)	Between Groups	55.615	7	7.945	2.398	.073
	Within Groups	49.689	15	3.313		
	Total	105.304	22			
Engagement (Trial 2)	Between Groups	56.744	8	7.093	1.551	.221
	Within Groups	68.589	15	4.573		
	Total	125.333	23			
Immersion (Trial 2)	Between Groups	62.203	8	7.775	1.181	.371
	Within Groups	98.756	15	6.584		
	Total	160.958	23			
Engagement (wall)	Between Groups	42.644	8	5.331	1.789	.158
	Within Groups	44.689	15	2.979		
	Total	87.333	23			
Immersion (wall)	Between Groups	46.569	8	5.821	.915	.530
	Within Groups	95.389	15	6.359		
	Total	141.958	23			
Engagement (3D)	Between Groups	31.513	7	4.502	1.503	.240
	Within Groups	44.922	15	2.995		
	Total	76.435	22			
Immersion (3D)	Between Groups	58.623	7	8.375	2.377	.075
	Within Groups	52.856	15	3.524		
	Total	111.478	22			

One can hypothesize that age brings about greater knowledge, a greater fondness for art, and that older students would show more enthusiasm for art due to their life experiences which would translate to higher scores on ratings of art enjoyment and the other responses used for the combined art score.

The participant's measured vividness ratings were significantly higher in both Trial 2 and in the Wall Gallery for participants with a higher combined art score ($p = .01$ and $p = .027$ respectively). The participant's measured realism ratings in the Wall Gallery were also significantly higher ($p = .038$). This could suggest either a parallel to the participant's real-life experience of visiting similar gallery/exhibit locations or a greater willingness to experience the featured art in a virtual setting if they have greater experience of real-world art.

CONCLUSION

Immersion is the state of consciousness where an immersant's awareness of physical self is transformed by being surrounded in an engrossing environment; often artificial, creating a perception of presence in a non-physical world. The term is widely used for describing partial or complete suspension of disbelief enabling action or reaction to stimulations encountered in a virtual or artistic environment. The degree to which the virtual artistic environment faithfully reproduces reality determines the degree of suspension of disbelief. This is best described by Murray (1997): *"A stirring narrative in any medium can be experienced as virtual reality because our brains are programmed to tune into stories with an intensity that can obliterate the world around us... The experience of being transported to an elaborately simulated place is pleasurable in itself, regardless of the fantasy content. We refer to this experience as immersion. Immersion is a metaphorical term derived from the physical experience of being submerged in water. We seek the same feeling from psychologically immersive experience that we do from a plunge in the ocean or swimming pool: the sensation of being surrounded by a completely other reality, as different as water is from air, that takes over all of our attention, our whole perceptual apparatus... "* This chapter described a series of experiments involving 24 participants who experienced virtual artworks in multiple gallery environments and utilizing different viewing perspectives. A number of positive correlations regarding the user experience were made from an analysis of the results. These results may identify key factors or guidelines that are useful to those attempting to design or create their own online virtual art environments:

- Engagement and immersion with the virtual experience can be increased by use of a 1st person perspective.
- The order in which different environments are experienced has a significant effect on the experience of the user.
- Increasing the amount of interaction will provide the user with a more engaging and immersive experience.
- Users who are more familiar with the technology, will be more comfortable in the virtual gallery environment.
- Users who have an existing appreciation of art will find the virtual artworks more stimulating (vivid and real).

Table 9. Measures of Age, Academic Year, Vividness and Realism ANOVA

ANOVA

		Sum of Squares	df	Mean Square	F	Sig.
Age	Between Groups	654.958	16	40.935	17.909	.000
	Within Groups	16.000	7	2.286		
	Total	670.958	23			
Academic Year	Between Groups	36.625	16	2.289	4.006	.035
	Within Groups	4.000	7	.571		
	Total	40.625	23			
Realism (Trial 1)	Between Groups	120.609	16	7.538	2.827	.103
	Within Groups	16.000	6	2.667		
	Total	136.609	22			
Vividness (Trial 1)	Between Groups	73.457	16	4.591	2.900	.097
	Within Groups	9.500	6	1.583		
	Total	82.957	22			
Realism (Trial 2)	Between Groups	91.500	16	5.719	1.232	.410
	Within Groups	32.500	7	4.643		
	Total	124.000	23			
Vividness (Trial 2)	Between Groups	113.833	16	7.115	6.225	.010
	Within Groups	8.000	7	1.143		
	Total	121.833	23			
Realism (wall)	Between Groups	120.125	16	7.508	3.893	.038
	Within Groups	13.500	7	1.929		
	Total	133.625	23			
Vividness (wall)	Between Groups	100.958	16	6.310	4.417	.027
	Within Groups	10.000	7	1.429		
	Total	110.958	23			
Realism (3D)	Between Groups	93.435	16	5.840	1.001	.541
	Within Groups	35.000	6	5.833		
	Total	128.435	22			
Vividness (3D)	Between Groups	77.370	16	4.836	3.868	.052
	Within Groups	7.500	6	1.250		
	Total	84.870	22			
Enjoyment of Visited Art	Between Groups	105.458	16	6.591	2.977	.074
	Within Groups	15.500	7	2.214		
	Total	120.958	23			
Prefered Location	Between Groups	3.500	16	.219	1.531	.293
	Within Groups	1.000	7	.143		
	Total	4.500	23			

This research work has attempted to explain a user's engagement with virtual art exhibits, which is dependent on such qualities of immersion. Following the insights provided by theorists including Milgram and Kishino, we find that increased engagement of the user can be achieved through the quality of graphics, interaction and content.

This analysis of the experimental data has provided an insight into the components that make up an engaging and productive virtual art experience for the user.

As Frank Rose states regarding the use of technology (2012):

> "People have always wanted to in some way inhabit the stories that move them. The only real variable is whether technology gives them that opportunity."

REFERENCES

Bailenson, J., Swinth, S., Hoyt, C., Dimov, S., and Blascovich, J. (2005). The Independent and Interactive Effects of Embodied Agent Appearance and Behavior on Self-Report, Cognitive, and Behavioral Markers of Copresence in Immersive Virtual Environments. *Presence*. 14(4), 379-393.

Berge, Z. (2008). Multi-User Virtual Environments for Education and Training? *A Critical Review of Second Life. Educational Technology.* May-June 2008. Retrieved November 16, 2011 from http://it.coe.uga.edu/ itforum/ETSecLife.pdf

Boulos, M. N. K., Hetherington, L. and Wheeler, S. (2007). Second Life: An Overview of the Potential of 3-D Virtual Worlds in Medical and Health Education. *Health Information and Libraries Journal*. 24, 233-245.

Bryce, J. and Rutter, J. (2002), Spectacle of the Deathmatch: Character and Narrative in First-Person Shooters, In: eds. G. King and T. Krzywinska (Eds), *ScreenPlay: Cinema/ Videogames/Interfaces*, London: Wallflower.

Hall, J. and Cooper, J. (1991). Gender, Experience and Attributions to the Computer. *Journal of Educational Computing Research*. 7(1), 51-60.

Dethridge, L. (2009). The magic realism of a virtual second life, In: *Literature and Aesthetics, Sydney Society of Literature and Aesthetics*, Sydney Uni., Sydney, Australia, vol. 19, no. 2, 262-278

Dethridge, L. (2011). Art and the Avatar in Virtual and Mixed-reality Exhibition Space, In: H. Yang and S. Yuen, (Eds), *The Handbook of Research on Practices and Outcomes in Virtual Worlds and Environments* (Volume 1), Hershey: IGI Global.

Eastwick, P. W. and Gardner, W. L. (2008) Is it a Game? Evidence for Social Influence in the Virtual World. *Social Influence*. 4(1), 18-32.

Goldberg, D. (Producer), Pytka, J. (Director), (1996), *Space Jam [Motion Picture]*. US; Warner Brothers Pictures.

Goldstein, A. (2009). Museum Attendance Rises as the Economy Tumbles. *The Art Newspaper*. 208.

Hauber, J., Regenbrecht, H., Hills, A., Cockburn, A., and Billinghurst, M. (2005). Social Presence in Two- and Three-Dimensional Videoconferencing. *Proceedings of PRESENCE 2005: The 8th Annual International Workshop on Presence*. London, UK.

Ivancic, D., Taylor, R. (2010). *The Java Affect Map* [Computer Software]. Oswego, NY: SUNY Oswego.

Latta, J. N. and Oberg, D. J. (1994). A Conceptual Virtual Reality Model. *IEEE Computer Graphics and Applications*, 14 (1).

Li, H. and Lee, K. C. (2010) Behavior and Participation in Virtual Worlds: A Triandis Model Perspective. *Proceedings of PACIS 2010 Conference*. Taipai, Taiwan.

MacDorman, K. F. (2006), Subjective Ratings of Robot Video Clips for Human Likeness, Familiarity, and Eeriness: an Exploration of the Uncanny Valley, In: *Proceedings of the ICCS/CogSci-2006 Long Symposium: Toward Social Mechanisms of Android Science*. Vancouver, Canada.

Metal Gear Solid [Computer software]. (1998). Japan: Konami.

Milgram, P. and Kishino, F. (1994). A Taxonomy of Mixed Reality Visual Displays. *Transactions on Information Systems*, E77-D(12).

Miller, G., Hoffert, E., Chen, S. E., Patterson, E., Blackkletter, D., Rubin, S., Applin, S. A., Yim, D., and Hanan, J. (2006). The Virtual Museum: Interactive 3D Navigation of a Multimedia Database. *The Journal of Visualization and Computer Animation.* 3(3), 183-197.

Montoya, M. and Massey, A. (2008). PVP; Measuring Perceived Virtual Presence in Collaborative Virtual Environment, *MIS Quarterly: Special Issue on New Ventures in Virtual Worlds*. 32(3).

Murray, J. (1997). *Hamlet on the Holodeck: the Future of Narrative in Cyberspace.* Cambridge: MIT Press.

Outlaw, D. (2011). 48 Mind-blowing Examples of Photo Manipulation Art. PsdTuts. Retrieved November 16, 2012 from http://psd.tutsplus.com/ articles/inspiration/photo-manipulation-art/

Photoshop [Computer software]. (2012). CA, US: Adobe.

Ratliff, E. (2007). How Google Maps is Changing the Way We See the World. *Whole Earth.* 1(5): 5-14

Robinett, W. (1992). Synthetic Experience: A Proposed Taxonomy. *Presence*, 1(2), 229-247.

Rose, F. (2012). The Art of Immersion: How the Digital Generation Is Remaking Hollywood, Madison Avenue, and the Way We Tell Stories. New York: W. W. Norton and Company.

Ryan, M. L. (1999). Immersion vs. Interactivity: Virtual Reality and Literary Theory. *SubStance*. 28(2).

Schofield, D. (2011a). Using Simulators for Training, In: Yang, H. and Yuen, S. (Eds), *The Handbook of Research on Practices and Outcomes in Virtual Worlds and Environments* (Volume 1), Hershey: IGI Global.

Schofield, D. (2011b). Playing with Evidence: Using Video Games in the Courtroom, *Journal of Entertainment Computing*, (Special Issue: Video Games as Research Instruments), 2(1), 47-58.

Schofield, D. (2012). Experiences with Virtual Learning: Using 3D Interactive Systems for Education and Training, *Journal of 3D Interactive Systems*, Society of Brazilian Computing, 3(1), 18-26.

Shashaani, L. (1997). Gender Differences in Computer Attitudes and Use Among College Students. *Journal of Educational Computing Research.* 16(1), 37-52.

Silver, S. (Producer), Wachowski, A. and Wachowski, L. (Directors), (1999), *The Matrix [Motion Picture].* US; Warner Brothers Pictures.

Slater, M., Sadagic, A., Usoh, M., and Schroeder, R. (2006). Small-Group Behavior in a Virtual and Real Environment: A Comparative Study. *Presence.* 9(1), 37-51.

Stallabrass, J. (2010). Can Art History Digest Net Art? In: D. Daniels and G. Reisinger (Eds), Netpioneers 1.0 - Archiving, Representing and Contextualising Early Netbased Art. Berlin: Sternberg Press.

Strickland, J. (2007). How Virtual Reality Military Applications Work. HowStuffWorks.com. Retrieved November 16, 2011 from http://science. howstuffworks.com/virtual-military.htm

Warburton, S. (2009). Second Life in Higher Education: Assessing the Potential for and the Barriers to Deploying Virtual Worlds in Learning and Teaching. *British Journal of Educational technology*. 40(3), 414-426.

Wheelan, T. J. (2008). Social Presence in Multi-User Virtual Environments: A Review and Measurement Framework for Organizational Research. North Carolina State University.

Retrieved November 16, 2011 from http://www4.ncsu.edu/~tjwhelan/presence_in_OB_research_2008_%28LAS_prelim%29.pdf

World of Warcraft [Computer software]. (2004). California: Blizzard Entertainment.

Yee, N., Bailenson, J. N., Urbanek, M., Chang, F., and Merget, D. (2007). The Unbearable Likeness of Being Digital: The Persistence of Nonverbal Social Norms in Online Virtual Environments. *The Journal of CyberPsychology and Behavior*. 10, 115–121.

In: Virtual Environments
Editors: Stephanie Trautman and Franchesca Julien ISBN: 978-1-62618-090-1
© 2013 Nova Science Publishers, Inc.

Chapter 4

WAYS OF VIEWING AND INTERACTING: USER EXPERIENCE IN A VIRTUAL ART GALLERY

Matthew Anderson[1], Damian Schofield[2] and Lisa Dethridge[3]
[1]Masters Student, Human Computer Interaction Program, SUNY Oswego, US
[2]Director of the Human Computer Interaction Program, SUNY Oswego, USA and Adjunct Professor of Forensic Computing, Edith Cowan University, Australia
[3]Senior Lecturer, School of Media and Communication, RMIT University, Melbourne, Australia

ABSTRACT

As computer-driven display technology becomes more powerful and accessible, the online, virtual art gallery may provide a new platform for artists to exhibit their work. Virtual exhibits may afford opportunities for both the artist and the patron to display, view and perhaps purchase various digital art forms.

The aim of this chapter is to examine user interaction with digital artworks inside a virtual gallery space along a metric based on a virtuality continuum. The chapter describes a number of experiments where users interacted with a virtual art gallery and were then extensively interviewed and surveyed. The gallery is a three-dimensional graphic digital construction within the RMIT University virtual campus in Second Life. Users take on the form of online avatars to access the Second Life online environment and experience various colourful art objects in a simulated gallery environment.

The experiment initially employs the taxonomy of Milgram and Kishino (1994) to assist the discussion of real, virtual and mixed-reality media. The chapter describes and delineates the user's navigation of space and compares their perception of art objects in the virtual environment to digital objects in a 'real world' gallery.

The data collected in this study provide the basis for a discussion of how the user may perceive and navigate virtual objects and spaces in the virtual art gallery environment. We observe levels of what Manovich (2002) describes as 'immersion' and what Slater (1994) would term 'presence' in relation to the user experience.

VISUAL ART

Visual artifacts, physical gestures, and color are common means for people to communicate with each other, whether the communication uses body language, hand signals, or art. Throughout history, visual art has served as a medium for expression of emotions, intellect and ideas. This expression allows humans to perceive the surrounding world around them as well exploring the mind's conception of abstract and concrete denotations of life and existence. This perception becomes a translation of our experience which can be gauged through our ability to communicate these ideas.

Over the centuries, visual artistic expression has captured emotion and affect perception. This expression has led to scientific principles of vision and color which were developed through studies of color in the 14th century, continuing with the use of optics in art in the 15th century, and leading to the mass-reproduction of colored objects during the industrial revolution (Douma, 2006). Scientific understanding of vision and color began to spark new forms of art such as impressionism and neo-impressionism. Artists such as Van Gogh (1853-1890) and Paul Signac (1863-1935) used modern concepts of color and vision to improve their visual expression of life and nature.

In the twentieth century modernist movement, the paradigm of political, mythological and spirtual abstraction in art became meshed with the power of the imagination itself. The meaning of art is now recognized as one that is shared between the viewer and the artist (Douma, 2006).

The visualization of art, be it paintings or sculpture, becomes 'visible speech' for the artist to capture the audience's attention whether that language is understood or not. Kenneth Clark (1981) suggested that : *"Modern art is a true and vital expression of our time and differs radically than from anything before it."* In a statement that predated digital artworks Grigson wrote (1970) : *"Art in its modern form will become more familiar and will be acceptable to more people than at present ... "*

Since the conception of computer graphics, the representation of art has allowed for images of more detailed realism. With the advent of the Internet, art is more familiar and accessible to a wide international audience. As digital technology continues to advance and becomes more accessible, artists are now able to create new ways of viewing and interacting with their artwork.

DIGITAL ART

Around the 1960's digital processing began its impact on the creation and visual representation of computer-generated visual media or digital art. The first Graphical User Interface (GUI) was created by XEROX in the 1970's. This led to computer animation and icons becoming widespread. Later, during the 1980's digital art began to blossom and digital art evolved as artists created interactive artwork using computer software. This practice would conceptually change the significance of the artwork, as microchips and processors were now doing the actual processing work. As Kuspit (2005) states : *"Essentially, the digital artwork becomes a second manifestation... of the abstract code, which becomes the primary vehicle for creativity."*

This creativity comes with a cost. Since the birth of visual art; the viewing and appreciation of artworks have been embedded in human experience. Humans have always used physical senses in proximity to the artwork itself to produce the haptic-gestural feedback of experiencing art works in person. An artist may create a sculpture that people can touch and feel. If the work is reproduced or displayed in a three-dimensional virtual environment the viewer may effectively lose that physical sensation. Alternatively, there may be gains as well. Virtual reproduction means that the precision and scale of an artwork may be manipulated much more finely than an artist could manage in real life.

Artists are utilizing digital technologies to augment and distribute their work in order to share and sell their creations. They are now able to reproduce, rescale and reproduce their artwork digitally as can the online viewer who may access it online. In addition, there may be cultural and social advantages to replicating and disseminating artwork over the Internet. No longer are paintings secluded in museums and prestigious art galleries which are often the domain of the educated classes. With the advent of digital simulations and computer driven technology, artists may create new forms of 'visible speech', new forms of interaction with the audience. The use of three-dimensional graphic tools for displaying visual art is evolving as an art form in itself. Virtual environments such as Second Life, allow users to immerse themselves and engage in expression and creativity. Such new forms of digital media may ultimately traverse traditional ideas of visual communication and lead to new and diverse models of conceptual artwork (Popper, 2007).

SECOND LIFE

Second life (www.secondlife.com) is a Massive Multi-player Online (MMO) three-dimensional environment that was launched in 2003. A client or viewer is downloaded to the user's computer which connects to a global bank of servers which form a vast matrix of online locations and spaces. As a "resident" of this online world, the user creates their own avatar, a 3D graphic version of themselves who moves around within the onscreen world. Residents are able to explore the Second Life world, meet other residents, travel to destinations by flying, walking, or teleporting; participate in social activities and learning environments; create and trade goods and services; own and create property, and access media (Figure 1). With ever growing content, there is an immense amount of virtual economic commerce and artistic generation. (Dethridge, 2009; Robbins and Bell, 2008). Through Linden Scripting Language, residents can create objects and manipulate their functions. For instance, a resident could create or upload a piece of art. This art work may then be displayed as a three-dimensional object in the world or as a flat painting on a wall. The affordances of such art creation allow residents to create or display visual art work that other residents can interact with. The creativity and manifestation of the visual art is a function of the artist's ability to operate and configure the Linden Scripting Language (Malaby, 2009). Traditionally, users view the virtual environment through a laptop or desktop screen, but technology is allowing users to immerse themselves into gaming worlds with bigger screens, three-dimensional displays and Head Mounted Display units at lower costs than ever before. Whichever interface metaphor is used, the residents who interact with the art work will have varying experiences.

Figure 1. Views from Second Life (www.second life.com).

The conditions of the resident's experience depend on their history or previous experience within the environment. The intrinsic characteristic of "engagement" is a threshold for measuring user experience in terms of visualization, embedded cognition and human computer interaction through the medium of Second Life (Walsh, 2009).

INTERACTION METAPHORS

Since people have interacted with paintings for thousands of years, this theme provides an opportunity to explore how these components – visualization, embedded cognition and human-computer interaction- may work together. A consideration of these themes may be useful to augment user experience in virtual environments. This chapter will consider a number of questions including:

- Is immersion necessary for viewing paintings in a virtual environment?
- Is a well-designed user interface important for enjoying a painting?
- Does the graphical power of the visuals play a role in determining how a user perceives a painting?

As we enter an era where visual art can be routinely experienced through three-dimensional virtual environments, this new dimension allows people to perceive art in ways unprecedented in the past. When a user engages with artwork through portals such Second Life, does this effect how they interact with and conceptualize the work? This rather novel experience is a function of several human processes; human visual behavior, embodied cognition and human computer interaction. Each of these components will alter the users experience with varying degrees. Research is limited regarding how each experience will vary.

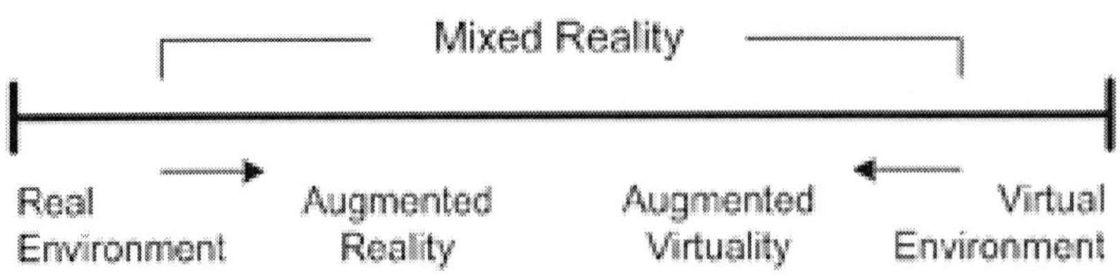

Figure 2. The Virtual Reality Continuum (Milgram and Kishino, 1994).

Therefore, analyzing the variables of each component may assist in our understanding of how a user defines their interaction and engagement. The Virtual Reality (VR) continuum (Figure 2) describes an object being viewed by defining the display mechanism being used to view the object (Milgram and Kishino, 1994).

- On the left side of the continuum, there are real environments, for instance, a real museum full of real paintings.
- Next is Augmented Reality (AR), which refers to physical spaces which are integrated with virtual technologies. For example, imagine walking through a museum using a video camcorder to record the experience. The viewer is looking at an actual painting, but through a video camera screen. Other extra (augmented, non-diegetic) visual information may be present on the screen display such as; time, display resolution, zoom depth, or framing alignment bars.
- Alongside augmented reality is Augmented Virtuality (AV) which refers to virtual spaces that are integrated within the physical world; for example, viewing a live podcast through Second Life.
- And finally, Virtual Environments (VEs) refer to entire simulated computer environments that stimulate the user through a combination of sensory information (such as most computer games.) Even this category may by further divided based on the display mechanisms used:
    - Virtual Environments (such as games played on a standard LCD screen or computer monitor) and
    - Immersive Environments that use more advanced interaction technologies, such as Head Mounted Displays (HMDs) or Cave Automated Virtual Environments (CAVEs).

Other taxonomies that are often used to categorize a virtual experience include :

- Sheridan (1992) measured "presence" using three factors: extent of sensory information, control of relation of sensors into the environment and ability to modify the physical environment. Difficulty of the task was also sometimes used to classify presence.
- Zeltzer (1992) classified graphic simulation systems by: components autonomy, interaction and presence. This scheme is widely used for classifying virtual environments.
- Naimark (1991) classified several ways in which a user can record and reproduce a visual experience. Such approaches are defined as: monoscopic imaging (two-dimensional), stereoscopic imaging (three-dimensional), multiscopic imagining (viewing multiple angles at once, i.e. turning your head to the left of the screen and viewing the right side of object), panoramic (wide angle view), surrogate travel (remotely controlling a robot to travel through an environment) and real time imaging (Magnetic Resonance Imaging or ultrasounds of a baby).
- Robinett (1992) classified different technological devices for simulation and interaction ranging from head mounted displays to microscopes and telephones. The taxonomy consists of classifying devices by nine components; "encompassing causality, model source, time, space, superposition, display type, sensor type, action measurement type and actuator type."

This chapter aims to describe experiments that examine and compare three attributes of human behavior when viewing virtual art gallery environments :

- Human Vision: Based on an understanding of how users visualize and conceive color and light.
- Embodied Cognition: Based on an objective definition of 'immersion' (diminished awareness of self) and measuring the effects of user 'presence' as they interact with the three-dimensional environment.
- Human Computer Interaction: Users of the virtual environment will examine art work in virtual galleries. Awareness and involvement should be suggested with avatar movement and time spent engaging with the art work.

The users will interact with the artworks across a range of displays, positioned at different points along the VR continuum including: Augmented Reality (PowerPoint) and Virtual Environments (Second Life on a screen) and Immersive Environments (Second life on a head mounted display).

ATTRIBUTE 1: VISUAL ANALYSIS

There exists a phenomenon in the field of human vision where observations can be perceived to be three-dimensional objects built up from the patterns of light that project onto the retina. Whereas objects in the real world, such as a painting, exist in a three-dimensional space and have atomic properties, the resulting optical image is encapsulated on an internal, personal, two-dimensional projection screen (Todd, 2004). Human vision is a function of an operation where we use our senses and brain to input and compile real world data in order to determine the nature of objects, including shape, material and roughness. Our perceptions will vary with experience and age. The physiological and cognitive processes that resolve our visual input also calculate the level of precision used to perceive a specific real world object. How the object appears to us is also directly influenced by the illumination and the shape of the object (Vangorp, 2009). While it is not possible to measure direct perceptual quantities, the perception of the properties can be observed and measured. It is important when quantifying an individual's experience of observing a visual artwork such as a painting, to note that color is not a construct of pure light frequencies. Color is a function from spectral reflectance that is constructed in the brain. Because of this complex processing, how a painting appears to us is a combination of the painting, the display mechanism and of our perception. Hence, the visual perception of a virtual artwork will ultimately be influenced by the display medium and the user's perception. This system of vision is also conditioned by the user's degree of engagement or immersion in the three-dimensional environment.

ATTRIBUTE 2: IMMERSION

Virtual Environments (in particular head mounted display technology) provide a unique opportunity for users to surround themselves visually with virtual space. This experience has driven many experts to attempt to define the phenomenon that Ivan Sutherland calls 'being there'. The common terms today are 'presence', which is an abbreviation of Telepresence suggested by Minksy (1980) and 'immersion', suggested by Murray (1997).

While there is a general consensus of the phenomena, there tends to be a variance in the actual definitions. Oliver Grau (2004) applied the term immersion to paintings, whereas with multimedia and digital media, immersion is often used to describe the overall interactive experience (Grau, 2004; Mäyrä et al, 2005; Schofield, 2011). There have been numerous and separate studies on immersion, presence, virtual environments and interface design. Many scholars continue to debate the definitions of presence and immersion (Slater, 1992; Manovich 2002), as well as their applications within virtual environments and conceptual interface designs.

Mel Slater (2003) suggests that presence is like form: *"the extent to which the unification of simulated sensory data and perceptual processing produces a 'coherent' place that you are 'in' and in which there may be the potential for you to act".*

For Slater, a high quality of immersion does not guarantee of a commensurate quality of content, *"a virtual environment system can be highly presence inducing and yet have a really uninteresting uninvolving content".*

Immersion in a three-dimensional environment may offer more possibilities for interaction. The user of a 3D graphic environment may effectively initiate tasks like differentiation, which require more data processing power than is available from a standard optical flow field (Schubert et al, 2008). Both presence (qualitative) and immersion (quantitative) drive the development of many three-dimensional online environments, such as virtual art galleries. Schubert et al stated in their 2008 paper that:

"When possibilities to act in a spatial environment are perceived or when dramatic events structure the interaction, presence emerges. Both spatial and dramatic conceptualization can be framed as meaning. Spatial and dramatic meaning determine how present we feel in a virtual environment".

Schubert's concept is useful when viewing online artwork. Space, presence and interaction of forms will determine the level of meaning in a virtual environment. The user's level of engagement or immersion may also depend on how interested they are in the content and objects within that virtual environment. (Calleja, 2011).

Embodied cognition describes how physical action is dependent on cognitive processing. For instance, vision requires bodily movement and the feedback from this movement is processed in the brain. The essential thesis of embodied cognition theory is that the mind is connected to the body and influences it directly just as the environment influences both mind and body. This process is embedded in our physiology and also helps explain how metaphors become meaningful.

Metaphors are useful devices in visual art to create meaningful subjects and express ideas. An individual may paint a bright morning sunrise and hang it in a place where they spend a lot of time in the mornings. The artist may do so to augment morning activity with a more positive emotion. This correlates with the idea of immersion, creating an environment that allows an individual the ability to facilitate or augment their own presence.

For any user to experience a visual artwork, they must observe it first hand with their own eyes. This conflation of art, environment and mind may be likened to a visual, symbolic discourse that enhances the planes of our physical reality. How we structure our interpretation of art, environment and interaction perhaps needs to be defined by the significant variables that are effecting the user's perception. By observing artwork in fixed virtual and real environments; it is possible to identify key elements which link immersion and presence to the larger concept of experience.

ATTRIBUTE 3: HUMAN-COMPUTER INTERACTION

In a three-dimensional environment, the entire world is essentially a visual metaphor created for the user to express an idea or emotion through affordances, visuals and sounds of the world. The degree of affordances in the 3D environment will affect the individual's sense of presence; his or her subjective sense of being in the virtual place (Schubert et al, 2008). Because immersion and presence are often viewed as functions of interaction, it is important to understand the modalities and interface types in which the artwork is being viewed and experienced.

Typically, Second Life is viewed from a user's account on a desktop computer monitor with a keyboard and mouse, or a laptop, which has the standard interface devices; screen, keyboard and mouse. The user creates an avatar which allows them to : *"experience vicarious vision, public visibility, physical motion and interactivity with other objects and entities in this world."* (Dethridge, 2011) Throughout the virtual world of Second Life, there are several ways to travel to destinations and interact with these objects. Avatars have the ability to walk, fly, teleport or use of vehicles such as; cars, bicycles, planes, boats, etc. The three-dimensional environment that the user controls is a function of the visual cues based on the avatar's onscreen proximity to objects. Essentially, the avatar is a pivot point for directing a virtual camera to interact with the three-dimensional world from a 1st (egocentric) or 3rd (exocentric) view (Byson, 1994).

This virtual camera perspective which allows the user to view of artworks within a three-dimensional environment is a: *"space where the real and virtual image merge; where time, 3D animation and the avatar's enhanced perspective"* interact onscreen to form images that the user may read as somehow real. (Dethridge, 2011). These forms of interaction may ultimately have an impact on the viewer and potentially have the ability to alter the user's conception of time, image and self.

EXPERIMENTAL DESIGN

To test these theories, this experiment will require a group of participants to directly view a work of art on computer screens. The same group will interact with virtual art galleries environments thus demonstrating a range of interaction across the spectrum of real and virtual environments and display conditions. After viewing the art work, the participants fill out surveys about their experiences and feelings regarding the artwork. Sessions will be video recording to the track time spent by the user viewing particular artworks and to monitor the movement of avatar in second life. The data collection is formatted to allow the analysis of three variables and how these affect the user experience : visual content, immersion and interaction.

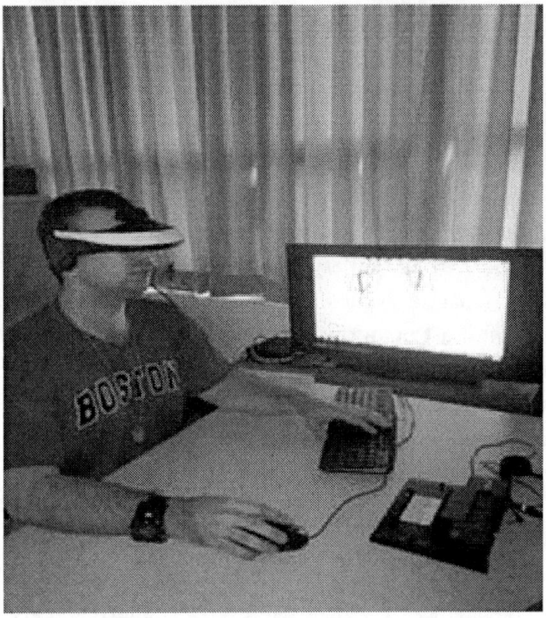

Figure 3. The Experimental Set-Up Showing the SONY HMZ T1 HMD.

Online virtual environments, such as the ones used in this experiment permit the scientific study of human behavioral responses in a controlled laboratory setting alongside ecologically valid contextual cues (Kim et al, 2012). The experiment is actually made up of two distinct components. The first part of the experiment required participants to view artworks on a computer monitor. The participants use the Second Life virtual environment to interact with four paintings. They then use a PowerPoint slide presentation to interact with 2D images of the same four paintings. The second part of the experiment collects data from users who viewed the same four paintings in Second Life wearing a SONY HMZ T1 head mounted display (www.sony.com).

As display screen technology continues to advance, Head Mounted Display (HMD) units are becoming more accessible in terms of cost as well as comfort and universal connectivity to home devices. They may be used concurrently with highly graphical user interfaces, such as computer games and virtual environments like Second Life.

There is a large amount of research on high-end uses of head mounted display technology. However very little work has been done at lower-cost end of the technology spectrum, examining everyday entertainment applications. A number of previous studies have tested HMD technology in relation to issues involving spatial navigation or visualization but studies involving the cognitive interpretation of real world objects (such as paintings) are very limited (Sharples et al, 2008).

By using HMDs in this experiment we ask whether participants become more immersed in the virtual gallery environment through the use of HMD technology. A number of researchers have noted that HMD technology has the potential create a different effect in relation to the emotional responses of the user (Kim et al, 2012). These effects are examined in this experiment which considers how the user interprets the virtual paintings from a visual standpoint, in addition to measuring how immersed they feel while interacting with the art gallery. The ultimate goal of this experiment is to generate data that may assist in developing guidelines to improve the display of artworks, such as paintings, in virtual galleries. The data collected may provide general assumptions of qualitative analysis for those designing interactive three-dimensional environments. Our results will be quantified for an objective understanding of how the properties of three-dimensional environments and objects may influence user experience. It is predicted that fluctuations of the user's sense of immersion and presence may be present and influenced by the changes in the dimensionality of the display technology. These changes may in turn influence the user's behaviour in relation to their engagement with the virtual gallery. The first part of the experiment used eight participants split into two separate groups. The participants observed four visual art pieces; two paintings and two digital art creations, on a laptop screen. One group viewed them on PowerPoint, controlling the slides at will. The other group viewed the artworks via an avatar in a virtual gallery in Second Life. These participants were gathered by means of social networking and academic announcements from the State University of New York, Oswego campus. The demographics of the sample were a predominantly male group between the ages of 18-35. The second part of the experiment gathered 21 participants; 14 male and 7 female. The experiment consisted of one group, each observing the same four visual art pieces; two paintings and two digital art creations. This time, participants interacted in the Second Life virtual space via the SONY HMZ T1 Head Mounted Display (Figure 3). The participants were again recruited by means of social networking and academic announcements from the SUNY Oswego campus. The age range of the participants was again between 18-35.

The experiments were carried out in a Human-computer interaction laboratory on the SUNY Oswego campus. Dell laptop computers based in the laboratory were used as the platform device which participants used to operate PowerPoint and Second Life. Default settings were used in Second Life to prevent color and contrast biases. Low external lighting helped with immersion and to eliminate unnecessary visual distractions. The second part of the experiment was held in the same location with the addition of a SONY HMZ T1 Head Mounted Display. Users were introduced to Second Life on the laptop screen, then shown how to properly attach and wear the HMD to complete the experiment.

Within each display modality, each participant viewed four pieces of artwork (Figure 4):

- Duke of Berry on a Journey by the Limbourg Brothers (1370-1416)
- Sunday Afternoon on the Island of Grand-Jatte by Georges Seurat (1884-1886)
- Digital Art rendition of Japanese game Okami (2006)
- Digital Art rendition of a Halo character from the Halo Wars game (2009).

One of the principle data collection instruments used in this study was questionnaires. Two different types of questionnaire were used in this experiment: a pre-test questionnaire, and a post-test questionnaire. The pre-test questionnaire is a survey given to each participant before they started the experiment and consisted of thirteen questions relating to demographic information. The pre-test questionnaire also gauges the user's level of experience of and usage of related technology, of gaming and their inherent familiarity with, and appreciation of art. The post-test questionnaire is a survey given to the participant after they had viewed the virtual artwork. It consisted of twenty six questions arranged in a specific manner to allow the collection of information relating to the user's visual analysis, embodied cognitive experience, and interaction experience.

Figure 4. The Four Artworks Used in the Experiment.

The questions are not categorized on the form and the participant wasn't aware of the motives behind the questions being asked. Each question belonged to a specific category. The categories were used for final analysis to compute differences between color, brightness, immersion, presence, engagement, and interactivity with the interface. Each question used a Likert scale for the response, with numerical values from 1 to 10. The experimental procedure involved each participant arriving at the laboratory individually. They were asked to have a seat and were briefly told about the nature of the study. The use of the three-dimensional environments and the visualization of paintings were explained. The users were then informed that they would be participating by either visualizing the paintings on a laptop screen or using a Head Mounted Display. Next, they were asked to sign an informed consent form. After doing so, the participants filled out the pre-test questionnaire to gather general demographic information. After completing the pre-test questionnaire each participant was given control of the laptop and allowed to begin. For the group viewing PowerPoint, the paintings were already visible on the screen. For the group using a Second Life environment, the onscreen avatar was positioned near the paintings so the participant could use the avatar to walk around and view the paintings with ease. The participants started the task until they were deemed to have finished, at their own discretion. The post-test questionnaire was given to all participants after they had finished viewing the virtual artworks. Finally, a short debriefing of the experiment was given to all participants and information sheets were given to each participant to explain about the purpose of the study and the hypothesis being investigated.

RESULTS

Initially, a number of paired T-Tests were conducted to compare the view of the art in PowerPoint on the laptop display screen with the screen view of the virtual art in Second Life. The T-Tests were based on the categorization of the survey results into visual, immersive and interactive facets of the experience.

Attribute 1: Visual

The first three questions on the post-test questionnaire asked participants how the how they perceived the color of the paintings on a scale from one to ten. Questions four through seven asked the participants how they perceived the brightness of the paintings. A paired T-Test was conducted to compare the overall visual quality of the screen view of the virtual art in Second Life with view of the art in PowerPoint on the laptop display screen (Figure 5).

Paired T-Test and CI: secondlife Visual, Powerpoint Visual

Paired T for secondlife Visual - Powerpoint Visual

	N	Mean	StDev	SE Mean
secondlife Visual	28	7.143	2.399	0.453
Powerpoint Visual	28	8.286	1.013	0.191
Difference	28	-1.143	2.031	0.384

95% CI for mean difference: (-1.931, -0.355)
T-Test of mean difference = 0 (vs not = 0): T-Value = -2.98 P-Value = 0.006

Figure 5. The Visual T-Test Results.

There was a significant difference in the scores for the visual component of the survey for the virtual environment (M=7.143, SD=2.399) and the PowerPoint experience (M=8.286, SD=1.013). There is enough evidence to suggest that when viewing the virtual artworks, the visual components related to the color and brightness of the artworks are affected by the display technology being used; this includes the medium of presentation. The implication is that the virtual environment of Second Life is interpreted by the viewer as a different mode of display to that used by a PowerPoint presentation.

The user's perception of the spectrum of colors and brightness is significantly altered with the change of medium. This can be explained using the theory of simultaneous contrast, which describes how the brain will perceive two identical colors differently when superimposed with a different contrasting background. This may explain why, for the viewer, the visual component in Second Life (which provides a juxtaposition of the artwork and virtual environment) differs from the full screen PowerPoint presentation of the artwork.

Attribute 2: Immersion

Questions 11-21 on the post-test questionnaire asked participants about their ability to predict actions in the environment and about their awareness of surrounding events. A paired T-Test was conducted to compare the overall immersive nature of the screen view of the virtual art in Second Life with view of the art in PowerPoint on the laptop display screen (Figure 6). There was no significant difference in the scores for the immersive component of the survey for the virtual environment (M=6.727, SD=2.697) and the PowerPoint experience (M=6.75, SD=3.279). There is not enough evidence to suggest any difference in the means. Hence, we can infer that the cognitive and immersive characteristics of viewing the paintings in a virtual art gallery remain similar as viewing the paintings full-screen on the laptop.

Attribute 3: Interaction

Questions 8-10 and 22-26 asked participants how they felt about their engagement and interaction with virtual environment and the PowerPoint experience of viewing the paintings.

Paired T-Test and CI: Second Life Cognitive, PowerPoint Cognitive

Paired T for Second Life Cognitive - PowerPoint Cognitive

	N	Mean	StDev	SE Mean
Second Life Cognitive	44	6.727	2.679	0.404
PowerPoint Cognitive	44	6.750	3.279	0.494
Difference	44	-0.023	4.321	0.651

95% CI for mean difference: (-1.337, 1.291)
T-Test of mean difference = 0 (vs not = 0): T-Value = -0.03 P-Value = 0.972

Figure 6. The Immersive T-Test Results.

Paired T-Test and CI: secondlife interactive, Powerpoint Interactive

Paired T for secondlife interactive - Powerpoint Interactive

	N	Mean	StDev	SE Mean
secondlife interactive	32	6.313	2.901	0.513
Powerpoint Interactive	32	7.688	2.620	0.463
Difference	32	-1.375	3.731	0.660

95% CI for mean difference: (-2.720, -0.030)
T-Test of mean difference = 0 (vs not = 0): T-Value = -2.08 P-Value = 0.045

Figure 7. The Interaction T-Test Results.

A paired T Test was conducted to compare the overall quality of the interaction experience of the screen view of the virtual art in Second Life with view of the art in PowerPoint on the laptop display screen (Figure 7).

There was a significant difference in the scores for the interactive component of the survey for the virtual environment (M=6.313, SD=2.901) and the PowerPoint experience (M=7.688, SD=2.62). The way the questions were formulated, the more difficult the interaction was, the lower the participant would rate the score. If interaction interfered with the viewing of the art, then participants would give a low rating. There is enough evidence to suggest that there is a difference in the mean scores of the interaction, with the PowerPoint experience being rated as easier to use. The easier the experience of interaction is for the user, the more analogous that experience will be to real life, and thus perhaps seem more natural to the user.

This will potentially have an effect on the user's perception of the painting in terms of immersion. Referring to Milgram and Kishino's taxonomy (1994), we may hypothesize that a painting would be perceived differently, and the user would experience varying degrees of immersion, if they were to experience the art at different points along the virtuality continuum. If the interaction with an interface becomes too complex, then the experience feels disjointed, breaking the feeling of immersion, and thus, attempting to enjoy the artwork becomes difficult and counterproductive.

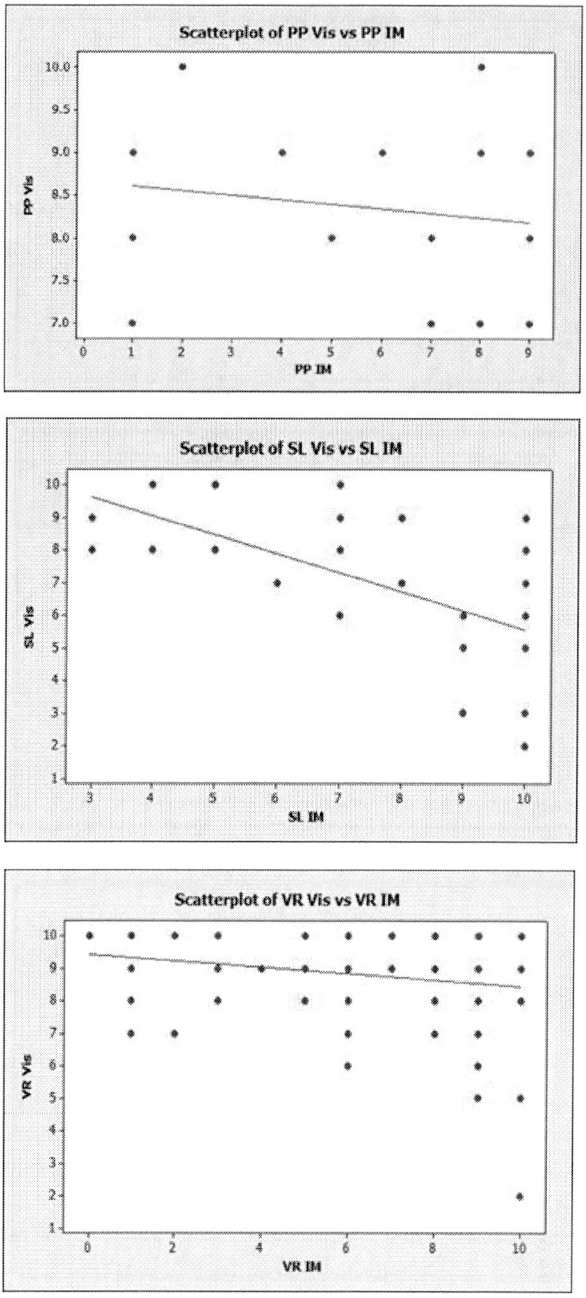

Figure 8. A Comparison of the Visual and Immersive Aspects of a Range of Displays.

Comparing Attributes 1 and 2: Visual and Immersion

For this section of the analysis, the post-test questionnaire results for both the visual attribute and the immersive attribute were collected for the PowerPoint screen experience

(PP), the Second Life screen experience (SL) and the Second Life HMD experience (VR). These attributes were plotted as a series of scatter plots demonstrating the relationship between the visual aspects of the experience and the immersive nature of the experience while using each of these different display mechanisms (Figure 8).

All three experiments revealed a negative slope when plotting visual aspects against the immersive aspects of the experience. It appears that as the levels of immersion increased, the perceived visual brightness and lightness would decrease. The PowerPoint slope is less negative, the visual rating never dropped below a rating of 7. The PowerPoint experience indicates a wide range of immersion ratings from 1-9. The Second Life chart displays a more negative slope. The visuals begin to decrease at a greater rate as the user perception of immersion increases. We know that the user understands that they are manipulating an avatar representation through a virtual environment, and their perception of the visual quality is being diminished. This implies that the increasing immersion experienced by the user in the virtual environment leads to a perception of decreased color and brightness quality, or acute visuals. Hence the virtual environment artwork is perceived to not be as realistic as a digital representation of a painting on a PowerPoint slide, even though the actual digital artifacts are identical in both environments.

The quality of visuals shows a significant drop when compared to the high ratings recorded for the PowerPoint experience. The Second Life chart clearly demonstrates an increased density of plot points on the scatterplot in the lower right region, where users recorded lower visual ratings in the more immersive environment in response to the relevant survey questions. The HMD chart displays a dense data area for high visuals, similar to the PowerPoint rating with a few additional outliers. However, once again as immersion increased, the perception of visual quality begins to decrease - a similar trend is seen in the data shown in the Second Life chart. The HMD displays the visuals at a greater quality than the Second Life screen option. As immersion increases within the HMD environment, the interpolated slope is negative. Hence, the visual quality (in terms of level of light and visual brightness) associated with the artwork as perceived by the user, appears to reduce at higher levels of user immersion.

Comparing Attributes 1 and 3: Visual and Interaction

For this section of the analysis, the post-test questionnaire results for both the visual attribute and the interactive attribute were collected for the PowerPoint screen experience (PP), the Second Life screen experience (SL) and the Second Life HMD experience (VR).

These attributes were plotted as a series of scatter plots demonstrating the relationship between the visual aspects of the experience and the interactive nature of the experience while using each of these different display mechanisms (Figure 9).

PowerPoint was the only experiment to display a negative slope for visuals and interaction. As ease of interaction and general feel of control increased, the user's perceived visual quality decreased.

It was noted during the experiment that some users did not like the control mechanism to view the slides in PowerPoint, while others seemed to feel accustomed to it and generally comfortable. Again, the visual quality never drops below 7 during the PowerPoint experience.

In the Second Life chart, the slope is almost flat, with a slight increase. As the interaction rating increased, the visual quality rating slightly increased. The highest clusters of interaction ratings were midrange, around 5. These clusters contributed to the balancing of the slope, to make it almost horizontal.

The HMD chart displays a slightly positive slope this time with the visual rating increasing as ease of interaction increases. Although the Second Life and HMD experiments utilize the same virtual interface in Second Life, the higher clusters in the 6-10 range of interaction on the HMD chart are not present on the Second Life screen chart.

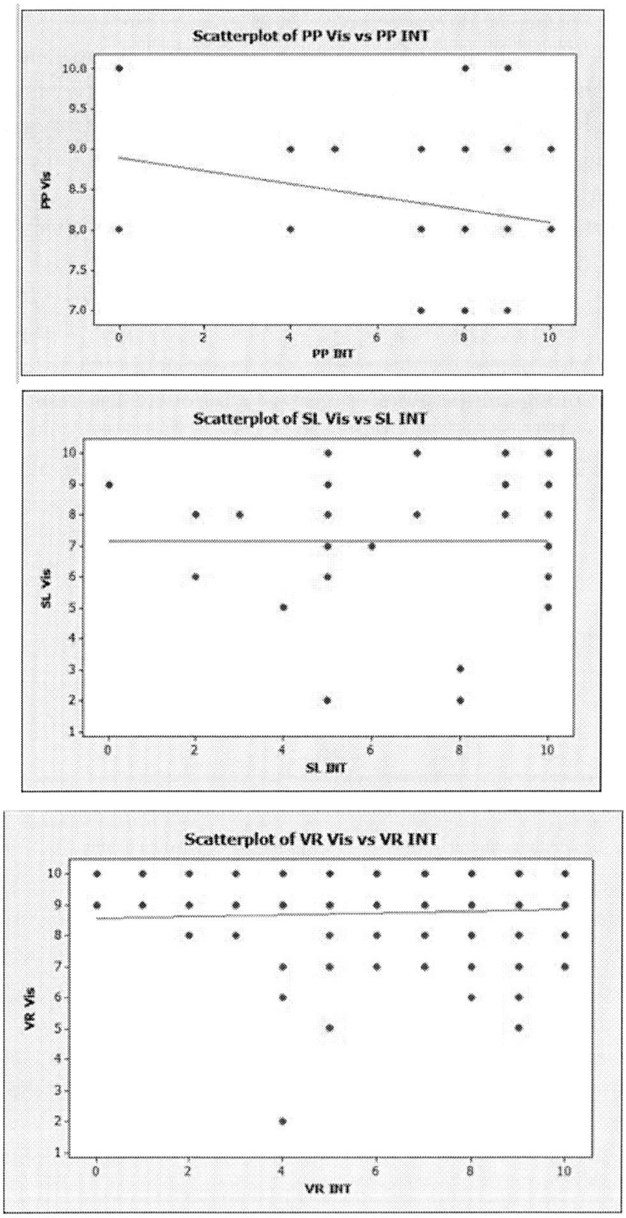

Figure 9. A Comparison of the Visual and Interactive Aspects of a Range of Displays.

Comparing Attributes 2 and 3: Immersion and Interaction

For this section of the analysis, the post-test questionnaire results for both the immersion attribute and the interactive attribute were collected for the PowerPoint screen experience (PP), the Second Life screen experience (SL) and the Second Life HMD experience (VR). These attributes were plotted as a series of scatter plots demonstrating the relationship between the immersive aspects of the experience and the interactive nature of the experience while using each of these different display mechanisms (Figure 10). The PowerPoint chart displays a relatively flat slope when interaction rating is plotted against user perceived immersion. This interpolated trend indicates that there isn't a substantial positive or negative correlation between these two components. This implies that users did not experience a change in how easy they felt the system was to use, as their perceived level of immersion varied. Interaction for the PowerPoint chart ranges from 0-10 and immersion ranges from 1-9. The fluctuations never lead to an increase or decrease; hence the results appear arbitrary when compared. The Second Life chart displays a slight positive slope between interaction rating and user immersion. The interaction rating for the Second Life screen experiment ranges from 0-10 and immersion ranges from 3-10. As immersion increases, the ease of interaction appears to increase.

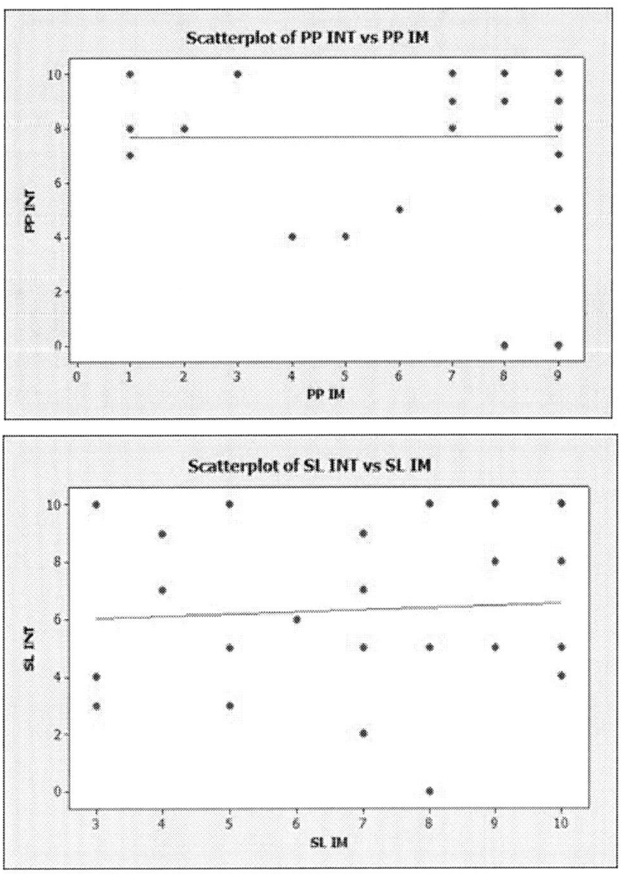

Figure 10. (Continued).

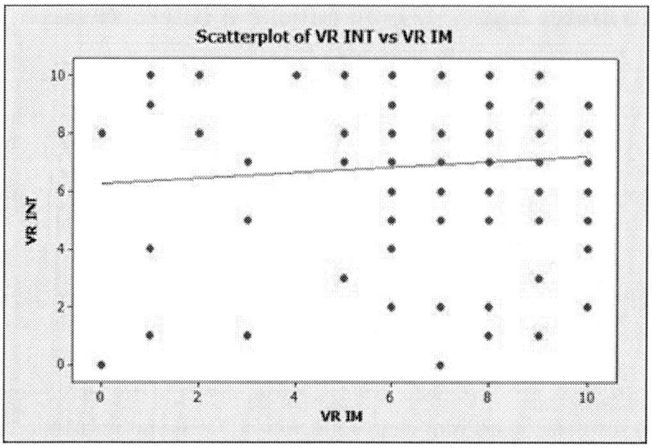

Figure 10. A Comparison of the Immersive and Interactive Aspects of a Range of Displays.

The HMD chart displays the most positive slope of the set for a plot of interaction rating against user immersion. This seems to suggest that the more immersive the experience, the easier the interaction and the easier the interaction, the more immersive the experience. The clusters are most dense in the ranges of 6-10, showing an overall ease of use with a high level of immersion when a HMD is used.

DISCUSSION

The experiment collected data comparing the screen view of the virtual art in Second Life with views of the art in PowerPoint on the laptop display screen. The survey results were categorized based on the visual quality of the experience as rated by the user, the immersive (cognitive) nature of the experience and the ease of interaction (Figure 11).

The first attribute to be considered was the optical quality. The first test compared art displayed with a surrounding virtual environment to art viewed directly on a computer screen. Results showed that the human eye will potentially perceive color and brightness differently when art in both cases. The lower score for the participant's viewing of the artworks in the virtual environment could suggest two things;

The size of the screen affected the viewer's perception. Although the size of the screen could be adjusted, the size of the typical computer monitor screen is typically between 13 and 20 inches. The images displayed using PowerPoint utilized all of the screen real estate whereas the Second Life environment itself utilized the entire screen real estate, with the painting displayed as an object within the environment being viewed on screen. Essentially, visiting the Second Life virtual gallery meant that the user was always viewing a smaller version of the artwork on the screen. The user does however have the ability, within the Second Life environment, to walk their avatar to an ideal position right in front of the painting and switch to a first person (egocentric) view and achieve a similar full screen view of the painting – but, even so, this requires expert navigation and often the view is still slightly angled or bordered when compared to the full screen PowerPoint images.

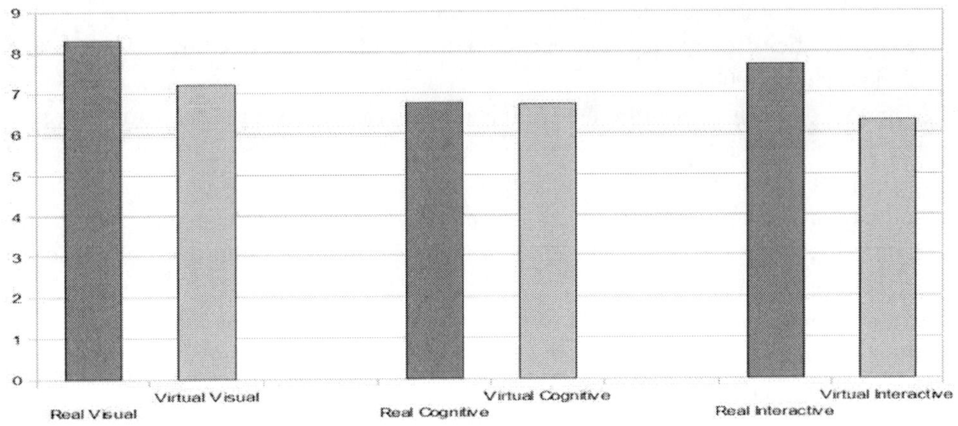

Figure 11. A Comparison of Mean Ratings for the Attributes Examined (Direct View vs Virtual Environment).

The HMD allows the user to view the interface on a perceived 70 inch TV, this potentially alleviates the reduction in artwork size experienced by users within the virtual environment.

The virtual environment created a poor color contrast. Poor color contrast could be a result of a simultaneous contrast of colors in the artwork interacting with adjacent colors in the three-dimensional environment. When using the PowerPoint screen to view artwork, there are no other interactions of color or brightness other than those within the frame of the laptop screen itself. One could see this simultaneous color contrast as unavoidable in virtual environments used for this purpose. The effect could be avoided within a Second Life virtual art gallery if there was an option to select a painting and have it appear on screen in full, but then then the user would potentially lose some of the immersive aspects that are enhanced within the virtual environment.

The second attribute to be considered was the immersive nature of the experience for the user. There appears to be no difference in the rated cognitive/immersive component when viewing art from a virtual screen in Second Life or via PowerPoint on the laptop screen.

Presence and immersion were not affected by either display type. The only significant variable worth noting that was different was the time the users spent looking at the paintings. Users spent significantly longer time in the virtual environment than they did looking at the paintings directly on screen. Time may be considered as a variable of engagement, but this discrepancy could also be a factor of the difficulty of navigating around the virtual environment compared to viewing the paintings directly on the screen.

Both the Second Life and PowerPoint viewing options provided the same level of presence and immersion in the controlled environment. This lack of difference between the measures could be interpreted as illustrating how the virtual art gallery environment may provide a realistic environment for the user to view the paintings. The similar means may also suggest that there was no significant metaphor for visual augmentation and that the natural mappings perceived by the users were similar when using both display mechanisms. Experimental results from human factors, perceptual studies, and cognitive science can help explain this effect. As the fidelity of digital images improves, enabled by technology, research has shown the user's ability to interpret and comprehend visual rhetoric increases. Users become able to see 'through' the interface, and their interactions become natural and more accurate as restrictions (due to previous technological limitations) are removed (Azuma et al, 2001; Davidson et al, 2003)

Perhaps Second Life is seen by the participants as a lower resolution environment when compared to other virtual worlds such as computer games. Or perhaps it seen as adequate quality, providing an experience that is analogous to viewing art directly on the laptop screen. A larger study involving more participants, examining the individual components that make up the immersion rating may allow a better understanding of this attribute and its effect on the user experience.

The third attribute to be considered was the ease of interaction experienced by the users. Controlling and navigating an avatar around in a virtual environment with a mouse and keyboard has more functionality issues than viewing consecutive slides on PowerPoint. Some of the participants in the study who used Second Life to view the art work were able to easily move around the environment. However compared to users who were using the PowerPoint slides, the Second Life viewers were less able to manipulate the view they wanted in order to enjoy the art work

The lower scores could mean that users were not as comfortable in the virtual art gallery or perhaps had difficulty controlling the movements and interactions. The pre-test questionnaire indicated that many of them were already familiar with computer software and virtual environments, and knew how to use both Second Life and PowerPoint. Hence, one would not have expected to see an issue with the control and navigation mechanisms in the virtual environment.

The rating for interactivity may tie into the ratings for attribute 1 (visual analysis). The actual view of the actual paintings in the virtual art gallery (the angles and sizes) is where the difference in the means may be significant. When analyzing the users in the gallery, it can be seen that some participants had difficulty viewing the paintings the way they wanted to, even though they had control over what angle they wanted to see it in contrast to the fixed position of the PowerPoint experience.

The results of tests comparing Second Life to PowerPoint indicate several things. Generally, as perceived visual quality increases, immersion decreases. The more immersed a user is in the virtual environment, the less visually acute the paintings were perceived to be. Milgrim and Kishino (1994) discuss this idea where they explain that: *"A person who is using a virtual environment knows they are in a virtual environment."*

This concept may explain the difference with the participant's perception of the visuals in the virtual environment compared to those viewed directly on screen. The paintings viewed directly on the PowerPoint screen had a less negatively correlated slope than the paintings viewed in Second Life. Perhaps since PowerPoint is less immersive, the visuals were perceived to be of higher quality and as the users interacted with Second Life, they felt less immersed in the gallery environment when interacting with the paintings that were perceived to be of lower quality.

The data showed that as immersion decreased the perceived visual quality increased, also the ease of interaction increased with increased visual quality. With the PowerPoint experience on a laptop screen, the interaction was low and a visual quality increase was noticed, while immersion decreased. In Second Life, the interaction appeared to be more engaging. As visual quality increased, the ease of interaction also increased. And finally as ease of interaction increased, immersion also increased. Increased visual quality only had a positive effect on immersion when ease of interaction was introduced as a factor.

These trends become particularly evident when comparing the Second Life user experience on the laptop screen to the Second Life user experience with the Head Mounted Display. The virtual interface and the artworks being viewed are the same. However users with the HMD noted an increased visual quality. There was also an increased slope indicating increased ease of interaction; a more positive slope for ease of interaction against level of immersion and a less negative slope for visual quality against level of immersion. It can be seen that an increase in visual quality allow for a greater ease of interaction, which in turn increases the level of immersion for the participant.

CONCLUSION

This study has shown that different modes of display offer very different user experiences. A user viewing that artwork viewing artwork in a virtual environment such as Second Life must navigate around the virtual gallery as well use more complex tools controlled by a keyboard and mouse to interact with objects in the environment. This additional layer of interaction creates a new experience in itself. The users in the experiments who viewed the artwork directly on a screen using PowerPoint had the easiest interaction metaphor. The paintings sat on the screen in front of them and they only had to use the left or right arrow keys to move between them. Thus, a user wishing to view art in a virtual environment may have a more complex experience than a user browsing online images in an art catalog. This study also showed that the cognitive elements of presence and immersion remain approximately the same for both experiences.

While there are many ways to increase immersion and presence felt by a user within a virtual environment, it should be remembered that for the user (Dethridge, 2011): *"Virtual experience is the sum of their experience and is not enhanced or augmented by an ability to compare the virtual with the real"*.

REFERENCES

Azuma, R., Baillot, Y., Behringer, R., Feiner, S., Julier, S. and MacIntyre, B. (2001). Recent Advances in Augmented Reality. *IEEE Computer Graphics and Applications,* 21(6): 35-47.

Bryson, S. (1994). Approaches to the Successful Design and Implementation of VR Applications. In Proceedings of SIGGRAPH Conference (Volume 94). Orlando, FL.

Calleja, G. (2011). In-Game: From Immersion to Incorporation. Cambridge, MA: The MIT Press.

Clark, K. (1981). Moments of Vision and Other Essays. New York: Harper and Row.

Davidson, A. J., Mayol, W. W. and Murray, D. W. (2003). Real-Time Localisation and Mapping with Wearable Active Vision. In Proceedings of the Second IEEE and ACM International Symposium on Mixed and Augmented Reality, 2003, Tokyo, Japan.

Dethridge, L. (2009). The Magic Realism of a Virtual Second Life, in Literature and Aesthetics, Sydney Society of Literature and Aesthetics, Sydney Uni., Sydney, Australia. 19(2): 262-278.

Dethridge, L. (2011). Art and the Avatar in Virtual and Mixed-reality Exhibition Space, in H. Yang, and S. Yuen, (Eds), The Handbook of Research on Practices and Outcomes in Virtual Worlds and Environments (Volume 1), Hershey: IGI Global.

Douma, M. (2006). Simultaneous Contrast, Color Vision and Art. WebExhibits, Institute for Dynamic Educational Advancement. Retrieved November 16, 2011 from http://www.webexhibits.org/colorart/contrast.html.

Grau, O. (2004). Virtual Art: from Illusion to Immersion. Cambridge, MA: The MIT Press.

Halo Wars [Computer software]. (2009). USA: Microsoft Game Studios.

Kim, K., Rosenthal, M. Z., Zielinski, D. and Brady, R. (2012). Comparison of Desktop, Head Mounted Display, and Six Wall Fully Immersive Systems Using a Stressful Task. Virtual Reality Workshops. London: IEEE.

Kuspit, D. (2005). The Matrix of Sensations. ArtNet. Retrieved November 16, 2011 from http://www.artnet.com/magazineus/features/kuspit/kuspit8-5-05.asp.

Malaby, T. M. (2009). Making Virtual Worlds: Linden Lab and Second Life. Ithaca, NY: Cornell University Press.

Manovich, L. (2002). The Language of New Media. Cambridge, MA: The MIT Press.

Mäyrä, F. and Ermi, L. (2005). Fundamental Components of the Gameplay Experience: Analysing Immersion. In Proceedings of DiGRA 2005 Conference: Changing Views–Worlds in Play. Vancouver, Canada.

Milgram, P. and Kishino, F. (1994). A Taxonomy of Mixed Reality Visual Displays. Transactions on Information Systems, E77-D(12).

Minsky, M. (1980). Telepresence. Omni. June 1980: 45-51.

Murray, J. (1997). Hamlet on the Holodeck: the Future of Narrative in Cyberspace. Cambridge: MIT Press.

Naimark, M. (1991). Elements of RealSpace Imaging: A Proposed Taxonomy. Proceedings of SPIE, Stereoscopic Displays and Applications II. 1457.

Okami [Computer software]. (2006). Japan: Capcom.

Popper, F. (2007). From Technological to Virtual Art. Cambridge, MA: The MIT Press.

Robbins, S. and Bell, M. (2008). Second Life for Dummies. Hoboken, NJ: Wiley Publishing, Inc.

Robinett, W. (1992). Synthetic Experience: *A Proposed Taxonomy. Presence,* 1(2), 229-247.

Schofield, D. (2011). Playing with Evidence: Using Video Games in the Courtroom, Journal of Entertainment Computing, (Special Issue: Video Games as Research Instruments), 2(1), 47-58.

Schubert, T., Friedmann, F. and Regenbrecht, H. (2008). Embodied Presence in Virtual Environments. In R. Paton and I. Neilson (Eds). Visual Representations and Interpretations. New York: Springer-Verlag.

Sharples, S., Cobb, S., Moody, A. and Wilson, J. R. (2008). Virtual Reality Induced Symptoms and Effects: Comparison of Head Mounter Displays (HMDs), Desktop and Projection Display Systems. *Displays,* 29(2): 58-69.

Sheridan, T.B. (1992). Musings on Telepresence and Virtual Presence. *Presence,* 1(1), 120-125.

Slater, M., Usoh, M. and Steed, A. (1994). Depth of Presence in Virtual Environments. Presence: *Teleoperators andVirtual Environment*, 3, 130-144.

Slater, M. (2003). A Note on Presence Terminology. Presence Connect. 3(3).

Todd, J. T. (2004). The Visual Perception of 3D Shape. Trends in Cognitive Science. 8(3).

Vangorp, P. (2009). Human Visual Perception of Materials in Realistic Computer Graphics. Doctoral Dissertation, Arenberg Doctoral School of Science, Engineering and Technology.

Walsh, K. (2009). Using Second Life for Educational applications. Emerging EdTech. Retrieved November 16, 2011 from http://www.emergingedtech.com/2009/06/using-second-life-for-educational-applications/.

Zeltzer, D. (1992). Autonomy, Interaction, and Presence. *Presence,* 1(1). 127-132.

In: Virtual Environments
Editors: Stephanie Trautman and Franchesca Julien
ISBN: 978-1-62618-090-1
© 2013 Nova Science Publishers, Inc.

Chapter 5

A Framework of Collaborative Virtual Environments for Design Research

***Figen Leman Gul*[1]*, Xiangyu Wang*[2] *and Mi Jeong Kim*[3]**
[1]TOBB University of Economy and Technology,
Ankara, Turkey
[2]Curtin University, Australia
[3]Kyung Hee University, Seoul, Republic of Korea

Abstract

Recent advances in Collaborative Virtual Environments (CVEs) have attracted noted research efforts in using it for assisting design and facilitating design collaboration.

This paper proposes a CVEs framework for design research that focuses on practicability of each variable for providing design assistances in specific projects. Although previous work in CVE in design has properly addressed the variables in an isolated manner, comprehensive issues in terms of CVE effectiveness in design assistance need to be further developed. The comprehensive CVE framework consists of three dimensions and thirteen categories, which further address the variables for theory and implementation. The paper further critically reviews each of the variables in its implication of design assistance based on the findings from representative literature. This framework provides a basis for evaluating potential and important research areas and identifying driving factors for future CVE research in design assistance.

Keywords: CVE, design assistance, design collaboration, analytic framework

1. Introduction

Using Collaborative Virtual Environments (CVEs) to assist design and design collaboration has been of great popularity in order to support the creativity and effectiveness of design in a geographical distributed multi-user scenario. Clearly, research with CVEs concentrated mostly in social life, training/education, entertainment, etc. This paper intends to expand the knowledge gained in those areas and adapts it to the needs and special requirements of design assistance and design collaboration. The work establishes a new taxonomy for the variables that can be investigated in CVEs adoption in design assistance. The taxonomy provides the scientific bases for the future adoption of CVEs to a large class of designers, at the same time, drastically improve design quality. However, the general concept and associated enabling technologies in CVE is broad (see Jabi, 2004, for an extensive review of the field). Formulating a comprehensive framework of CVEs in the context ground of design assistance, therefore, would effectively facilitate the strategic utilization and adoption of CVEs for design assistance.

The developed framework is a systematic set of relationship and its purpose is to categorize the existing research streams, guide research efforts, and review the critical issues. There are many concepts that either under the broad concept of CVE or overlap with it. There have been limited efforts in systematically defining or positioning these concepts in CVE as a framework for theory and implementation. This framework provides a basis for evaluating potential and important research areas and identifying driving factors for future CVE research in design assistance.

2. Research Methodology

Recently, there is a large quantity of work in CVE for design. It is necessary to have a comprehensive and thorough review of the recent significant work in this area. The main objectives of this review are:

- To provide a framework for the integration and classification of the state-of-the-art work in CVE in design and design assistance;
- To reveal the research concentration and paucity;
- To summarize the issues and challenges, and suggest how they can be pursued; and
- To forecast future research and development trends

The Selection Criteria

Each paper is reviewed by the authors to determine its eligibility and level of relevance based on the following criteria:

- Only articles published from 2000 to 2012 are considered to assure the recent work, except papers concentrated on theory from earlier date are included.
- The selected paper must be CVE for design. Those articles that concentrated solely on technical aspect of CVE or CVE in other areas rather than their applications in design were not included.
- Considering CVE for design is an emerging area and there are not significant body of journal articles, wc also looked into the leading design research conferences.

Data Sources

In order to not miss the relevant articles, we have also searched the following six online databases in additional to the leading computer-aided (architectural) design conferences and journals. The number of articles by each online database is as follows: Science Direct, IEEE Xplore, Springer Link Online Libraries, ACM Digital Library, Wiley InterScience, Ingenta Journals, and EBSCO (Electronic Journal Service). Journals that are more computer science focused, narrow in focus to a specific niche, were excluded from the list.

Research reviews of a specific paradigm are an established form of enquiry within the information systems discipline. The identification of articles within the journal and conference list involved keyword searches and an exhaustive search on the title of the journals and conferences. The search was initialized using the keywords "CVE", "digital design", "collaborative design support", "distant collaborative design", and "shared design representation". Articles that appeared to fit into the category were verified by firstly reading the abstract and then the entire article to extract the main findings and emphasis of the article. Many articles that are initially identified via the title or keywords might be discarded in this process if either the abstract or the article itself did not primarily focus on CVE in design. For example, although having the keyword "virtual", or "collaborative", papers in pure CVE area are not eligible because they have no design context.

3. CVE Framework and Taxonomy for Design Assistance

A CVE framework should be comprehensive enough to address all relevant concepts, methods, models, techniques, technologies and issues. In the context of design assistance, the CVE framework focuses on practical implementation with 13 major variables classified into three dimensions in a hierarchical structure. The three dimensions include 'CVE technology', 'CVE perspective', and 'design task requirements' as depicted in Figure 1. Among the three dimensions, 'CVE technology' is then further divided into nine categories; 'modelling (M)', 'relation (R)', 'functionality (F)", "service (S)" "implementation (I)" , "usability (U)", "communication assistance (C)", "spatial computing for design (SC)", and "evaluation (E)".

For the convenience of discussion and identification, we have a simple coding method to name each dimension, category and variable. For example, "geometric" (M1.1) is a constituent under the variable of "parametric" (M1), which belongs to the category "modeling" (M). "Modeling" is a sub-category of "CVE technology". Therefore, this taxonomy effectively incorporates CVE technologies in terms of modelling, relation, functionality, service, implementation, usability, communication assistance, spatial computing for design evaluation across work task, collaboration and transition tasks throughout individual, project, organization, and industry perspectives.

It should be noted that the variables in this framework are fully independent and will be critically reviewed, analyzed and discussed in the subsections. Each of the category and variables in the taxonomy of Table 1 will be explained in details, be critically reviewed based on the recent literature and their implications in design assistance will be presented into subsections. The state-of-the-art methods, issues, challenges, limitations, and future trend of the work in each variable will be presented in the paper.

Table 1. Framework of CVE for design research

Dimension	Category	Variable	Constituents	Ref.
CVE Technology	M. Modelling	M1. Parametric	M1.1. Geometric	Wang 2003 Jason 2001
			M1.2. Non-geometric	Jason 2010
		M2. Level	M2.1. Data	
			M2.2. Information	
			M2.3. Knowledge	
	R. Relationship	R.1 Composition	R.1.1. Link	
			R.1.2. Group	
			R.1.3. Layer	
		R.2 Ontology	R.2.1. Reasoning	
			R.2.2. Hierarchy	
			R.2.3. Object	
	F. Functionality	F.1. Individual		
		F.2. Collaborative	F.2.1. Social interaction	
Assessment of CVEs	U. Usability	U.1. Presence / telepresence	Vividness and interactivity	Kalawsky 1993 Steuer 1992
		U.4. Awareness	Peripheral awareness	Gül and Maher 2009
	C. Communication Assistance	C.1.Communication Channels	C.1.1.Public-Private C.1.2. Text-video C.1.3.Com. Modes	Milne 2005 Herbsleb 2000 Gabriel 2000
	SC. Spatial computing for design	SC.1. Supporting external representation		Arias et al 2000 Robertson 1996
		SC.2. Supporting visuo-spatial properties		Tversky 2005 Gül 2007
		SC.3. Shared visual space		Gül 2007 Kvan 1997 Engestrom 1992
	E. Evaluation	E.1. Affordance	E.1.1. Usability	
			E.1.2. Collaboration and embodiment	
			E.1.3. Cultural affordance	
		E.2. Communication/Collaboration	E.2.1. Protocol analysis	

Dimension	Category	Variable	Constituents	Ref.
		E.2.2. Presence		
Design Task Requirements	W. Work task	W.1. Fit for purpose	W.1.1. Planning task	
			W.1.2. Creativity and Brainstorming	
			W.1.3. Intellective tasks	
			W.1.4. Decision making task	
			W.1.5. Cognitive conflict tasks	
			W1.6. Competitive performance task	
			W1.7. Information Dissemination tasks	
	C. Collaboration	C.1. Social protocol		
		C.2. Group characteristics		

4. The Usefulness and Implication of the Framework

Predominant previous research efforts in CVE have largely focused on issues of technology itself. The framework could allow us to consider systematically, in very technical details, what applicable CVE techniques and technologies are and what aspects should be evaluated. In order to achieve effective CVE implementation, a comprehensive framework can facilitate the identification of promising areas and influencing driving variables. The CVE framework developed in this paper supplements practical issues for real-world implementation across different levels of perspective.

The relative research frequency of each category or variables in the literature of CVE for design assistance will be calculated based on the recent relevant literature. The research areas which current CVE research has concentrated on will be identified and sorted out. Those areas, which are still in a developing stage towards a higher maturity, will be identified and analyzed as well. Those areas of great potential will be identified and expected to be increasingly developed for practical applications.

Assessment of CVEs

Assessment of CVEs is directly related to HCI and usability standards which are reviewed by (Bevan 2001, Preece 1993). Many technical reports have published suggesting metrics for effectiveness, productivity, satisfaction and safety as vital components of product quality (see Bevan 2001 for a detailed review of the standards). However, the assessments of CVEs in design activity require several components which have direct relevance to design activity, such as affordability of design assisting tools, design context and phase, and communication assisting tools etc. Therefore, we summarized the main areas in the assessment of CVEs in design domain as follows: usability, communication and spatial computing for design.

Usability: Designing is already a complex task, when it includes employing digital tools and collaboration with other parties in a remote location, it becomes even more complicated. In terms of evaluating a collaborative system, several usability tests such as performance testing, participatory evaluation and satisfaction questionnaire have been conducted. Usability has many definitions as described in (Bevan, 2001) but in this chapter, one of the international definitions of usability is employed: "the extent to which a product can be used by specified users to achieve specified goals with effectiveness, efficiency and satisfaction in a specified context of use" (ISO 9241-11). In the context of CVE in design domain, the specified users are 'designers', and the specified goals include collaboration and design work. In a collaborative design activity, monitoring actions and locations of each other, inspecting the design artifact and creating a shared understanding of the design task are vital. In the development of the CVE in design domain should afford sense of being there and peripheral awareness, as summarized in the following section:

Measuring Presence

Presence, is defined as "a psychological state or subjective perception in which even though part or all an individual's current experience is generate by and /or filtered through human-made technology, part or all of the individual's perception fails to accurately acknowledge the role of the technology in the experience" (International Society for Presence Research 2000). Social presence refers to the feeling of being together with a virtual or remotely located communication partner (Riva et al. 2003). Providing sense of presence is considered important in VE applications. In VEs the concept of presence which is extremely subjective and behavioral (Steuer, 1992) has a ubiquitous component of 'the sense of being in a place'. Clearly, the sense of 'being there' in computer-mediated platforms is associated with varies of factors that are perception, content, cognitive processes and affordability. Witmer and Singer (1998) state that presence is brought about by focusing the attention on a 'meaningful coherent set of stimuli'. Researchers point out one of the challenging problems today is the achievement of a sense of presence in virtual environments which might replicated, replace, or enhance the human sense of 'being there'(Oxman, Palmon et al. 2004).

Focus of presence research diversifies into the concerns of various kinds of visual displays, human interaction technologies, and psychological factors to determine the sense of presence (Davies, 2003; Heeter, 2003; Hogue et al., 2003). Studies in the field ask the question of how can presence be maximized? What characteristics does a virtual environment must have in order to increase the experience a high degree of presence? In particular in the area of collaborative virtual environments, the research question is to ask: how does the technology affect by the way we relate to others? And what would be the impact of new interaction technologies on social dynamics and social networks?

In the field of presence, the method of measuring presence which has been considered as a very fuzzy area (Knight et. Al., 2003; Slater et. Al.2009; Slater, 2004) could be based on subjective, behavioral and physiological measures (Insko, B., 2003). Subjective measures rely on participant's self-reported sense of presence. The most common method is the post-immersion questionnaire. The behavioural method measures participant's responses to objects or events in the VE, while the physiological method attempts to measure presence by gauging changes in heart rate, skin temperature, and breathing rate, etc. trying to avoid the subjective bias. Similar to Insko's (2003) view, Sadowski and Stanney (1999) argue that there would be two sets of data which can be gathered regarding the experiences of people in virtual worlds: Objective and subjective (Sadowski and Stanney,1999). Subjective measure can be gathered through post-experiment questionnaires. Some researchers argued that post-experiment questionnaires as the method of the measurement have demonstrated the inherent instability (Slater,2004; Freeman et al. 1999). Objective data can be gathered throughout the testing procedure measuring the reflexive motor responses of the user (as cited in Knight et al, 2003; Lepecq, et al.,2008).

According to Sadowski and Stanney (1999), a valid measure of presence should be a)Relevant-have a direct connection with presence and its components, b)Reliable- have proven test-retest repeatability, c) Sensitive- to variations in variables affecting presence, d)non-intrusive- to avoid intentional degradation of performance and/or sense of presence and e) convenient-portable, low-cost and easy to administer. Those measurement requirements may help to develop a scientific approach to measure presence.

The qualitative analysis methods such as think-aloud and protocol analysis are also employed to determine presence in VEs. In a think aloud study, Chan and Weng (2005) reported several methodological problems: "the most intriguing issue was that it is difficult to interpret what you are thinking and how you really feel" (p.192). They observed that subject's personality, controlling problems, navigating skill and cognitive load are the factors affecting the subject's externalisations. The results of the study show that the factors of sensory stimuli (visual, audio, and haptic) and the cognitive mechanisms utilized in the process (perception, feature mapping for recognition, searching for orientation, attention paid to focus points, and the problem solving exercise for navigation) are all attributed to the generation of the feeling of "being there" (Chan and Weng, 2005).

Peripheral Awareness

Most 2D-based multi-user systems support shared interfaces by presenting exactly the same image of the representation to all users: What You See Is What I See (WYSIWIS) (see He and Han, 2006 for a review on WYSIWIS). In contrast, most 3D-based multi-user systems, etc. virtual worlds, that can be considered as shared three-dimensional interfaces provide a shared 3D space and all the users have a different viewpoint. In virtual worlds, team members involve parallel and independent actions need to be able to coordinate and inform their activities through peripheral awareness of one another's activities (Mary, 2011). Peripheral awareness includes:

1. consequential communication, which is the characteristic movements of an action communicate its character and content to others (Segal, 1995) and
2. feed-through which is produced when artifacts are manipulated provides others with clues about that manipulation (Dix et al., 1993).

In collaborative work, providing peripheral awareness is seen as an important topic, as evidenced in ethnographic studies. Gül and Maher (2009) measured different levels of awareness while designers worked and collaborated across three different CVE. In this study, designers were given similar design tasks in a 3D CVE and a remote sketching environment, required to work together. The protocol analysis is applied as the method which requires a customized coding scheme calculating the behavioral changes of the users of CVEs. The analysis of the protocol data demonstrates that remote sketching supports the WYSIWIS approach, except that the users have the ability to configure their shared user interface to best suit their working needs. The dynamic interface of the 3D virtual worlds encourages the designers to work in the individual mode. The findings of this research indicate that there is a potential benefit to be gained from further research on the relationship between collaborative design activities and shared representation in collaborative virtual environments.

Assessment of Communication Assistance

In general, communication imposes a challenge in collaborative work. Early researchers put most emphasis on simulating face-to-face co-presence as much as possible (Redfern and Naughton, 2002). Recent studies show that this is not required for a successful collaborative work in computer mediated environments.

Synchronous and Asynchronous Mode

Online communication tools commonly used to support collaborative work provide for both synchronous and asynchronous communication. Synchronous communication means that all members of a team are working on the same product at the same time simultaneously to search for new innovative design solutions or routine design solutions (Scherer 2004). Asynchronous communication means that each team members can provide and contribute a part, which is necessary for solving the problems without direct and immediate communication in a formalised way by exchanging the ideas and suggestions (Scherer, 2004). Common asynchronous tools include email, listserv and web bulletin boards. Synchronous tools include chat rooms, application sharing such as whiteboards, tele and video conferencing and text-based multi-user domains.

Recently, in a collaborative design learning context, a protocol study which explores the use of asynchronous and synchronous communication tools during design activity is conducted (Gül et al 2012). The results of the protocol analysis show that in the synchronous communication mode, the students were working together with their peers for the development of the design ideas staying in joint decision-making mode of negotiation and evaluation. In the asynchronous mode, the same students spent most of their time for coordinating their collaborative activities for effective time management and task monitoring. The results also suggest that working in synchronous communication mode encourage students to work collaboratively on the development of the design ideas, on the other hand, asynchronous communication mode encourages students to plan their collaborative activities, monitoring the processes and work individually. The results also show that the students proposed more design ideas and stayed more on the analysing the design problem and clarifying the design concepts in the synchronous communication mode. The same students stayed more on the discussions that are related to the 'setting-up' goals to each other in the asynchronous communication mode.

Communication Channels

There has been a long history of research on the assessment of the communication channels in distributed collaborative work (Siegel et al.1986; Chapanis et al. 1977; Baltes et al. 2002; Diamant et al. 2008; Balakrishnan, 2008; Dong and Fu, 2012). Media richness has been identified as one of the most prominent antecedents of performance in distributed collaborative work via different communication channels (Daft et al. 1984). Several factors such as anonymity, uninhibited behavior, task types, culture and other contextual factors play a role in moderating the effectiveness of communication channels in distributed collaboration context (Anderson 2007; Baltes, 2004, Setlock et al. 2007). Studies also show that collaborative virtual environments present some advantages when communicating over distance as they often allow more focused and concise information exchange between team members (Gabriel and Maher 1999; Maher and Simoff 2000), and assist team members keeping to their task (Cleland and Ireland 2002).

A fundamental difference between text and audio-video based channels is whether information exchange is done verbally or textually. Ethnographic studies are conducted comparing face-to-face, text-based and video-based communication channels. Dong and Wu (2012) conducted a comparative study to investigate how different communication channels affect the process of information exchange and negotiation in a collaborative work. The study reveals interesting results: Participants who used the video-based communication method were more likely to agree on solutions that were equally good to both parties than participants who used the text and audio based channels. Specifically, time information was exchanged in a more condensed format in text condition and smaller chunks of more specific time information was discussed in audio and video conditions.

An early study done by Vera et al. (1998) comparing video- conferencing with a chat line demonstrated that there was negligible influence of the communication channels on the collaborative problem-solving. The results showed that designers worked on their collaborative design tasks using the same collaborative process, regardless of the communication channel. On the other hand, changing the communication channels had an effect on the ratio of low-level and high-level design exchanges. Although the change in communication channels did not influence the design outcome, which was evaluated by a group of professional architects, in text-based communication experiments, the level of low-level exchanges dropped compared to the video-conferencing category. Vera et al. (1998) concluded that: "[…] designers adapt the nature of their communication to the bandwidth of the channel available without compromising their collaborative strategy or expert contributions". Kvan and Wong (1999) reported that text-based participants compensated perfectly for the narrower bandwidth interface.

Similarly, Gabriel et al. (2000) compared the effectiveness of above channels in collaborative design context underlining differences of them. He reported that communication channels should be selected on the basis of the type of communication considered being the most effective for the stage and task of the design project (Gabriel 2000). Gabriel and Maher (1999) pointed out that simply mimicking co-located settings such as teleconferences may result in fewer social interactions between team members as well as difficulties in sharing visual information.

Benford et al. (1995) reported that video-conferencing does not create a feeling of co-location: you cannot place people in relation to one another, other than knowing that someone is looking at the camera; you cannot tell what they are looking at. When video conferences are used, team members' abilities to communicate through non-verbal interactions (such as body language) can be inhibited (Hoyt 2000). This occurred mostly because the collaborator's focus is on the design artifact, not on the faces of their partner. On the other hand, Evard et al. (2001) pointed out that text-based social communication supported the development of effective collaborative work-related problem solving.

Public - Private

With the increasing use of CVEs in variety of tasks, the ability of maintaining the levels of visibility in media sharing activities become an issue. Particularly, social networks, which are defined as websites allowing participants to construct a public or semi-public profile within the system, are articulated the participant's relationship to other users in a way that is visible to anyone who can access their profile (Boyd and Ellison, 2007). In terms of communication context, there are a great deal of work which defines, classifies and evaluates public and private in common social networks (see, Lange, 2007 for a review on the subject).

Assessment of Spatial Computing for Design

Supporting External Design Representation

For communicating design ideas to the designer her/himself or to others, designers rely on external design representations in several overlapping ways, that is, through at variety of types of sketches, physical and digital models, diagrams, graphs and notations. An extensive review of literature shows that external design representations have many functions: First, they act as memory aids, for both short-term working memory and long-term working memory. They decrease working memory load by offering external tokens for the objects that must otherwise be kept in mind and freeing working memory to perform mental calculations on the objects, instead of both keeping objects in mind and operating on them. (Goldschmidt, 1994; Suwa and Tversky, 2002). Second, external representations carry information that can be directly perceived and utilised without being interpreted and explicitly formulated, such as visuo-spatial and metaphoric calculation, inference and insight (Cox and Brna, 1995; Larkin and Simon, 1997; Suwa and Tversky, 1996). Next, they function as an aid in organising cognitive activity (Chandrasekaran et al., 1993). In addition to supporting the design activities of iteration and problem formulation, external representations support the communication of design decisions (see Cardella et al., 2006; Römer et al., 2001) with clients, team members, and other related parties.

In the field of collaborative design, one of the topics of research is the provision of a more efficient communication process. Thus, representations that have a significant role as communicative resources are the objects of interaction (Robertson, 1996). When design thoughts are externalised through objects, each object contains properties of future interpretations that designers can negotiate during further developments to the design. Objects that can be pointed to, talked about or sketched on (Perrya and Sanderson, 1998) play an important role both in one's conversation with her/himself and with others. Most importantly, these external representations become the ground on which conflicts and collaboration take place. Arias et al. (2000) put forward that the externalisations were especially important for collaborative design, because externalisations in collaborative design: (1) create a record of the mental efforts, one that is "outside us" rather than vaguely in memory, (2) represent artefacts that can talk back to us (Schön and Wiggins, 1992), and (3) form the basis for critique and negotiation (Arias et al., 2000).

Supporting Visuo-spatial Properties

Researchers have studied how designers used design representations to facilitate design thinking, and the relationship between the design process and design outcome has been studied (Atman and Bursic 1998). Ullman et al. (1990) reported that sketches had different levels of abstraction and provide an external memory to aid the designer. External representations, sketches in particular, serve as visual aids for design thinking in a variety of ways (Laseau 1989).

Tversky (2005) defined four types of space in which human activities occur: (1) the space of the body, (2) the space around the body, (3) the space of navigation, and (4) the space of external representations. Each of them is experienced and conceptualised differently. The space of the body has a perceptual side, the sensations from outside and inside the body, and behavioural side, the actions the body performs. The space around the body includes the space in which it acts and sees, including surrounding objects. The space of navigation is the space for travel, depending on the knowledge and memory, not the concurrent perception. Finally, the space of external representations includes a space on paper meant to represent an actual space, as in a map, diagram or architectural drawing (Tversky 2005). In the field of psychology, studies show that diagrams and models promote participants to take the perspective of a character surrounded by objects (Bryant and Tversky 1999). In their study, Bryant and Tversky (1999) pointed out that with models, participants adopted the character's perspective, and with diagram, participants took an outside perspective. We are interested in the views of the designers when they are designing in the physical and the virtual space and how the space around the body (physical and virtual) affects their interactions with the design representations.

In relation to the space around the body, design research examines the designers' reasoning on the visuo-spatial representations that "captures visuo-spatial properties of the world" (Tversky 2005). This includes visual and spatial information. The spatial relations include the properties that are "close or above or below" in the world to preserve those relations of the representations. The visual information includes static properties of objects, such as shapes, textures, colours, or between objects and reference frames, such as distance and direction (Tversky 2005).

In the field of design, researchers also investigate the relationship between body and design tools, particularly looking at the impact of virtual design environments on designer's perception of presence (Gül, 2008). Gül (2008) suggests that the experience of being immersed in a virtual world while designing is very distinct from interacting with real-world artefacts. Each virtual environment studied provides different experiences of embodiment.

Shared Visual Space

Another interest of the CVE studies is to characterise the use of the shared representation in collaborative design. Engeström (1992) pointed out that the nature of collaboration is dependent on the shared representation. In his framework, there are three types of collaboration: co-ordination, co-operation and communication. According to Engeström (1992), in co-ordination designers are carrying out individual design tasks without having a shared object, whereas in co-operation, designers focus on a shared problem and try to negotiate a jointly satisfactory way of solving it. In the highest form of collaboration, communication, they are not only sharing a design object but also managing their collaborative efforts by developing a shared writing of joint actions.

Most 2D-based multi-user systems support shared interfaces by presenting exactly the same image of the representation to all users: What You See Is What I See (WYSIWIS) (see He and Han, 2006 for a review on WYSIWIS). The remote sketching applications, such as Groupboard, also supports the WYSIWIS approach, except that the users have the ability to configure their shared user interface to best suit their working needs. In contrast, 3D virtual worlds that can be considered as shared three-dimensional interfaces provide a shared 3D space and all the users have a different viewpoint, which is notanalogous to the use of WYSIWIS interfaces. Having their own viewpoint and work-space in the collaborative virtual environments might have an effect on designers' collaborative design process, as it allows them to be apart and work separately (Gül, 2007). The research findings suggest that the shared visual spaces have an impact on designers' collaborative process (Gül, 2007). The shared visual space includes the communication channel, and the 2D-3D visual information that allows designers to work together on the shared representation. The observations show that designers seem to be interested in the view of the design representation and the avatar and the designing tools and interfaces in the remove virtual environments, rather than seeing each other's face on the video screen (Gül, 2007). Thus, they closed the video channel window for resizing their working space.

Evaluation

Affordances

Affordances theory was developed by Gibson (1977) who suggests that humans perceive in order to operate on the environment. The theory was introduced to HCI field by Norman (1988) and further developed by Gaver (Gaver, 1991, Bærentsen and Trettvik, 2002) with others. Norman (1988) believes "[...] that affordance results from the mental interpretations of things based on our past knowledge and experience applied to our perception of the things about us" [p.219]. According to Norman (1988), "the term affordance refers to the perceived and actual properties of the thing [...] that determines just how the thing could possibly be used" [p.9]. Later studies differ from Gibson's conception of affordances which is based on visual perception. In these later studies, researchers (Vyas et al., 2006, Bærentsen and Trettvik, 2002) conceptualised affordances "in interaction" which suggest that affordances emerges during a user's interaction with environment. In this view, users are actively taking part in the interaction with the artefact and constantly interpreting the situation and constructing and re-building meaning about the artefact (Vyas et al., 2006). A study in affordances in the design of VEs points out "(1) that substituting designed cues via sensory stimuli in available sensory modalities for absent or impoverished modalities may enable the perception of affordances in VEs, (2) that sensory stimuli substitutions provide potential approaches for enabling the perception of affordances in a VE, and (3) that affordances relating to specific action capabilities may be enabled by designed sensory stimuli" (Gross, 2004).

Communication/ Collaboration

In the field of CVE, design researchers investigate the effects of communication and information technologies on design thinking and collaboration using protocol analysis. Protocol analysis that allows the characterisation of the processes in designing has been used in different design disciplines, such as architectural design, interior design, industrial design, mechanical engineering and software design. Early studies focused on protocol's verbal aspect (Ericsson and Simon, 1984). For example, in the engineering domain, verbal protocol analysis is a well-documented approach to understanding what a designer is thinking while solving a problem; it has been applied to the experts' (Cross et al., 1996) and to the novices' (Atman and Bursic, 1998) design cognition. On the other hand, later studies acknowledged the importance of the design drawings that are associated with the design thinking which can be interpreted through verbal descriptions (Suwa et al. 1998, Akin 1996). In addition, early design studies were usually single-subject; think-aloud protocol studies that required the externalisation of the thoughts during designing.

In the late 1980s, a rapid change occurred in the protocol studies by extending single-subject design activity to the team's design activity (Schön, 1984; Gabriel and Maher, 1999; Scrivener et al., 1992; Cross et al., 1996; Kvan et al., 1997). Cross et al. (1996) said that a team's design protocols resembled the "think aloud" method, since a joint task seemed to provide data indicative of the cognitive abilities that were being undertaken by the team members. Consequently investigating the team's design protocol was not substantially different from investigating single-subjects' design thoughts.

Gabriel (2000) called the team's design protocols "design communication protocols", which provided information about the natural process of communicating design ideas, and did not interfere with the main design activity. According to Gabriel (2000), the design activity was the high-level cognitive processes while the subjects were externalising what they thought was adequate to communicate their ideas to their collaborator.

Design Task Requirements

CVEs have transformed ways of collaboration for people to design in social play. To effectively facilitate the strategic utilization of CVEs for design assistance, appropriate design tasks should be determined in the context of CVE. The dimension for design task requirements, consisting of work task and collaboration, builds on the requirement level of the framework by Cugini et al. (1997) that adopted McGrath's work (1984). We went through design tasks that teams performed in the context of CVEs to reveal the fundamental characteristics required in achieving successful collaborative design in CVEs.

Work Tasks

Fir for Purpose

CVEs have brought a paradigm shift in data representation and information access, from 2D to 3D representation, from the real to the virtual space (Benford et al. 2001; Caneparo 2001). To address adequate capabilities of the shared workspace, what works and what does not need to be tested through the design tasks in empirical studies of CVEs (Schnabel 2002a). According to the purpose, work tasks can be categorized into six types of tasks: planning task, creativity and brainstorming task, decision-making tasks, cognitive conflict tasks, competitive performance tasks and information dissemination tasks. In our framework, these types of tasks are reinterpreted in the design context rather than generic collaborative works, which is different from Cugini et al.'s framework (1997).

Planning Task

Planning is essential in designing, thus modeling tools such as CAD software and database have been emphasized in CVEs. With the rise of Web 2.0, the ways designers explore and engage with spatial design in CVEs has been transformed (Yun et al. 2007; Wang et al. 2012). Many CVEs models for supporting planning started from Virtual Design Studio (VDS) (Kvan 2001; Reffat 2007). The recent 3D virtual world approach in VDSs allows so called "design within the design" (Maher et al. 2000; Figen et al. 2009). Modifying a 3D design in a networking system has been introduced through 3D virtual world platforms such as Secondlife and Active worlds (Wael 2009; Gu et al. 2009). Understanding and description of volumes is improved within a 3D CVE, making planning more dynamic and engaging.

Creativity and Brainstorming

There has been research examining the benefits from brainstorming in CVEs for the better quality and quantity of ideas in the early stages of design (Kvan 2001; Maher, 2010). Through an empirical study, Schnabel (2002b) noted that the interaction within the CVE was direct through a model-based (virtual) channel, thus acts as a 'shortcut' from idea to creation. While designers worked three-dimensionally, they engaged in intense discussion, which improved the design outcomes in their creativity. Using linkographs, Kvan and Gao (2006) identified that the pattern of design activities in the remote digital setting is richly interlinked, enhancing design exploration. CVEs support idea development, further creative exploration by allowing multiple perspectives, more active participation and design reflection.

Decision Making Tasks

Many research demonstrated that the synchronous nature of CVEs has improved the design review process. Virtual prototypes initially provided simple interactivity like walkthroughs and the ability to zoom in and out (Liston, 2000; Garcia, et al. 2003; Issa, 2003; Gopinath 2004). More recently, CVEs enable participants to manipulate shared 3D models in real-time from their own viewpoint, thus facilitating decision-making and coordination of the collaborative design (Benford et al. 2001; Woksepp et al. 2005; Reffat 2006; Majumdar et al. 2006). CVEs enable designers to communicate in the objects as shared workspaces effectively, thus facilitating more rapid consensus on issues among team members.

Cognitive Conflict Tasks

CVEs provide an immersive sense of place in a multi-user 3D virtual world, where teams hold different viewpoints in designing. Recent research has shown that designing in CVEs has an impact on design cognition (Maher et al. 2005; Gul et al. 2007; Gu et al. 2011). Developments in HCI have brought to interaction technologies that immerse the designer in the digital world. More recently, augmented reality (AR) provides new variations on the visualization of design by enabling seamless interactions (Kim and Maher 2008). To compromise cognitive conflicts caused by HCI and interdisciplinary perspectives, CVEs need to afford multimodal interaction leading to intuitive manipulation and communication tools enabling clarification of team members' ideas or opinions in collaboration sessions.

Competitive Performance Tasks

Montoya et al. (2011) indicate that distinct patterns of collaborative behaviors are related to the performance of remote teams in a 3D CVE. They found that higher-performing teams coordinated better teamwork and exhibited more equality of participation than lower-performing teams. Sas et al. (2004) highlights the relationship between cognitive style and the level of sense of presence and then discovered a negative relationship between sense of presence and task performance, which should be considered in terms of task characteristics. The continuous visual cues and environmental feedback of the CVEs allow equal contribution by team members, which is essential in supporting collaborative performance tasks.

Information Dissemination Tasks

CVEs act as a communication spaces and shared database, supporting information exchange and indirect interactions among team members. Designers in CVEs share task-related information or provide feedback to other members by updating design developments in the shared workspace (Rousseau et al. 2006). Maher et al. (2006) explores ways of integrating CVEs with an external database of objects and project information in DesignWorld. The shared understanding of information and simulation is important for team collaboration, thus the integration of collaborative tools such as whiteboards or shared views with communication tools is emphasized in CVEs (Bravoe et al. 2006).

Collaboration

Working as a member of a team introduces different problems and possibilities in comparison with working alone, i.e. roles and relationships, information gathering and sharing, and conflict avoiding and resolving (Cross 1995). It is important that collaborators know what is currently being done in context of the goals through interdependent tasks (Maher 2010).

Social Protocols

Social protocols, related to interpersonal interactions, roles and relationships, have been acknowledged more recently since they may influence the team design activities (Cross and Cross 1995; Benford et al. 2001). Social protocols support coordination behaviors by allowing awareness of members, activities, objects; and meeting activities (Cugini et al. 1997). However, key aspects of social interaction such as visual cues, a sense of presence of others and objects are often attenuated in remote teams (Dennis et al. 2008). Many researchers tried to support user engagement in CVEs by emphasizing avatar representation of users and personalization (Ashraf et al. 2001; Montoya et al. 2011). Avatars make team members aware of each other and what team members are doing while discussing objects.

The social relational affordances of CVEs support rich communication and interaction in designing.

Group Characteristics

CVEs offer a new form of teamwork, where communication is enhanced affecting the process of thinking, creation and understanding (Schnabel 2002). Teams may have different characteristics depending on the makeup of the team, the social relations, formality, the location of the members, and the time constraints for tasks, which affect how different types of tasks perform (Cugini et al. 1997). In collaborative design, studies have shown that designers move fluidly from working individually to working together, in which different stages of collaborative design are characterized as a closely coupled or loosely coupled (Kvan 2000; Maher et al. 2005). The use of CVEs facilitates the seamless movement from working closely on the same task to working individually on a complex shared design task.

SUMMARY

The recent literature on CVE in design assistance have been intensively reviewed and analyzed in this paper in order to address CVE variables for theory and technology implementation. This taxonomy effectively incorporates CVE technologies in terms of modelling, relation, functionality, service, implementation, usability, communication assistance, spatial computing for design evaluation across work task, collaboration and transition tasks throughout individual, project, organization, and industry perspectives. This framework can provide a solid basis for evaluating promising areas and identifying driving factors for practical CVE effectiveness such as effectiveness of CVE technology. In the full paper, many discussions, arguments, and analysis will be conducted based on the framework.

REFERENCES

Abdelhameed, W. 2009, Urban Wiki and VR applications, 9th international conference on construction applications of virtual reality.

Ashraf, N., Anderson, J. N., Douther, C. L., McKay, I. G., Jack, M., and Platt, P. 2001, Longitudinal Study of Habituation and Participatory Design for Multi-User Shared Virtual Environments. *International Journal of Virtual Reality*, 5(1).

Benford, S, Greenhalgh, C, and Rodden, T. 2001, Collaborative virtual environments, Communications of the ACM, 44(7): 79.

Boyd, d. m., and Ellison, N. B. (2007). Social network sites: Definition, history, and scholarship. *Journal of Computer-Mediated Communication*, 13(1), article 11.

Bravo, C., M. A. Redondo, M. Ortega and M. F. Verdejo. 2006, "Collaborative distributed environments for learning design tasks by means of modelling and simulation." *Journal of Network and Computer Applications* 29(4): 321.

Caneparo, L. 2001, "Shared Virtual Reality for Design and Management: The Porta Susa Project." *Automation in Construction* 10(2): 217-228.

Cross N., and Cross, A.C. 1995, Observations of teamwork and social processes in design, *Design Studies* 16, 143-170.

Cugini J., Damianos, L., Hirschman, L., Kozierok, R., Kuzierok, R., Kurtz, J., Laskowski, S., Scholtz, J. 1997, Methodology for Evaluation of Collaboration Systems, The Evaluation Working Group of the DARPA Intelligent Collaboration and Visualization Program.

Davies, C. 2003, Rethinking VR: Key Concepts and Concerns, in Hal Thwaites (ed), Hybrid Reality: Art, Technology and Human Factor. International Society on Virtual Systems and Multimedia, Montreal, Canada. pp. 253–262.

Dennis, A.R., Fuller, R.M. and Valacich, J.S. 2008, Media, tasks, and communication processes: a theory of media synchronicity. *MIS Quartely* 32 (3), 575-600.

Dix, A., J. Finlay, et al. (1993). Human-Computer interaction Europa, Printice Hall. International Society for Presence Research (2000). The Concept of Presence: Explication Statement http://ispr.info/.

G. Riva, DAvide F. WA IJsselsteijin 2003 being there: concepts, effects and measurement of user presence in synthetic environments. Amsterdam: Ios Press 2003.

Garcia, A. C. B., Kunz, J., and Fischer, M. 2003, "Meeting details: methods to instrument meetings and use agenda voting to make them more effective," CIFE Technical Report #147, Stanford University, Stanford, CA.

Gu, N., Kim, M.J. and Maher, M.L. 2011, Technological Advancements in Synchronous Collaboration: The Effect of 3D Virtual Worlds and Tangible User Interfaces on Architectural Design, *Automation in Construction* 20 (3), pp 270-278.

Gul et al. 2007, A new approach to design education: evaluations of 3D virtual worlds on design teaching and learning, 7th International Conference on Construction Applications of Virtual Reality, October 22-23, pp. 40-49.

Gul, LF and Maher, ML. 2009, Co-creating external design representations: comparing face-to-face sketching to designing in virtual environments, *CoDesign International Journal of CoCreation in Design and the Arts*, 5(2): 117-138.

Gul, L.F., Wang, X., Bulbul, T.T., Cagdas, G., and Tong, H. 2009, Global Teamwork: A Study of Design Learning in Collaborative Virtual Environments. In: Undisciplined! Design Research Society Conference 2008, Sheffield Hallam University, Sheffield, UK, 16-19 July 2008.

Heeter, C. 2003, Reflections on Real Presence by a Virtual Person, Presence, vol. 12 no. 4, pp. 335–345.

Hogue, A., Robinson M., Jenkin M. R., and Allison R. S. 2003, A vision-based head tracking system for fully immersive displays, in J. Deisinger, and A. Kunz (eds), International Immersive Projection Technologies Workshop. *Eurographics Workshop on Virtual Environments*, pp. 179–187.

Horne, M. and Hamza, N. 2006, Integration of virtual reality within the built environment curriculum. *ITCon*, 11, 311-324.

Issa, R. R. A. 2003, "Virtual reality: a solution to seamless technology integration in the aec industry." 4D CAD and Visualization in Construction: Developments and Applications, R. R. A. Issa, I. Flood, and W. J. O'Brien, eds., Lisse : Exton, PA :A.A. Balkema Publishers, 243-260. Gopinath, R. (2004).

Kalay, Y. E. (2004). Contextualization And Embodiment In Cyberspace. Caadria 2004 [Proceedings Of The 9th International Conference On Computer Aided Architectural Design Research In Asia], Seoul Korea.

Kim, M.J. and Maher, M.L. 2008, The Impact of Tangible User Interfaces on Designers' Spatial Cognition, Human-Computer Interaction 23 (2), pp 101-137.

Kitchens, K., Shiratuddin, M.F. 2007, Interactive Home design in a virtual environment, 7th international conference on construction applications of virtual reality, October 22-23, 10-19.

Knight, M., Brown, GP, Hannibal, C. Noyelle, C. and Steer, O., 2003, Measurement of Presence in Large Scale Virtual Environments, 21th eCAADe Conference Proceedings / ISBN 0-9541183-1-6] Graz (Austria) 17-20 September 2003.

Kvan, T. 2001, The Pedagogy of Virtual Design Studio, *Automation in Construction* 10, 345-353.

Kvan, T., and Gao, K. 2006, Comparative Study of Problem Framing in Multiple Settings, *Design Computing and Cognition* 2006, pp 245-263.

Lange, P. G. (2007). Publicly private and privately public: Social networking on YouTube. *Journal of Computer-Mediated Communication*, 13(1), article 18.

Lepecq JC, Bringoux, L, Pergandi, JM, Coyle T, Mestre D, 2008, afforded actions as a behavioral assessment of physical presence, Presence 2008, Proceeding of the 11th International Workshop on Presence, eds. Spagnolli and Gamberini, L., Padova, Italy, 16-18 October 2008.p.202-208.

Liston, K. 2000, "Assessing and characterizing the use of visualization techniques for AEC decision making tasks," Ph.D. Thesis Proposal, Stanford University, Palo Alto, CA.

Maher, M.L. 2010, Designers and Collaborative Virtual Environments, in X. Wang and J.J.-H Tsai (Eds): Collaborative Design in Virtual Environments, ISCA 48, pp.3-15.

Maher, ML, Bilda, Z and Marchant, D. 2005, Comparing collaborative design behavior in remote sketching and 3D virtual worlds, Proceedings of International Workshop onHuman Behaviour in Designing, Key Centre of Design Computing and Cognition, University of Sydney, pp. 3-26.

Maher, ML, Rosenman, M, Merrick, K and Macindoe, O. 2006, DesignWorld: An augmented 3D virtual world for multidisciplinary collaborative design, in A Kaga and R Naka (eds), CAADRIA '06: Proceedings of the 11th Conference on Computer-Aided Architectural Design Research in Asia, Osaka, Japan, pp. 133-142.

Maher, M. L. and Simoff, S. 2000, Collaboratively Designing within the Design. Proceedings of Co-Designing 2000.

Majumdar, T., Fischer, M.A., and Schwegler, B.R. 2006, "Conceptual Design Review with a Virtual Reality Mock-Up Model," Building on IT: Joint International Conference on Computing and Decision Making in Civil and Building Engineering, Hugues Rivard, Edmond Miresco, and Hani Melham, editors, Montreal, Canada, June 14-16, 2902-2911.

McGrath, J.E. 1984, Groups: Interaction and Perfomance, Englewood Cliffs, N.J., Prentice-Hall.

Montoya, M.M., Massey, A.P. and Lockwood, N.S., 2011, 3D Collaborative Virtual Environments: Exploring the Link between Collaborative Behaviors and Team Performance, *Decision Sciences* 42 (2), 451-476.

NIGEL BEVAN, (2001) International Standards for HCI and Usability, *International Journal of Human Computer Studies*, 55(4), 533-552.

Oxman, R., O. Palmon, et al. (2004). Beyond the reality syndrome: Designing Presence In Virtual Environments. Sigradi 2004 - [Proceedings Of The 8th Iberoamerican Congress Of Digital Graphics], Porte Alegre - Brasil.

Jabi, W. (2004), A Framework for computer-supported collaboration in architectural design, PhD thesis, University of Michigan.Jenny Preece, David Benyon, and Open University. 1993. A Guide to Usability: Human Factors in Computing (1st ed.). Addison-Wesley Longman Publishing Co., Inc., Boston, MA, USA.

Rabbe M. Reffat. 2006, Computing in architectural design: reflections and an approach to new generations of CAAD. *ITcon* 11, 655-668.

Reffat R. 2007, Revitalizing architectural design studio teaching using ICT: reflections on practical implementations, International journal of education and development using information and communication technology (IJEDICT) 3(1), 39-53.

Rousseau, V., Aube, C. and Savoie, A. 2006, Teamwork behaviors: a review and an integration of frameworks. *Small Group Research* 37(5), 540-570.

Sas, C., G. M. P. O'Hare and R. Reilly. 2004, Presence and task performance: an approach in the light of cognitive style. *Cognition, Technology and Work* 6(1): 53.

Sadowski, W., and Stanney, K. (1999). Measuring and Managing Presence in Virtual Environments, Handbook of Virtual Environment Technology, K. M. Stanney, ed., Publisher: Lawrence Erlbaum Associates, Inc., University of Central Florida.

Segal, L. (1995). Designing team workstations: the choreography of teamwork. Local applications of the ecological approach to human-machine systems. P. Hancock, J. Flach, J. Caird and K. Vicente. Hillsdale, NJ., Lawrence Erlbaum: 392-415.

Schnabel M.A. 2002, Collaborative studio in a virtual environment, Proceedings of the international conference on computers in education (ICCE'02).

Shao, Y.J., Daley, L., and Vaughan, L. 2007, Exploring Web 2.0 for virtual design studio teaching, *Proceedings of ascilite Singapore* 2007.

Slater, M., Lotto, B., Arnold, MM and Sanchez-Vives, MV, 2009, How we experience immersive virtual environments: the concept of presence and its measurement, Anuario de Psicologia, Vol.40, No.2,p.193-210, Facultat de Psicologia, Universitat de Barcelona.

Slater, M. 2004, How colourful was your day? Why questionnaires cannot assess presence in Virtual Environments, Presence, Vol.13, No.4, August 2004, 484-493, by the Massachusetts Institute of Technology.

Slater, M and Usoh, M. (1993), Presence in Immersive Virtual Environments, IEEE Virtual Reality Annual International Symposium (VRAIS), September 18-22, Seattle, Washington, 90-96.

Steur, J.S., 1992, Defining Virtual Reality: Dimensions determining tele-presence, *Journal of communication*, 42(4),73-93.

Wang, X., Love, P.E.D., Klinc, R., Kim, M.J., Davis, P.R. 2012, Integration of E-learning 2.0 with Web 2.0, *Journal of Information Technology in Construction* Vol 17, pp 387-396.

Wittmer, G. and Singer, M., 1998, Measuring Presences in Virtual Environments: A Presence, Questionnaire, Presence: Tele-operators and Virtual Environments, 7(3),225-240.

Woksepp, S., Olofsson, T., and Jongeling R. 2005, Design Reviews and Decision-making Using Collaborative Virtual Reality Prototypes: A Case Study of the Large-scale MK3 Project [online]. In: Kenley, Russell (Editor). 13th International Group for Lean Construction Conference: Proceedings. Sydney: International Group on Lean Construction, 2005: 145-152.

In: Virtual Environments
Editors: Stephanie Trautman and Franchesca Julien
ISBN: 978-1-62618-090-1
© 2013 Nova Science Publishers, Inc.

Chapter 6

VIRTUAL ENVIRONMENTS IN EDUCATION: DEVELOPMENTS, APPLICATIONS AND CHALLENGES

Haisen Zhang[1,*] and David Kaufman[2,†]
[1]School of International Studies, University of International Business and Economics, Beijing, China
[2]Faculty of Education, Simon Fraser University Burnaby BC, Canada

ABSTRACT

Virtual environments have witnessed a considerable growth over the past decade. They have been applied in diverse domains and for a variety of purposes. While they have been shown to enhance learning and performance in educational contexts, the landscape of virtual environments in terms of developments, applications, and challenges still remains relatively unexplored. The purpose of this study is to address this lack by exploring how far virtual environments in the educational sphere have come over the past 11 years. Data were collected from peer-reviewed journal articles in the ERIC database, which claims to be the "world's largest digital library of education literature." The database was searched on the basis of keywords "virtual environments." The time span of the publications reviewed ranged from 2001 to 2011. There were 155 articles identified in the search. These were then grouped into four categories based on the purpose of this study: patterns of yearly publications; fields of applications; themes of research; and challenges of applications of virtual environments in education. The qualitative data were analyzed through content analysis. Results are discussed and suggestions proposed for future research.

* Haisen Zhang: School of International Studies, University of International Business and Economics, Beijing, China 100029. E-mail: haisenzhang@uibe.edu.cn.
† David Kaufman: Faculty of Education, Simon Fraser University Burnaby BC Canada V5A1S6. E-mail: dkaufman@sfu.ca.

Keywords: Virtual environments; virtual learning environments; immersive virtual learning; virtual worlds

1. INTRODUCTION

Virtual environments (VEs) are a 3D computer-generated simulated representation of real-world physical environments. As they are a virtual representation of the real-life world or physical reality, VEs are often called virtual worlds or virtual reality. In these VEs, objects are visually identical to what we can see in the physical world, though they may be enhanced in some way, and users are virtually represented by graphical embodiments called avatars, which are in effect a digital embodiment of humans and their behaviors. Within VEs, multiple users are able to interact and collaborate with each other in real time.

Historically, the current VEs originate from the single-user head-mounted display systems, which were developed in the 1990s (Schroeder, 2002). Nevertheless, only with the advent and popularity of the Internet have multi-user VEs been made possible, where distributed users around the globe are linked together and can gather together under the same roof of a building in an immediate manner with just the click of a mouse. To a larger extent, VEs have transformed the way we live and work by reducing our living world to the size as small as fingertips. Some of our routine activities are able to be carried out in a more convenient, less costly, and more efficient fashion. For instance, business professionals at multinational companies are able to attend a business meeting without having to travel from branch offices to headquarters. They can simply sit in a chair at their physical office and then gather around a table in a virtual headquarters conference room without the cost and hassles of traveling to a meeting place thousands of miles away. Pre-service health professionals can also equally well benefit from such environments in term of enhancing their surgical and clinical practices without the risks of harming their patients when practicing procedural and clinical tasks.

Likewise, research shows that VEs can also benefit educational endeavors. VEs can "provide highly collaborative, immersive environments that promote interactions among students and with the instructor" (Jones, Morales, and Knezek, 2005, p. 221). Zhang (2010) found that VEs afford "an authentic, situated, immersive, low-stress and complementary learning environment for spoken English learning in traditional learning contexts" (p. 227). In a meta-analysis of previous studies, Perterson (2010) found that "participation in gaming and simulation may facilitate aspects of SLA [second language acquisition] and the development of communicative competence" (p. 89) due to the fact that negotiation of meaning and modified interaction are facilitated in such environments. Schwienhorst (2002) also posited that VEs are conducive to second language acquisition in terms of their affordances such as reduction of the affective filter, enhancement of linguistic and cognitive awareness of the learning process, support of interaction;, and enabling of collaboration.

Similar findings can also be seen in other disciplines. For instance, in medical education, Wiecha, Heyden, Sternthal and Merialdi (2010) claimed that VEs offer ample pedagogical opportunities for medical education that are intended to enhance learning outcomes. Their claims have been supported by Creutzfeldt, Hedman, Medin, Heinrichs, and Felländer-Tsai's

(2010) empirical study, demonstrating that VEs can engage students' learning, facilitate knowledge construction, and enhance their self-efficacy in cardiopulmonary resuscitation.

Although VEs have been employed in a multitude of contexts and for diverse purposes, the landscape of VEs in educational contexts in terms of developments, applications, and challenges to date still remains relatively unexplored. There is therefore a need to enrich the current literature by presenting a panorama of the landscape so that both future practitioners and researchers can be better informed of how VEs can be more effectively adopted to enhance teaching and learning.

1.1. Research Questions

The goal of this study is to address the gap in our understandings by exploring how far virtual environments in the educational sphere have come over the past 11 years, namely from 2001 to 2011. In order to achieve the goal, this inquiry is guided by addressing the following five questions:

1 What are the trends in research on VEs in educational contexts over the past 11 years?
2 What are the fields of education that VEs have been mostly applied to over such a period of time?
3 What are the major themes in research on VEs in the educational arena?
4 Do VEs contribute to the enhancement of learning?
5 What are the challenges in the applications of VEs in education?

The remainder of the chapter is structured as follows: Section 2 gives an overview of the methods employed in this research, which centers on the issues such as research design and data collection as well as data analysis. Section 3 presents and discusses the statistical results relating to the research questions. The last section presents the conclusion of this inquiry, which summarizes the major findings and proposes directions for future applications and research.

2. Methods

2.1. Research Design

This study employed an archival design. According to Vogt, Gardner, and Haeffele (2012), archival design refers to the fact that a researcher collects data from existing sources instead of generating primary data on their own from the use of specific research instruments such as surveys, interviews, observations, and/or experiments. In the current research scenario, data were collected from an educational database, and the findings of this inquiry were built upon analyses of these database archives.

Such a design is appropriate for this study due to the fact that this study is in nature a review of literature.

2.2. Data Sources and Selected Data

The data came from published research articles available from the ERIC database, which claims to be the "world's largest digital library of education literature." A selection of the archives on VEs from such a database can well cover what practitioners and researchers have done in terms of the applications of VEs in the educational sphere. According to the goal of this study, the selected archival data were the articles published between 2001 and 2011. The following data selection criteria were observed:

1 The articles were published in peer-reviewed journals;
2 The articles were published between 2001 and 2011;
3 The database was searched based on the keyword: "virtual environments."

On the basis of the above criteria, there were 156 articles identified via "virtual environments," which were included in the analysis.

2.3. Data Collection Procedures

ERIC Advanced Search was first set up. The first keyword "virtual environments" was keyed into the "Search for" box. Then, "Keyword" was selected from the drop-down list. The "Year" was set from 2001-2011. There was no limitation to "Language Phrase." "Document Type Phrase" was confined to "Article (EJ)." "Yes" was selected in "Peer Reviewed" drop-down list. "Date" was selected in the "Rank by" top-down list. After the first round of search was conducted, identified articles were downloaded for analysis.

After the articles were identified from a search with the keyword "virtual environments," they were downloaded into a folder for further reading and analysis. Meanwhile, the records of all the identified articles were exported from the database via EndNote X4 for ease of making sure that there were no overlapping articles, which were also checked against date, author, and title of the respective individual articles. One of the articles was overlapping and consequently removed from the analysis, with the total number of articles reduced from 156 to 155. Thus, all of these 155 articles were included in the analysis.

2.4. Data Analysis

Content analysis was done by employing the grounded theory method (Glaser and Strauss, 1967), which involves constantly "comparing incidents applicable to each category," "integrating categories and their properties," "delimiting the theory," and "writing theory" (pp. 105-113).

In this specific scenario, each of the articles under study was carefully read and re-read by the first author, with an emphasis on the coding, which "is the ascription of a category label to a piece of data … either decided in advance or in response to the data that have been collected" (Cohen, Manion, and Morrison, 2007, p. 480) or categorizing of the themes.

The themes that corresponded to the research questions included "academic disciplines of applications," "types of research methods," and "re-emerging themes of the studies."

"Academic disciplines" were defined as "a branch of knowledge that is taught and researched at the college or university level" (Wikipedia, 2012, para. 1). They were further classified into branches and subject matter so that subjects that are covered in the curriculum of elementary, secondary, and postsecondary schools could be revealed. "Academic disciplines of applications" referred to the disciplines to which virtual environments were applied. Accordingly, a discipline that was involved in a research study on the use of virtual environments in a subject such as biology, chemistry, or engineering was identified as an academic discipline of science. When there was no obvious identifier of a discipline, the discipline in which a study was involved was attributed to the "education-general" category. The "types of research methods" were defined as one of the research methods, namely, quantitative, qualitative or mixed research approaches (Creswell, 2009; Lodico, Spaulding, and Voegtle, 2006). For the articles that failed to fall into any of the three categories, they were classified into the "none" category. The "theme of the study" is the "focus of the study," namely, "what is researched" (Paltridge and Startfield, 2007, p. 100).

When the coding was being done, an investigator triangulation was employed. The first researcher and an external experienced researcher read and re-read all of the articles independently to have the data coded. The coded data were compared, and discrepancies of the outcomes were discussed until agreements were reached.

3. Results and Discussion

3.1. Dynamic Patterns of Use of Virtual Environments in Education

Figure 1 shows VEs have been researched and utilized in educational contexts at a steadily rising pace from 2001 to 2007. However, in most recent years, especially as of 2008, the increase jumped sharply and reached the peak in 2009. Though the trend experienced a downturn in 2010, the momentum of increase was maintained in 2011. Overall, the trend of applying VEs in education is expected to continue to rise. In fact, the increase of VE applications in education may have coincided with the outbreak of the financial crisis that swept across the entire globe in 2008. As most of the countries in the western world suffered heavy financial burdens, fundings for educational endeavors at both schools and university levels plummeted. The financial constraints pushed educational institutions to seek opportunities of enhancing learning and teaching through technology so as to maintain educational quality in a cost-effective fashion. As a consequence, taking education virtual became one of the ways to achieve the goal at the times of financial difficulty, in addition to being able to meet the needs of millennial learners of the digital generation (Qian, 2009).

3.2. Academic Disciplines of Applications in Educational Virtual Environments

Virtual environments have been applied to multiple academic disciplines across the elementary, secondary, and post-secondary spectrum.

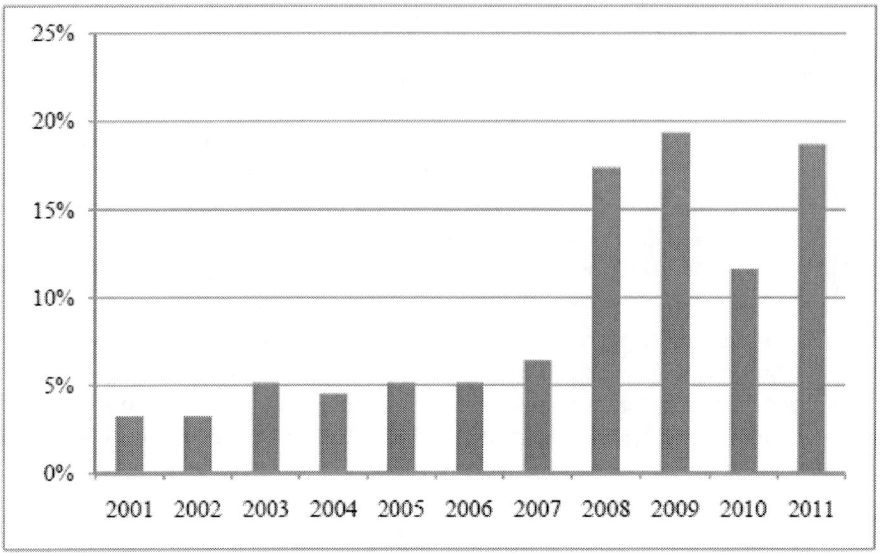

Figure 1. Yearly percentage of the identified articles published from 2001 to 2011.

However, the applications of VEs in the disciplines have been disproportionally distributed. Figure 2 exhibits that the top five disciplines that virtual environments were applied to are science education (11%), psychology (9%), computer science (7.7%), language education (5.2%), and educational technology (3.9%). The applications to these diverse disciplines are mainly due to the characteristic affordances of the environments for the educational endeavor. Also, these disciplines, among others, require an environment that is unavailable in the physical environment or too costly or risky to experiment or practice in the physical environment. For example, Qian (2009) argued that virtual environments provided a beneficial tool for learners to learn science in an informal setting beyond the brick and mortar scenario and enabled them to be engaged in authentic learning "in an enjoyable and fervent gamelike environment" (p. 28). Due to the inherent simulative and representative nature of virtual environments, scientific concepts that are too abstract or complex to be comprehended in a two-dimensional space can be presented in a visually enhanced fashion (Trindada, Fiolhais, and Almeida, 2002; Weusijana, Svihla, Gawel, and Bransford, 2009).

More strikingly, the unavailability in a physical setting be addressed by simulating reality in a virtual setting (Cooper, Ding, Simpson, Fitzgerald, Spaeth, Guo, Koontz, et al. (2005; Good, Howland, and Thackray, 2008; Jansen-Osmann, 2002; Kennedy-Clark, 2011; Mamo, Namuth-Covert, Guru, Nugent, Phillips, Sandall, Kettler, et al., 2011). Scientific demonstrations or experiments that are difficult to be performed in the physical world can be replicated and conducted in the virtual world (Jansen-Osmann, 2002).

For instance, Mühlberger, Bülthoff, Wiedemann, and Pauli (2007) tested fear of driving in a virtual tunnel by utilizing virtual environments to simulate a driving environment without exposing the drivers to hazardous driving conditions.

Just as Mamo, et al. (2011) put it, virtual environments provide a supplementary tool for an instructor to be able to accomplish the impossible "because of the time required, student safety, liability issues, cost, and difficulty in transferring the activity to other faculty or teachers" (p. 121).

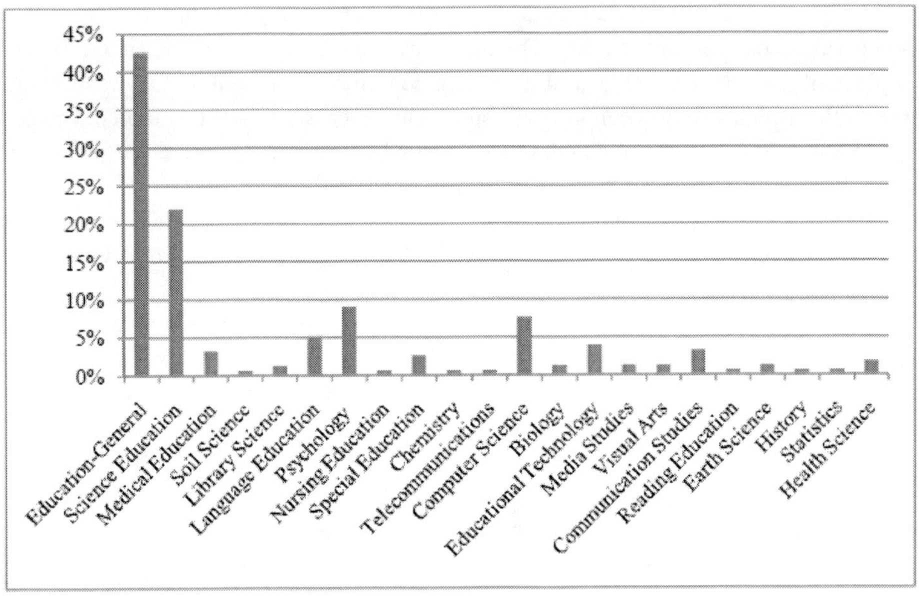

Figure 2. The percentage of each discipline involving applications of virtual environments among the identified research studies.

In the discipline of psychology, most of the researchers and/or practitioners have employed VEs in an investigative manner, and few signs can be revealed that VEs have been integrated into the psychology curriculum. For instance, Brawn, Fenn, Nusbaum, and Margoliash (2008) examined the role of sleep in consolidating sensorimotor skill learning by engaging the participants in a VE to perform tasks requiring the production of "novel bimanual motor responses" (p. 815). Likewise, Fields and Shelton (2006) used VEs to investigate individual skill differences in large-scale environmental learning. They recruited 20 male and 20 female volunteer participants (N=40) in a psychology course, with extra credit awarded to each participant. The participants in equal numbers of different gender were randomly assigned to one of four conditions: Park-Route/Zoo-Survey, or Park-Survey/Zoo-Route and undertook the virtual learning task with limited exposure to two navigation movies in the order of route and survey, or vice versa. Then, they were tested on the judgments of relative locations of objects. Along the same line, Kelly and Bischof (2008) used a VE "to examine the relative importance of featural and geometric information for men and women orienting in a virtual environment" (p. 103). Participants (N=35) were randomly assigned to one of the two groups: group Beacon and group Landmark. The former group was presented with images depicting Rectangular-Boundary environments while the latter group with images depicting Rectangular-Segment environments. They found that "the relationship between geometric and featural information depends strongly one's initial experience with an environment and relative cue informativeness. [They] also found that men and women rely on featural and geometric information to differing degrees" (p. 103).

The use of virtual environments in the discipline of computer science has been mainly oriented toward the development of virtual environments-based learning platforms. For example, Livingstone, Kemp, and Edgar (2008) examined how Sloodle can be developed by integrating the Second Life virtual world with the open-source VLE Moodle. Also, Lamotte,

Quax, and Flerackers (2008) described the architecture and applications of large-scale networked virtual environments. Stuer, Broeckhove, and Arickx (2003) presented the design and implementation of a reliable multipeer protocol for distributed virtual environments. Dozens of other similar studies can also be found. However, studies of this kind have had one thing in common: many of them claimed that the newly developed virtual environments were meant to address educational problems and proven to be effective in addressing the problems. Nevertheless, these environments have rarely been used or tested by other researchers or practitioners. Therefore, whether the environments can help deliver the educational agenda still remains unknown.

A contrast can be seen in use of virtual environments in second language (L2) education. L2 learners have been benefited from virtual environments in terms of "extended periods of language socialization, adaptation, and creative semiotic work that illustrate vibrant communicative practices" (Thorne, Black, and Sykes, 2009, p. 815) as well as "countless opportunities for language learners to gain oral, aural, and cultural proficiency through interactions with native speakers in life-like settings" (Cooke-Plagwitz, 2008, p. 555), due to the vanishing of physical boundaries (Zhang, 2012). Miller and Hegelheimer (2006) also found that The Sims virtual world could help the students of English enhance their grammar and vocabulary when such virtual environments were integrated into the language classroom. Their findings were supported by Ranalli's (2008) study of the same type of virtual environments, revealing that the students generally had a positive attitude toward L2 learning in such a scenario and that the students' vocabulary knowledge could be significantly improved. However, the researcher argued that virtual environments can only be used "as a supplementary source of linguistic exposure to complement regular coursework" (p. 453) instead of using them to teach specific vocabulary. In other words, they should be pedagogically used "under certain conditions" (p. 453).

In the sphere of educational technology, virtual environments have been applied to examine the potential of using virtual environments or to develop a conceptual framework for enhancing learning and teaching in such an environment. For instance, Omale, Hung, Luetkehans, and Cooke-Plagwitz (2009) conducted a case study of the role of attributes of virtual environments in a problem-based learning scenario by integrating the environments into the teaching of an introductory educational technology course. Tsiatsos, Andreas, and Pomportsis (2010) developed an evaluation framework for supporting learning in the environments.

Nonetheless, virtual environments do not always fit into pedagogical needs naturally, and thus changes are required in order to maximize pedagogical effectiveness (Ryan, Porter, and Miller, 2010). Also, the knowledge and skills acquired from virtual environments in a particular discipline may not be able to be automatically transferred to a real-life experience (McKerlich and Anderson, 2007). The affordances of virtual environments "[need] to be supported by sound pedagogical practice to facilitate the transfer of knowledge and skills gained in the MUVEs into the real world" (Kennedy-Clark, 2011, p. 2233). Moreover, successful applications "[require] a timely elimination of technical problems and a systemic optimization of learning environments from both pedagogical and administrative perspectives" (Zhang, 2012, p. 9).

Even though virtual environments were identified as being applied to a range of salient disciplines, the largest percentage of the studies (43.2%), which involved virtual environments, did not fall into the saliently identifiable discipline categories but into

"Education-General" (See Figure 2), which ended up with a prevailing exploration of virtual environments in the enhancement of learning and teaching without being set in a discipline context. These studies were more focused on a researcher's conceptual framing of virtual environments for education or the subjects' perceptions of the potential of virtual environments from a perspective of a non-specific discipline.

For instance, Warburton (2009) presented a full picture of the affordances and challenges of virtual environments for education, concluding that "virtual worlds are attractive spaces for education, yet they present particular [pedagogical] design challenges to educators" (p. 424). His findings were echoed in the findings of Dickey's (2003) study, which investigated the affordances and constraints of virtual environments for distance education, arguing that pedagogical approaches should be carefully considered in order to more effectively take advantage of the affordances and circumvent the constraints. Along this line, Whitton and Hollins (2008) explored the pedagogical advantages of virtual environments in the context of higher education, stressing that the adoption of virtual environments for education should be based not on the following of a passing fad or "a perceived motivational effect" but on "a sound pedagogic rationale" (p. 228). Similarly, Gamage, Tretiakov, and Crump (2011) examined teachers' perceptions of the affordances for teaching and learning in a broader sense, yielding that the teachers were "positive with respect to the usefulness of MUVEs as a learning environment" (p. 2412). They further claimed that virtual environments were expected to witness "a wider acceptance as a teaching tool" (p. 2413) based on the similar views of the teachers with and without experience of utilizing virtual environments in teaching and learning.

The fact that a large majority of the researchers have failed to relate their studies to a particular discipline is due to the following three reasons: Firstly, the adoption of virtual environments in education still remains to be technically a challenging task (Cooke-Plagwitz, 2008; Mamo, et al., 2011). The technology of virtual environments was "developed by the US Department of Defense in the late 1980s" (Dede, 1995, p. 46), and it was not used in education until the early 1990s. Since it was born, it has been evolving rapidly. Technical, pedagogical, and administrative challenges for an effective adoption of virtual environments in a particular subject domain are enormous, especially for the people who are in the lack of tech-savvy (Kanuka, Rourke, and LaFlamme, 2007; Zhang, 2012). Even though 20 years has elapsed, most of the adopters of educational virtual environments still remain to be innovators (Rogers, 2003) and hence few in number. These innovators are teachers, researchers, and/or practitioners who are not only innovative in pedagogy but also highly skilled in and enthusiastic about technology. They are also self-motivated to explore how to integrate virtual environments into their curriculum pedagogically and practically without caring much about the influence of external factors such as rewards and policy inplications. In contrast, other practitioners may feel discouraged due to the lack of "institutional support and recognition of their efforts" (Yadgir, 2011, p. 666).

Secondly, the applications of virtual environments to a particular discipline can be costly. For teacher practitioners, their workload can be huge and the time involved can be tremendous (Santilli and Beck, 2005; Zhang, 2012). In addition, due to the technical complexity, the task of applying virtual environments may involve more than one person (See Herold, 2010; Mamo, et al., 2011). Thus, the investment in human capital can be significant (Whitton and Hollins, 2008). Moreover, if a piece of land is purchased in a readily available virtual world such as Second Life, which is viewed as the most widely used virtual world in education (Herold, 2010; Mayrath, Traphagan, Jarmon, Trivedi, and Resta, 2010; Mazar and Nolan, 2008; Ryan, Porter, and Miller, 2010; Shen and Eder, 2009; Wiecha, Heyden, Sternthal, and Merialdi, 2010), or if a special virtual world is developed for a particular course, the financial cost can be overwhelmingly substantial. Without support or funding, the integration of virtual environments into a discipline on a continual basis is rarely possible.

Finally, hardware problems could be another barrier. The running of virtual environments normally requires more up-to-date and sophisticated configurations of a computer. Such configured technologies are normally costly and rarely available in all campus computer labs or at many students' homes (León and Guzner, 2011; Yadgir, 2011; Zhang, 2012). Such an existing problem lessens the chance that teachers will take their classes into virtual environments, not to mention the resistance of cultural conceptions to the teaching and learning in virtual environments (Herold, 2010).

3.3. Compelling Themes of the Studies on Virtual Environments in Education

Over the past eleven years, researchers have mainly focused on three re-emerging themes in relation to the applications of virtual environments (see Figure 3): potential (36.8%), effectiveness of learning (27.1%), and development of VEs (16.8%).

As seen in Figure 3, most of the studies have given more attention to the potential of utilizing VEs in education, especially the Second Life virtual world (Ryan, Porter, and Miller, 2010).

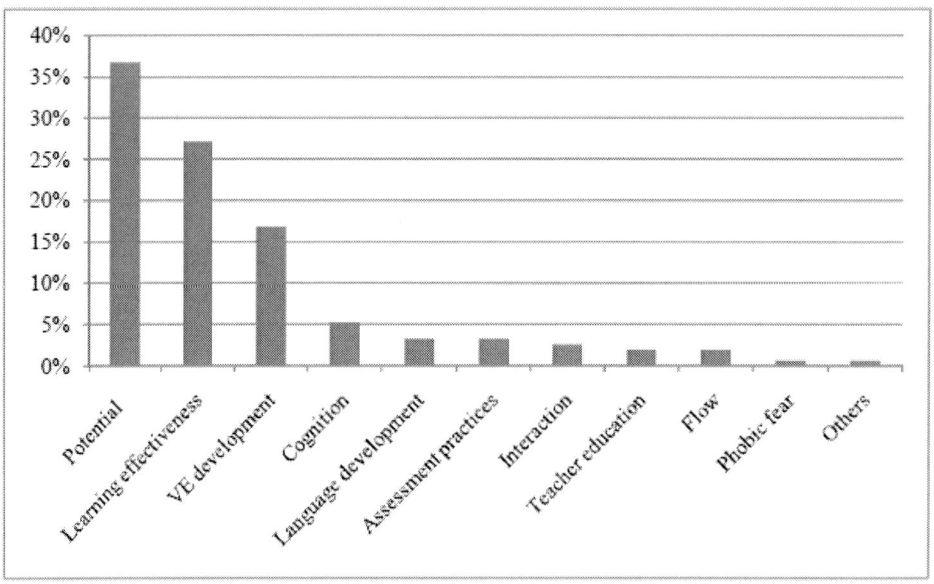

Figure 3. Major themes related to the applications of virtual environments in the articles published in 2001-2011.

Take the case of Second Life, due to the affordances of the environments such as immersion (Dede, 1995; Larach and Cabra, 2010; Salmon, 2009), anonymity (Yee, 2006), flow (Jones, Morales, and Knezek, 2005), low stress (Chester, 2006; Zhang, 2010), rich contextual cues (Warburton, 2009) , and instantaneous feedback (Ryan, Porter, and Miller, 2010; Richardson, Hazzard, Challman, Morgenstein, and Brueckner, 2011), learners are able to learn in an engaging, motivating, and learner-centered as well as exploratory, experiential, cross-culturally collaborative, and interactive fashion. Such a learning opportunity is not always accessible otherwise in physical environments (Antonacci and Modaress, 2005).

According to Jones, Warren, and Robertson (2009), virtual environments can afford the facilitation of student interactions, enhancement of student engagement, and enabling of deeper learning, and establishing a community of practice (Wenger, 1998). Qian (2009) also argued that these environments can "provide [students and teachers with] an experience that is not accessible, possible, or practical in reality" (p. 28) and "a unique extension to online learning, as students are not only able to view the content but also interact virtually with one another as they view the same material in the same virtual room, despite the real physical distance between them" (Richardson, Hazzard, Challman, Morgenstein, and Brueckner, 2011, p. 42). Learners in these environments can "experience life-like social interaction while at the same time engaging in meaningful learning activities" (Cooke-Plagwitz, 2008, p. 547). Additionally, learners of an introvert personality can feel more comfortable with virtual environments and be more inclined to participate in activities and thus are able to benefit a great deal more in these less stressful environments than in physical classroom settings (Zhang, 2010).

As Figure 3 illustrates, another widely discussed theme is the effectiveness of learning, namely, the effectiveness of utilizing virtual environments to enhance teaching and learning. Such a theme has been explored mostly through a qualitative study of participants' perceptions of a particular pedagogical approach or through a quantitative or mixed methods investigation into the effects of a particular pedagogical approach on learning and teaching. For instance, In the findings of one mixed methods study conducted by Charles, Charles, McNeill, Bustard, and Black (2011), their proposed game-based feedback approach could "[empower] a learner to establish and understand their educational identity within the context of a course of learning within higher education" and can "further enhance educational feedback and student engagement" (p. 653). In science learning, Moreno and Mayer (2004) found that feedback through personalized messages was more effective than that through nonpersonalized messages. In other words, students performed better when messages were communicated in conversational style than in formal style in high-immersion environments. This is due to the fact that "personalization leads to an increased sense of social and physical presence and to improved learning outcomes" (p. 171).

The effectiveness of learning in virtual environments can be influenced by both pedagogical approaches and student individual learning styles (Hauptman and Cohen, 2011). For instance, in a study on science learning, Nelson and Ketelhut (2008) found that when students scaffolded with individualized guidance messages performed better when carrying out tasks, regardless of the level of their individual self-efficacy. Their findings have been supported by Chen, Ismail, and Mohd's study (2008), claiming that guidance can help reduce learner cognitive load and therefore exert considerable impact on learning outcomes. Moreover, McKethan, Rabinowitz, and Kernodle's (2010) study demonstrated that students with different multiple intelligences performed differently in virtual environments. They found that the students with strong verbal/linguistic skills did better in virtual environments when performing tasks that demand skill and accuracy. There is also a cohort of other studies that assert that virtual environments are contributive to the enhancement of the effectiveness of learning (see Ketelhut and Nelson, 2010; Vergara, Caudell, Goldsmith, and Alverson, 2008).

However, even though student and teacher participants in the studies generally have had a positive attitude toward the utilization of VEs in education (Mikropoulos and Natsis, 2011) and encouraging results have been found, it is still too early or abrupt to conclude that learning in virtual environments is more effective than in physical environments. There are a number of studies (see Dalgarno, 2002; Lim, Nonis, and Hedberg, 2006) that supported the claim that "learning [in VEs] was not enhanced and that the technology became a distraction rather than an enabler" (Omale, Hung, Luetkehans, and Cooke-Plagwitz, 2009, p. 492). Davis and Smith (2009) also made similar findings that VEs did not help improve students' literacy competencies and their confidence levels. As we know, the effectiveness of learning is not determined by technology per se but by the way of how technology is used pedagogically (Clark, 1983). As Dalgarno and Lee (2010) put it, "it is the tasks, activities and underpinning pedagogical strategies supported or facilitated by the technology rather than the technology itself that have an impact on learning" (pp. 17-18). Moore and Pflugfelder (2010) further pointed out that the effectiveness of learning was dependent upon the effective scaffolding of pedagogy and technology, and the role of the teacher in facilitating student learning is vitally important (Bailenson, Yee, Blascovich, Beall, Lundblad, and Jin, 2008). Obviously, the effectiveness of learning in virtual environments may still require more data-driven empirical testing in a pedagogically innovative setting.

Apart from the two mostly discussed themes mentioned above, the development of VEs is another focal theme. Generally speaking, the environments were developed by catering to the needs of a particular endeavor, the examples of which include Lamotte, Quax,and Flerackers, 2008; Peng, Chou, and Chang, 2008; etc., just to name a few. They have been presented mainly from case studies, and some of them may originate from a one-time project while others may be rooted from a multiple-year project. These studies are generally characterized by either proposing a conceptual framework or creating a design model for effective development of such environments. In the meantime, these newly developed environments have generally been claimed to be effective by the authors. However, such effectiveness largely remains to be self-claimed. In other words, most of the environments developed, if not all, have not been applied to other scenarios or adopted by educational institutions beyond where they were originally tested. As a consequence, there is a lack of evidence that these environments can truly help deliver the intended educational goal in multiple educational contexts.

3.4. Research Methods Employed in the studies on VEs in Education

The conceptual classification of research methods is based on Creswell (2009). Figure 4 shows that 29.7% of the studies have employed the quantitative research approach and that the studies that have involved qualitative and mixed methods account for 16.1% and 11.6% respectively. Evidently, of the three research approaches, the quantitative research approach has been employed most.

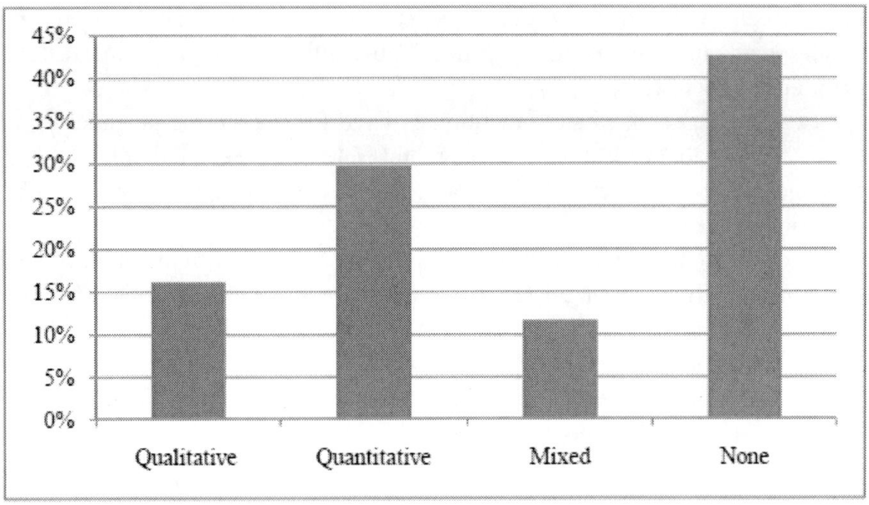

Figure 4. The number of research methods employed in the identified articles.

However, there are a large proportion of the studies that have fallen into the category of "none" (42.9%), which refers to those that have failed to adopt any of the qualitative, quantitative or mixed research methods.

As can be seen, most of the studies on VEs used in educational fields are simply the inquirers' personal perceptions or views on the adoption of VEs in education due to the lack of a research design and empirical data. To a larger extent, research with a rigorous research design is still highly desirable. As Gamage, Tretiakov, and Crump (2011) put it, "most of the articles are either conceptual and thus mainly express their authors' opinions, or are experience reports detailing authors' first-hand experience in conducting teaching in multi-user virtual environments (MUVEs), sometimes involving data collection via surveys or interviews" (p. 2406). Similarly, Good, Howland, and Thackray (2008) also found that "[t]here is a growing use of immersive virtual environments for educational purposes. However, much of this activity is not yet documented in the public domain, or is descriptive rather than analytical" (p. 163).

Conclusion

The enquiry under discussion is aimed at shedding light on the use of VEs in education within a recent 11-year period, with an emphasis on exploring where we are now and where we are going in terms of using VEs in education. The study concludes with the following findings:

1 The number of the research studies on virtual environments for educational purposes has been increasing, but the breadth and depth of the applications across the educational domains are still limited.

2 Most of the applications of VEs in education have been research-oriented whereas widespread applications to a particular discipline or in a school district have remained very few.
3 Most of the researchers and practitioners have focused on the potential of VEs for transforming the educational agenda, but few have explored how VEs can be pedagogically and practically integrated into a curriculum or discipline to enhance learning and teaching.
4 Most of the studies are cross-sectional in nature, and empirical longitudinal studies of rigorous design with triangulated data sources are highly desirable both for validating an individual investigator's self-claimed effectiveness of learning and for promoting more quality research.
5 The challenges of applying VEs in education remain in cost, technical, administrative, and pedagogical areas.

In anchoring the findings of this inquiry in the larger literature, some of its limitations must be acknowledged, which may offer opportunities for future research. First, generalization of the findings should be cautious. Due to the fact that the data used in this study are obtained from one database only, the studies that are not included in this single database may have been excluded in the current study. Future studies may include studies from multiple databases such as ERIC, ScienceDirect, Wiley Online Library and others so that a more complete picture of the research topic can be painted. Second, the articles that have been covered in this study are those identified with the keyword "virtual environments," which may have limited the range of relevant studies. Future studies may locate the articles by expanding the sample size through a combination of keywords such as "virtual environments," "virtual worlds" and "virtual reality." In this way, more articles can be included. Finally, the archival data used in this study are exclusively peer-reviewed journal articles. No conference articles and monographs have been included. Future studies may include these works so that a wider perspective of the current status of utilizing VEs in education can be better presented.

References

Antonacci, D. and Modaress, N. (2005). Second life: the educational possibilities of a massively multiplayer virtual world (MMVW). In: *The proceedings of EDUCASE, Southwest Regional Conference*. Austin, Texas.

Bailenson, J. N., Yee, N., Blascovich, J., Beall, A. C., Lundblad, N., and Jin, M. (2008). The Use of Immersive Virtual Reality in the Learning Sciences: Digital Transformations of Teachers, Students, and Social Context. *Journal of the Learning Sciences,* 17(1), 102-141.

Brawn, T. P., Fenn, K. M., Nusbaum, H. C., and Margoliash, D. (2008). Consolidation of sensorimotor learning during sleep. *Learning Memory,* 15(11), 815-819.

Charles, D., Charles, T., McNeill, M., Bustard, D., and Black, M. (2011). Game-based feedback for educational multi-user virtual environments. *British Journal of Educational Technology,* 42(4), 638-654.

Chen, C. J., Ismail, F. W. and Mohd, W. (2008). Guiding exploration through three-dimensional virtual environments: A cognitive load reduction approach. *Journal of Interactive Learning Research,* 19(4), 579-596.

Chester, A. (2006). Text-based MOOing in educational practice: Experiences of disinhibition. *Campus-Wide Information Systems,* 23(3), 128-137.

Clark, R. E. (1983). Reconsidering research on learning from media. *Review of Educational Research,* 53(4), 445-459.

Cohen, L., Manion, L. and Morrison, K. (2007). *Research methods in education* (6th ed.). Abingdon, Oxon: Routledge.

Cooke-Plagwitz, J. (2008). New directions in CALL: An objective introduction to Second Life. *CALICO Journal,* 25(3), 547-557.

Cooper, R. A., Ding, D., Simpson, R., Fitzgerald, S. G., Spaeth, D. M., Guo, S., Koontz, A. M, et al. (2005). Virtual reality and computer-enhanced training applied to wheeled mobility: an overview of work in Pittsburgh. *Assistive Technology,* 17(2), 159-70.

Creswell, J. W. (2009). *Research design: Qualitative, quantitative and mixed methods approaches* (3rd ed.). Los Angeles: Sage.

Creutzfeldt, J., Hedman, L., Medin, C., Heinrichs, Wm. L., and Felländer-Tsai, L. (2010). Exploring Virtual Worlds for Scenario-Based Repeated Team Training of Cardiopulmonary Resuscitation in Medical Students. *Journal of Medical Internet Research,* 12(3): e38. doi: 10.2196/jmir.1426

Dalgarno, B. (2002). The potential of 3D virtual learning environments: A constructivist analysis. *Electronic Journal of Instructional Science and Technology,* 5(2), 1-19. http://ascilite.org.au/ajet/e-jist/docs/Vol5_No2/ dalgarno.html

Dalgarno, B. and Lee, M. J. W. (2010). What are the learning affordances of 3-D virtual environments? *British Journal of Educational Technology,* 41(1), 10-32.

Davis, M. and Smith, C. (2009). Virtually embedded: Library instruction within Second Life. *Journal of Library and Information Services in Distance Learning,* 3(3-4), 120-137.

Dede, C. (1995). The Evolution of constructivist learning environments: immersion in distributed, virtual worlds. *Educational Technology,* 35(5), 46-52.

Dickey, M. D. (2003). Teaching in 3D: Pedagogical Affordances and Constraints of 3D Virtual Worlds for Synchronous Distance Learning. *Distance Education,* 24(1), 105-121.

Fields, A. W. and Shelton, A. L. (2006). Individual skill differences and large-scale environmental learning. *Journal of Experimental Psychology: Learning, Memory, and Cognition,* 32(3), 506-515.

Gamage, V., Tretiakov, A. and Crump, B. (2011). Teacher perceptions of learning affordances of multi-user virtual environments. *Computers and Education,* 57(4), 2406-2413.

Glaser, B. and Strauss, A. (1967). *The discovery of grounded theory: strategies for qualitative research.* Chicago: Aldine.

Good. J., Howland, K. and Thackray, L. (2008). Problem-based learning spanning real and virtual words: a case study in Second Life. *ALT-J, Research in Learning Technology,* 16(3), 163-172.

Hauptman, H. and Cohen, A. (2011). The synergetic effect of learning styles on the interaction between virtual environments and the enhancement of spatial thinking. *Computers and Education,* 57(3), 2106-2117.

Herold, D. T. (2010).Mediating media studies–Stimulating critical awareness in a virtual environment. *Computers and Education,* 54(3), 791-798.

Jansen-Osmann, P. (2002). Using desktop virtual environments to investigate the role of landmarks. *Computers in Human Behavior,* 18(4) 427-436.

Jones, J. G., Morales, C. and Knezek, G. A. (2005). 3-Dimensional online learning environments: examining attitudes toward information technology between students in internet-based 3-dimensional and face-to-face classroom instruction. *Educational Media International,* 42(3), 219-236.

Jones, J. G., Warren, S. J. and Robertson, M. (2009). Increasing student discourse to support rapport building in web and blended courses using a 3D online learning environment. *Journal of Interactive Learning Research,* 20 (3), 269-294.

Kanuka, H., Rourke, L. and LaFlamme, E. (2007). The influence of instructional methods on the quality of online discussion. *British Journal of Educational Technology,* 38(2), 260-271.

Kelly, D. M. and Bischof, W. F. (2008). Orienting in virtual environments: How are surface features and environmental geometry weighted in an orientation task? *Cognition,* 109(1), 89-104.

Kennedy-Clark, S. (2011). Pre-service teachers' perspectives on using scenario-based virtual worlds in science education. *Computers and Education,* 57(4), 2224-2235.

Ketelhut, D. J. and Nelson, B. C. (2010). Designing for real-world scientific inquiry in virtual environments. *Educational Research,* 52(2), 151-167.

Lamotte, W., Quax, P. and Flerackers, E. (2008). Large-scale networked virtual environments: architecture and applications. *Campus-Wide Information Systems,* 25(5), 329-341.

Lamotte, W., Quax, P. and Flerackers, E., (2008). Large-scale networked virtual environments: Architecture and applications. *Campus-Wide Information Systems,* 25(5), 329-341.

Larach, D. U. and Cabra, J. F. (2010). Creative problem solving in Second Life: an action research study. *Creativity and Innovation Management,* 19(2), 167–179.

Lim, C. P., Nonis, D. and Hedberg, J. (2006). Gaming in a 3D multiuser virtual environment: engaging students in science lessons. *British Journal of Educational Technology,* 37(2), 211-231.

Livingstone, D., Kemp, J. and Edgar, E. (2008).From Multi-User Virtual Environment to 3D Virtual Learning Environment. *ALT-J, Research in Learning Technology,* 16(3), 139-150.

Lodico, M. G., Spaulding, D. T. and Voegtle, K. H. (2006). *Methods in educational research: from theory to practice.* San Francisco, CA: Jossey-Bass.

Mamo, M., Namuth-Covert, D., Guru, A., Nugent, G., Phillips, L., Sandall, L., Kettler, T., et al. (2011). Avatars go to class: a virtual environment soil science activity. *Journal of Natural Resources and Life Sciences Education,* 40, 114-121.

Mayrath, M. C., Traphagan, T., Jarmon, L., Trivedi, A., and Resta, P. (2010). Teaching with Virtual Worlds: Factors to Consider for Instructional Use of Second Life. *Journal of Educational Computing Research,* 43(4), 403-444.

Mazar, R. and Nolan, J. (2008). Hacking say and reviving ELIZA: Lessons from virtual environments. *Innovate,* 5(2). Retrieved October 6, 2012, from http://www.innovateon line.info/index.php?view=articleandid=547

McKerlich, R. and Anderson, T. (2007). Community of inquiry and learning in immersive environments. *Journal of Asynchronous Learning Networks,* 11(4), 35-52.

McKethan, R., Rabinowitz, E., and Kernodle, M. W. (2010). Multiple intelligences in virtual and traditional skill instructional learning environments. *Physical Educator,* 67(3), 156-168.

Mikropoulos, T. A. and Natsis, A. (2011). Educational virtual environments: A ten-year review of empirical research (1999–2009). *Computers and Education,* 56(3) 769-780.

Miller, M. and Hegelheimer, V. (2006). The SIMS meet ESL: Incorporating authentic computer simulation games into the language classroom. International Journal of Interactive *Technology and Smart Education,* 3(4), 311-328.

Moore, K. and Pflugfelder, E. H. (2010). On Being Bored and Lost (in Virtuality). *Learning, Media and Technology,* 35(2), 249-253.

Moreno, R. and Mayer, R. E. (2004). Personalized messages that promote science learning in virtual environments. *Journal of Educational Psychology,* 96(1), 165-173.

Mühlberger, A., Bülthoff, H. H., Wiedemann, G., and Pauli, P. (2007).Virtual reality for the psychophysiological assessment of phobic fear: responses during virtual tunnel driving. *Psychological Assessment,* 19(3), 340-346.

Nelson, B. C. and Ketelhut, D. J. (2008). Exploring embedded guidance and self-efficacy in educational multi-user virtual environments. *International Journal of Computer-Supported Collaborative Learning,* 3(4), 413-427.

Omale, N., Hung, W.-C., Luetkehans, L., and Cooke-Plagwitz, J. (2009). Learning in 3-D multiuser virtual environments: Exploring the use of unique 3-D attributes for online. *British Journal of Educational Technology,* 40(3), 480-495.

Paltridge, B. and Startfield, S. (2007). *Thesis and dissertation writing in a second language: A handbook for supervisors*. Abingdon, Oxon: Routledge.

Peng, H., Chou, C. and Chang, C.-Y. (2008). From virtual environments to physical environments: Exploring interactivity in ubiquitous-learning systems. *Educational Technology and Society,* 11(2), 54-66.

Perterson, M. (2010). Computerized games and simulations in computer-assisted language learning: a meta-analysis of research. *Simulation and Gaming,* 41(1), 72-93.

Qian, Y. (2009). 3D multi-user virtual environments: promising directions for science education. *Science Educator,* 18(2), 26-29.

Ranalli, J. (2008). Learning English with The Sims: Exploiting authentic computer simulation games for L2 learning. *Computer Assisted Language Learning,* 21(5), 441-455.

Richardson, A., Hazzard, M., Challman, S. D., Morgenstein, A. M., andBrueckner, J. K. (2011). A "Second Life" for gross anatomy: Applications for multiuser virtual environments in teaching the anatomical sciences. *Anatomical Sciences Education,* 4(1), 39-43.

Rogers, E. M. (2003). *Diffusion of innovations* (5th ed.). New York: Free Press.

Ryan, J. and Porter, M. and Miller, R. (2010). Academic library services in virtual worlds: an examination of the potential for library services in immersive environments. *Journal of Information Technology Education: Innovations in Practice,* 9, IIP253-275.

Salmon, G. (2009). The future for (second) life and learning. *British Journal of Educational Technology,* 40(3), 526-538.

Santilli, S. and Beck, V. (2005). Graduate faculty perceptions of online teaching. *The Quarterly Review of Distance Education,* 6(2), 155-160.

Schroeder, R. (2002). Social interaction in virtual environments: Key issues, common themes, and a framework for research. In: R. Schroeder (Ed.), *The social life of avatars: Presence and interaction in shared virtual environments (pp. 1-18)*. London: Springer-Verlag.

Schwienhorst, K. (2002). Why environments? Implementing virtual reality concepts in computer-assisted language learning. *Simulation Gaming,* 33(2), 196-209.

Shen, J. and Eder, L. B. (2009). Intentions to Use Virtual Worlds for Education. *Journal of Information Systems Education,* 20(2), 225-233.

Stuer, G., Broeckhove, J. and Arickx, F. (2003). The design of a reliable multipeer protocol for DVEs. *Internet Research,* 13(2), 80- 85.

Thorne, S. L., Black, R. W. and Sykes, J. M. (2009). Second language use, socialization, and learning in internet interest communities and online gaming. *The Modern Language Journal,* 93, 802-821.

Trindada, J., Fiolhais, C. and Almeida, L. (2002). Science learning in virtual environments: a descriptive study. *British Journal of Educational Technology,* 33(4). 471-488.

Tsiatsos, T., Andreas, K. and Pomportsis, A. (2010). Evaluation Framework for Collaborative Educational Virtual Environments. *Educational Technology and Society,* 13(2), 65-77.

Vergara, V., T. Caudell, T. Goldsmith, P., and Alverson, D. (2008). Knowledge-driven design of virtual patient simulations. *Innovate, 5*(2). Received October 8, 2012, from http://www.innovateonline.info/pdf/vol5_issue2/Knowledge-Driven_Design_of_Virtual_Patient_Simulations.pdf

Vogt, W. P., Gardner, D. C. and Haeffele, L. M. (2012). *When to use what research design.* New York, NY: The Guilford Press.

Warburton, S. (2009). Second Life in higher education: Assessing the potential for and the barriers to deploying virtual worlds in learning and teaching. *British Journal of Educational Technology,* 40(3), 414-426.

Wenger, E. (1998). Communities of practice: Learning, meaning, and identity. Cambridge, UK: Cambridge University Press.

Weusijana, B., Svihla, V., Gawel, D., and Bransford, J. (2009). MUVEs and experiential learning: Some examples. *Innovate: Journal of Online Education,* 5(5). http://www.innovateonline.info/pdf/vol5_issue5/MUVEs_and_Experiential_Learning-__Some_ Examples.pdf

Whitton, N. and Hollins, P. (2008). Collaborative virtual gaming worlds in higher education. *ALT-J, Research in Learning Technology,* 16(3), 221-229.

Wiecha, J., Heyden, R., Sternthal, E., and Merialdi, M. (2010). Learning in a virtual world: experience with using Second Life for medical education. *Journal of Medical Internet Research,* 12(1): e1. doi: 10.2196/jmir.1337

Wikipedia (2012). *List of academic disciplines.* Retrieved November 2, 2012, from http://en.wikipedia.org/wiki/List_of_academic_disciplines

Yadgir, S. A. (2011). Leading in a technological age. *Educational Research and Reviews,* 6 (10), 664-670.

Yee, N. (2006). The demographics, motivations and derived experiences of users of massively-multiuser online graphical environments. *PRESENCE: Teleoperators and Virtual Environments,* 15, 309-329.

Zhang, H. (2010). *Spoken English teaching in multi-user virtual environments: Theory and practice.* Beijing: University of International Business and Economics Press.

Zhang, H. (2012). Pedagogical challenges of spoken English learning in the Second Life virtual world: A case study. *British Journal of Educational Technology*. doi:10. 1111/j. 1467-8535.2012.01312.x

In: Virtual Environments ISBN: 978-1-62618-090-1
Editors: Stephanie Trautman and Franchesca Julien © 2013 Nova Science Publishers, Inc.

Chapter 7

THE VIRTUAL ENVIRONMENTS AND SOCIAL NETWORKS FROM AN ADOLESCENT'S POINT OF VIEW: RELIABILITY AS A KEY ISSUE

Isabel Novo-Corti,* María Barreiro-Gen and Laura Varela-Candamio

Department of Economic Analysis and Business Administration, University of A Coruña, Spain

ABSTRACT

The importance of virtual spaces has been revealed in all the orders of the life and has concerned, in one way or another, to all groups and ages.

However, young people, especially adolescents, are those who have received this impact to a greater extent, to the point that on some occasions have been raised a negative impacts.

This work is based on research conducted among young teens that were enjoying their vacation in southern of the province of A Coruña (North West of Spain), during the summer of 2012. They have been asked about their relationship with virtual environments and their assessment of them in two respects: its usefulness as a means of acquiring knowledge and the utility as way to make friends, special attention has been paid to the relationship of teenagers with social networks and the purposes for using them.

We have developed an quantitative research using structural equation method. The results suggest that age and educational level are essential variables in assessing internet reliability.

Keywords: Teenagers; virtual environments, structural equation; internet use

* Isabel Novo-Corti: E-mail: Isabel.novo.corti@udc.es.

INTRODUCTION

Virtual environments are becoming increasingly important for many tasks. Learning or social relations are activities that have been already actually performed by Internet, which is a radical change on our lifestyles and on general society.

Internet is considered a revolution compared to the industrial revolution (Pérez de Silva, 2002). If the wheel and fire were the fundamental discoveries of rural society and the engine of industrial society, the computer and virtual networks are the key element for digital society. The scenario has changed, relationships are technologically mediated and we find new concepts of communication, space and time.

According to the report National Observatory of Telecommunications and Information Society, Ministry of Industry, Energy and Tourism Spanish, it is estimated that there were over 2,400 million Internet users worldwide in 2011, representing an increase of 18.2% compared to 2010. This means that for every 100 inhabitants, 34.7 were surfing the Internet. Most of these Internet users are in Asia or the Pacific (41.3%), while Europe concentrates the 19.2% of global Internet users. However, the European territory highlights the number of fixed lines per 100 inhabitants, with 74.4 Internet users per 100 inhabitants, compared with 27.2 Internet users per 100 people in Asia and the Pacific.

In Spain, 57% of the population in 2010 acceded to internet every day, according to a study by the European Interactive Advertising Association (EIAA). The time spent on the computer (social networks, information retrieval, computer games ...) continues to increase. In fact, in 2010, almost 30% of people were engaged in activities related to the "Hobbies and computing", compared to 17.9% in 2003 (INE, 2010).

In addition to learning through the Internet or making friends, there are many other tasks that can be carried out via online, as enrolling at a university, or establishing relations with any level of Public Administration. Governments, for example, have been able to use the Internet to reduce their costs of printing and distributing government publications or reports (Garcia-Marco, 2010). Many of these publications are distributed through Internet, allowing both of libraries and public offices the task of solving the problems that could arise from this change. In many countries it is now possible to establish more dynamic and interactive relations with public administrations via online forms or particular platforms.

In fact, the European Union calls on the Digital Agenda for Europe a number of goals for 2015, some of most notably of them are the intention that 50% of citizens will be using e-government and that 25% of them will complete forms online. It also seeks to achieve the online availability for all the key cross-border services (ONTSI, 2012).

Older people have also adapted to new technologies, as an entirely new element that has appeared in their lives, although the performance of these tasks seems cost them more (and for oldest ones we can't always be certain of that). But the younger people are born with technology and internet (Novo-Corti, Varela-Candamio and Ramil-Diaz, 2013). They are known as "digital natives", aged between 18 and 24 years.

In fact, the digital natives can't imagine life without the Internet. They are "multi-tasking". This means that while they are on the Internet, they listen music and watch television or attend their smartphone, all this simultaneously (Herman, 2010). In Spain, young people aged between 16 and 24 are connected to the Internet for 41% of the whole time of a week, which is 9.8 hours a day online on average (EIIAA, 2011).

For this group, social networks have shown spectacularly successful. Proof of this is that, in Spain, according to the Study of Social Networks in the IAB Internet (2011) 75% connected people, during that year, were users thereof.

Also, nine out of ten Internet users aged from 16 to 24 years are participating in social networks (INE, 2011) and 80% of the users of these networks with ages between 18 and 24 years engages network daily (ONTSI , 2012). But if we focus on lower ages, the figures are also high. The 87.1% of children / as aged 10 to 15 are Internet users and 65.8% have a mobile phone (INE, 2011). The spread of smartphones increases the role of networks, because the allowing use anytime, anywhere.

So social networks are not only well consolidated but also accompany the user wherever he goes. In 2011, the average per person visited networks increased 70% over the previous year. Therefore, users coexist with three social networks and, on average, Facebook always being one of them (IAB, 2011).

It so usual engaging to the Internet, specially social networks, by young people, who in some cases have generated various addictions and negative effects. There is already talk of "Internet addiction" pathological computer use or, in general, new technologies (García del Castillo et al., 2008). These addictions seem to be associated with certain demographic characteristics, personality and/or psychosocial, which could act as predispositions for use and / or abuse of the Internet. In fact, 11% of people who are not yet users of the Internet and social networks have as their main reason for not join or registering the fear of getting hooked by the network (IAB, 2011).

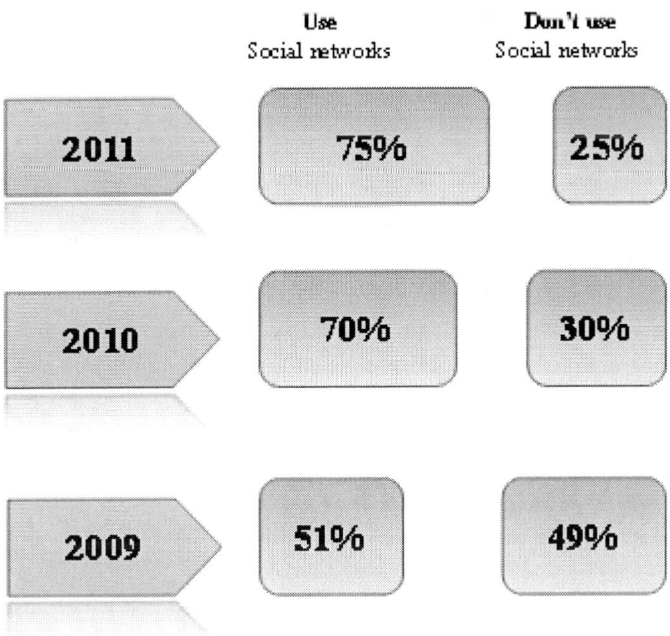

Source: Compiled from III Study of Social Networks in the IAB Internet (2011).

Figure 1. Social networks insight.

The amount of information used on the Internet, moreover, is really great and comes from many different sources. Anyone who wants to is able to write a blog or another website and, then, can make all kind of publications, without its reliability proof, so that nobody can be sure of confidence of the source of information. Therefore it is important to know "filtering", but this is not always the case with teens.

Our propose in this chapter is to analyze how the Internet is valued by young people. Taking account all we said before, on basis on the theoretical studies, we will measure this value by two items: its assessment of its effectiveness as a means of learning (knowledge) and a its means for people relations (friendship) considering other variables such as age, studies, etc., at the same time, we have taken as explanatory variables the use of social networks and the way that young people trust the Internet. We have analyzed some Spanish teen opinions about use and assessment of social network and internet as a way to relate and learn.

Life of Teen's on Internet Age

Younger generations have grown up with new technologies. Internet, computers, digital cameras or smart mobile phones are part of their daily lives and are essential tools to communicate, share, consume, participate or create (Tabernero, Aranda, and Sanchez, 2010). Therefore, it is essential to explore the practices of young people on the Internet and in particular social networks, given the increasing importance that they have, so important that it's impossible to imagine their own lives out of internet age.

According to the Pfizer Foundation study "Youth and social networks on the Internet" (2009), comparing Internet use by parents, mothers and sons/daughters, confirms the existence of a generation gap with nearly 27 percentage points difference in the level of use of parents/mothers (71.4%) and their children (98.1%). If we compare the frequency of use, we also found differences between the two groups of Internet users due to the existence of 14.1 points difference in the percentage of daily use of the Web. But, if we focus on social networking, the differences are even greater cause the proportion of users is almost 2.5 times higher among adolescents than among parents. Besides, the daily frequency of Internet usage rate is 39 points higher for teens.

Teens widely used instant messaging, online videos, listening to the music, seeking information for jobs or for their own leisure, sending e-mails, and so on. Social networking not only allows them to perform most of these activities, but also it is a way of enjoying the company of their peers while they are learning or having fun. According to the Report Generation 2.0, 2010, elaborated by the University Camilo José Cela, 91% of young people aged between 11 and 20 years have known, for their first time, social networks through their friends. The success of "word of mouth" shows that this is a real "social boom".

From all the social network Facebook is the world leader. In 2004 it had a million users and currently has over 500 million members. In Spain it is the most widely used network, for all age groups as a whole. However, the boom of Spanish social network Tuenti among teenagers is impressive. Tuenti is made by and for Spanish people and its success among this group is also exceptional. 80% of teens have qualified Tuenti as its preferred network.

The management of both network (Faceebook and Tuenti) is similar. The users can create their own profile, add friends, write private messages, chat, or write to the home page, etc. However, there are notable differences. A Tuenti's member require to have an explicit invitation. This might seem like a contradiction if the aim is to expand the network but serves as a good marketing tool and it increases the desire to become part of the closed group.

Also, Tuenti profiles do not appear in search engines and there is a commitment to the local phenomenon. We are conscious of the importance of several other social networks, with huge impact worldwide which is increasing users in Spain, for example, Tweeter (Twitter in Spain). The used system is different. It is a social network for sharing professional interests which began being primarily literary. Nevertheless, this network is revolutionizing journalism today because it offers an immediacy between sender and receiver never reached so far on the Internet that is suitable for monitoring conferences, meetings, world premieres, events, sports, etc. (Caldevilla, 2010).

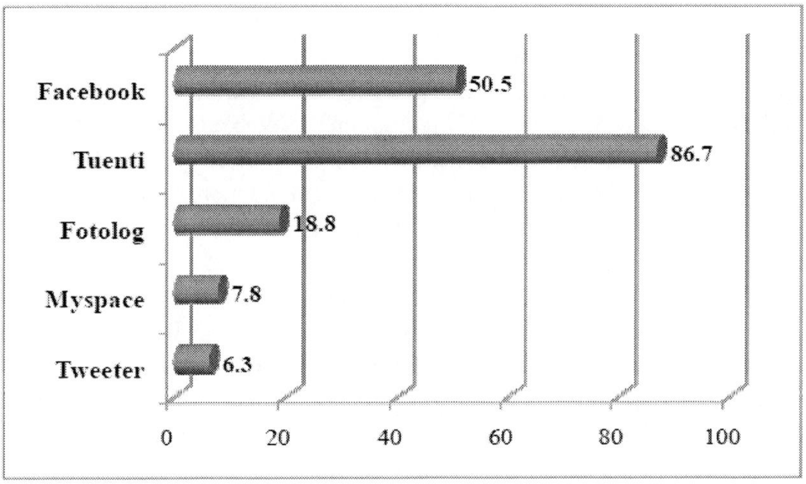

Source: Compiled from the "Generation Inform 2.0 2010" (University Camilo José Cela).

Figure 2. Percentage of social networks in which teenagers have entered their profile.

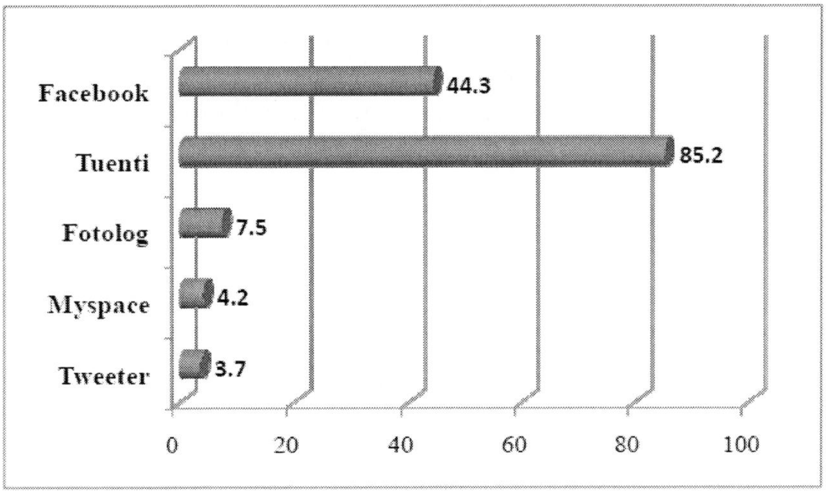

Source: Compiled from the "Informe Generación 2.0 2010" (University Camilo José Cela).

Figure 3. Percentage of social networks that adolescents remain active.

However, due to the important role played by Facebook and Tuenti for young Spanish people, we have focused our study mainly over them. Teens use social networks for different reasons. Among them, maintaining contact with friends, find people who is possible the don't contact in frequently in person, but that they feel comfortable making fun to make jokes, telling gossip or sharing their photos or music. The use of social networks are mainly focused on sharing or uploading photos, posting all kind of materials uploaded by their friends, sending private messages and updating their own profile.

INTERNET AS A SOURCE OF KNOWLEDGE

Rubio (2003) quotes Roserberg (2001) to define the e-learning as "the use of Internet-based technologies to provide a wide way of solutions to improve the acquisition of knowledge and skills." Internet has changed many of the traditional power relations in education. Teens can access all kind of information on the Web, and, on the other hand, some tasks that were only assumed formerly by teachers are now under the control of the students. Moreover, they can find information, create spaces for interaction, learning networking, etc. (Gomez and Tapia, 2011). Teens can access content from academic and research sources worldwide.

However, there is also a lot of misinformation or belonging to unreliable sources. It is therefore essential to distinguish the source of each knowledge but not all of them are trustworthy,so that it is very important to verify the origin of that information. In fact, you might be suspicious of the source of information on the Internet. It is widely accepted that one of the common problems in the analysis of Internet content is the lack of a procedure for checking the reliability of the documents exposed (Fornás, 2003).

Much of the information arose from confident sources, that is to say, from a guaranteed source (not free), but this kind of information is often out of of most teens due to budget restrictions.This information is located in databases or e-books, and its cost, in many cases, is not affordable to adolescents. By contrast, the "free knowledge" forces the user to decide on the veracity and credibility of the information. The debate on whether all knowledge is free is facing against defenders who remain copyright. This is a debate remains open yet.

Moreover, doctrine suggests that the level of expertise of the user, such as their level of education or social context, influences the individual's ability to discern between reliable and unreliable information.

MAKING FRIENDS ON THE NETWORK

Anybody needs to acquire an identity. We all need to differentiate and become aware of ourselves. But these identities do not arise independently of the rest of society. We are influenced by others' opinions or by social ties (Moral, 2004).

Nowadays, social networks contribute to draw our digital identity, which is a new part of our own identity. Friendly relations are vitally important for the teenager since integration and acceptance by peers and the group influences actually on the formation and consolidation of personal identity.

Therefore, the use of social networks influences highly socialization habits of users. In the past it was necessary to call one by one to invite friends to a celebration, but now, is enough to create an event on a social network to inform (ONTSI, 2011).

As we have seen, the most important reasons why teens use social networks are related to friendship. Keeping in touch with friends, hearing from people who you have not seen, meeting new people or flirting, are some of these reasons. In social networks everybody has a "peer group", which determines particular behavior and attitudes. It is a space of self-management, self-realization, in which, in principle, that they trust and it is an comfortable space where each one feels important and really valuated by friends.

While teenagers believe that social networks allow them to communicate with "friends", his parents refer instead to "people." Both points of view are in concordance with generational gap which we allude before. It is not a semantic difference due to a grammatical expression, it's a deep difference hidden under different words. It changes the concept used, which is very significant (Pfizer Foundation, 2009).

Trust and Security on Virtual Environments

Social networks have many advantages, but also containing some risks. Among the main advantages of social networking cited by users, according to the ONTSI (2011), we can include:

- Communication among friends.
- Communication between people who are far away.
- Communication free or very low cost.
- The immediacy in communication.
- The possibility of sharing photos or videos.
- The simplicity of use.
- Saving time and meet new people.
- Group Membership.
- Organizing events and meetings.
- The ability to express yourself more openly.

Regarding major risks:

- Privacy
- The identity spoofing.
- The chance of someone may know or spy what you're doing.
- Using social networks in an addictive way and wasted time.
- The criminal use.
- Risk of misinformation when talking about knowledge

With the goal of reinforce Internet security, the European Commission is working to stand out some of the major obstacles that hinder the full exploitation of ICTs, the increasing cybercrime and risk of low trust in networks. Therefore it seeks to promote safety through regulatory actions that increase the confidence of users.

There are many risks that may arise from online activities, since it is impossible to ensure 100% reliability. Then everybody is at risk, for example, of being deceived for example if you are making a purchase to a nonexistent company. Also be received malicious e-mails from false provenance, mailed by those who want swindle you. Therefore it makes necessary to know these hazards and establish appropriate precautions.

If we focus on social media, despite the positive assessment that overall, teenagers make them, are aware that they can be hazardous. 43.7% of young people highlighted as the main reason to negatively evaluate these networks which can be dangerous or open to damage, while 14.7% points to the lack of privacy.

Since the deal through the network stops being personal, the risk establish a friendly relation with the wrong partner is, in some sense, always present. On average, a teenager has 116 friends / as aggregates, while the average of the parents is 20 people (Pfizer Foundation, 2009). Then, teens may be confuse having someone on the social network as a friend and really it not is a true friendship. It is also possible that the person who has made the corresponding profile, their data has been invented or impersonates to another. Therefore, the risks of the Internet in general and social networks in particular, are many and varied, so that teens must have the tools and the necessary precautions for them to avoid them or, at least, to escape.

Assessing the Value of Internet and Social Networks by Adolescents

A survey of 75 young people has been conducted during the vacation time in a resort town in Galicia. The ages of the respondents ranged between 13 and 19 years. 48% of them are 18. Regarding the level of education, who is attending secondary school (65.3%) or university (34.7%). Table 1 lists the description of the sample.

The questionnaire with which we have worked includes questions related to the valuation of Internet as a means to acquire knowledge and to establish friendships. The proposed items were valued by young people using a Likert scale through which showed how much you agree with the proposed claims, on a scale of 1 (completely disagree) to 7 (completely agree). The values of the age and educational level didn't follow this pattern, so that we have used their standardized values for the quantitative analysis. In basis to the items used in the survey, we have built a structural equation model, that is show in figure 4. Thus, we can measure relationships between abstract variables, such as reliability, so called latent variables or constructs. These variables can't be measured directly, but we can "construct" them basing on the answered items on the inquiry. Therefore, we are using items or indicators that can be measured directly itself, then we can elaborate the latent variables.

In our model we try to explain the dependent variable, That We have called "assessment", referring to the view that young people has in the virtual environment, in terms of three independent variables, that, are themselves another constructs or latent variables. Of course all of these variables or constructs are determinate by the measured variables, corresponding to each item asked to adolescents on the questionnaire. The first is *reliability*, which is configured from observable variables, such as confidence in the Internet, knowledge of the source or age. The second latent variable is called *Facebook* and is constructed on the basis of aspects relating to knowledge, the ability to make friends through these networks, age or education level. The same happens with *Tuenti* variable, that is the third latent variable that we deal with. The composition of the constructs are shown in Table 2. As regards the measures of reliability and internal consistency of the scales, the Cronbach's alpha values re satisfactory and for the assessment variable and acceptable to all other latent variables. We also shown, in Table 2, coefficients of composite reliability and convergent validity.

OBTAINED RESULTS

The model meets all the requirements to be considered to work properly, with values for $\chi 2$ (freedom degrees = 46, N = 75) = 0,874, α = 0,036; CFI = 0,943 y RMSEA = 0,074, that supports our confidence is to explain assessment of internet by adolescents. Although assessment it is the only construct that is shown statistically significant in an individual way, we must assume that the other constructs' interaction is as important as to make the model works properly, even they be not individually significant.

Age and level of education is relevant to low significance levels (below 5%) both to explain the assessment that young people have of virtual environments in general, and the Facebook and Tuenti, in particular, and also for the their opinion about Internet reliability. These two variables that appear transversally in all constructs, remain relevant throughout.

Moreover, adolescents considered that relying on the information available on Internet is one of the most important factors, and the knowing of the source of information, with an average response of 5.64 points over the searchers efficiency (with 3.03 points average) or semantic webs (3.45 points). However, these variables is also relevant to explain the reliability of the network.

Table 1. Description of the sample

VARIABLE	CATEGORY	FRECUENCY	PERCENTAGE
Age	13	4	5,3
	14	5	6,7
	15	9	12,0
	16	8	10,7
	17	12	16,0
	18	36	48,0
	19	1	1,3
	Total	75	100,0
Studies	High school	49	65,3
	College	26	34,7
	Total	75	100,0

Table 2. Latent variables

Latent Variable	Item	Mean	Std error	Cronbach's Alpha	Composite reliability	Convergent validity
Reliability	Semantic Web	3,45	2,39	0,578	0,8112	0,4069
	To Know The Source	5,64	1,59			
	Confidence In Internet	3,28	1,18			
	Search Efficiency	3,03	1,97			
	E-Learning Use	4,91	2,33			
	Age	16,75	1,60			
	Studies Level	2,35	0,48			
Facebook	To Learn	2,16	2,11	0,594	0,8873	0,5634
	To Make Friends	3,37	2,50			
	Search Efficiency	3,03	1,97			
	E-Learning Use	4,91	2,33			
	Age	16,75	1,60			
	Studies Level	2,35	0,48			
Tuenti	To Learn	4,91	1,76	0,442	0,8358	0,4519
	To Make Friends	6,36	1,09			
	Search Efficiency	3,03	1,97			
	E-Learning Use	4,91	2,33			
	Age	16,75	1,60			
	Studies Level	2,35	0,48			
Assessment	Friendship	3,85	1,39	0,842	0,8615	0,7610
	Knowledge	5,33	1,55			
	Search Efficiency	3,03	1,97			
	E-Learning Use	4,91	2,33			
	Age	16,75	1,60			
	Studies Level	2,35	0,48			

Young people's value both social networks, Facebook and Tuenti, not only to make friends, but also for learning, since the coefficients associated with these variables are both significant at 99%.

The average response learn about Facebook is of 2.16 and 4.91 for Tuenti. As for making friends, have answered 3.37 points on average in the case of Facebook and a 6.36 in the Tuenti.

However, as already discussed, the kind of social network used is not relevant to explain the value of performing Internet (in an individual way).

However, the coefficient associated with the latent variable which measures the reliability itself is significant. In addition, other variables influence the valuation, which is also relevant, such as age, the efficiency of search engines or the use of e-learning.

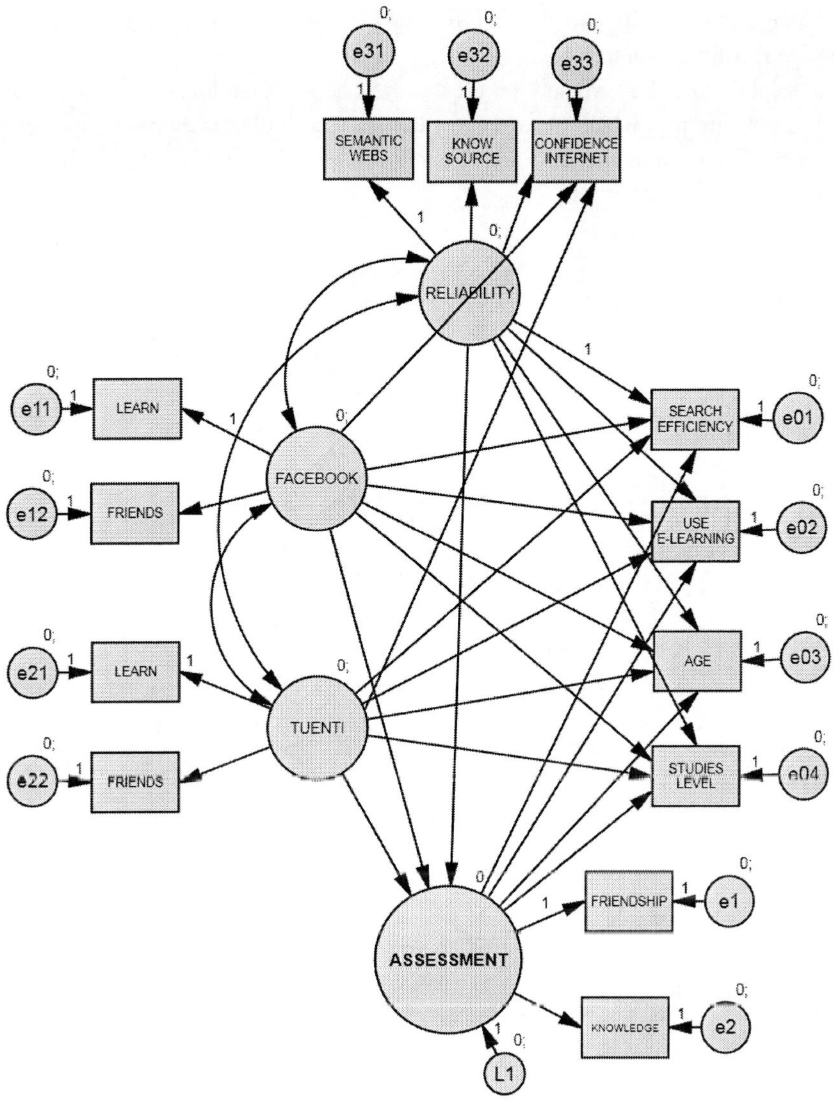

Figure 4. Proposed model.

Confidence in the Network Is Crucial for Teens

In line with the discussion in the main studies on youth and social networks in Spain, these tools are used by this group, both to learn and to establish and maintain friendships. However, undoubtedly dominates the latter use, being the most widely used network Tuenti. The age is what makes this preference, since teens surveyed are aged between 13 and 19 years. Our work indicate a probably change while the time goes by, founded on the differences that we have found among younger and older adolescents, over the years, we predict a change their habits and that drive young people to increase the use on Facebook while they are fulfilling years.

Moreover, the older they are and the greater their educational level is, the lower valuation they make of the Internet, which may suggest the need to protect children and guide them in the use of virtual environments, to have fewer mechanisms, for example, to distinguish the most reliable information sources.

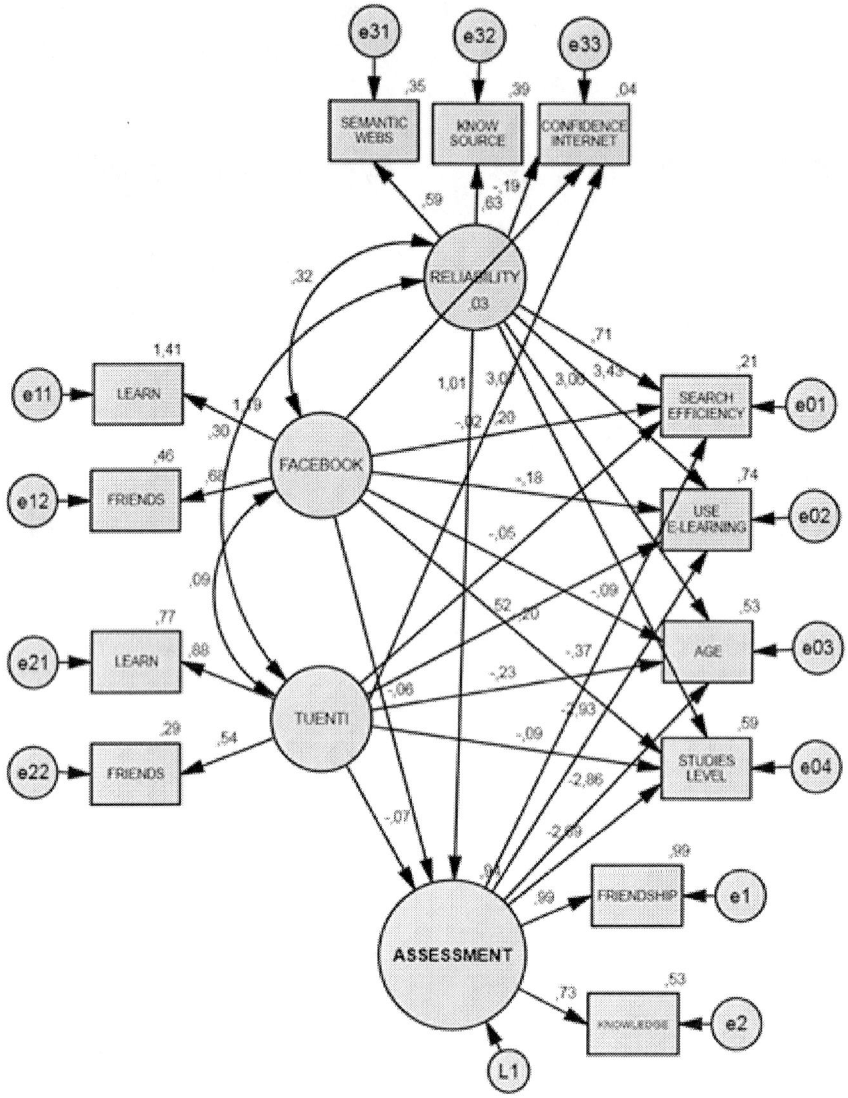

CFI:, 943.
RMSEA:, 074.
CHI:, 874- DF:, 46- DROB:, 036.

Figure 5. Output AMOS.

None of the networks has shown that use relevant to explain the general assessment that perform Internet. This result seems to show that the key matter to value positively the virtual network is not which one is the net used, but the confidence or rely on using it. If this is so, that is to say, if teens are confident on networks, their performing the subsequent assessment is positive. We can't, therefore, emphasize the Facebook or Tuenti as generators of greater confidence among young people, although, as we have explained in the beginning, Tuenti has security mechanisms and strict data protection.

Therefore, the main conclusion we can draw from the analysis is, first, the relevance of the age and level of education and, second, the importance of trust in the Internet in the subsequent assessment of the network by adolescents.

REFERENCES

Caldevilla Domínguez, D. (2010). Las redes sociales. Tipología, uso y consumo de las redes 2.0 en la sociedad digital actual. *Documentación de las ciencias de la información*, (33), 45-68.

European Interactive Advertising Association (2010). Mediascope Europe 2010. Resultados de España. February 2010.

Fornás Carrasco, R. (2003). Criterios para evaluar la calidad y fiabilidad de los contenidos en Internet. *Revista española de documentación científica*, 26, (1) 75-80.

Fundación Pfizer. (2009). *La juventud y las redes sociales en Internet.* Informe de resultados de la encuesta. November, 2009.

García del Castillo, J. A., Terol M. del C., Nieto, M., Lledó, A., Sánchez, S., Martín-Aragón, M. and Sitges, E. (2008). Uso y abuso de Internet en jóvenes universitarios. Adicciones, 20 (2) 131-142.

García Marco, F. J. (2010). El reto de la transparencia y la Web 3.0. Un nuevo contexto para las publicaciones oficiales. In: *O governo eletrônico e suas múltiplas facetas*, 239-262.

Germán Muñoz, G. (2010). Las redes sociales: ¿Fórmula mediática contra la soledad y el aburrimiento? *Revista latinoamericana de ciencias sociales, niñez y juventud*, 8(1) (separata): 51-64. Avaliable: http://www. umanizales.edu.co/revistacinde/index.html

Gómez Nieto, B. and Tapia Frade, A. (2011). Facebook y tuenti: De plataforma de ocio a herramienta e-learning. *Prisma Social: Revista De Ciencias Sociales*, (6), 238-260.

Instituto Nacional de Estadística (2010). *Encuesta de empleo del tiempo*. Madrid: Instituto Nacional de Estadística.

Instituto Nacional de Estadística (2011). Encuesta sobre Equipamiento y Uso de Tecnologías de Información y Comunicación en los Hogares. 2011. Avaliable: www.inebase.es

Interactive Advertising Bureau Spain Research (IAB) (2011). III Estudio sobre Redes Sociales en Internet. Avaliable online: http://www.slideshare.net/ IAB_Spain/iii-estudio-sobre-redes-sociales-en-internet

Moral Jiménez, M. de la V. (2004). Youth, Friendship social nets and psychosocial identity: the construction of Young identities peer-group. *Revista Galego-Portuguesa de Psicoloxía e Educación*. 9 (11) 183-206.

Novo-Corti, I., Varela-Candamio, L. and Ramil-Díaz, M. (2013). E-Learning and face to face mixed methodology: Evaluating effectiveness of e-learning and perceived satisfaction for a microeconomic course using the moodle platform. *Computers in Human Behavior*, (29), 410–415

Pérez de Silva, J. (2002). *La televisión ha muerto: la nueva producción audiovisual en la era de Internet: la tercera revolución industrial*. Barcelona: Gedisa.

Rubio, M. J. (2003). Enfoques y modelos de evaluación del e-learning. *Revista Electrónica de Investigación y Evaluación Educativa*. Avaliable online: http://www.uv.es/RELIEVE/v9n2/RELIEVEv9n2_1.htm

Observatorio Nacional de las Telecomunicaciones y la Sociedad de la Información (ONTSI) (2012). *La sociedad en red. Informe anual 2011*. Ministry of Industry, Energy and Tourism.

Tabernero, C., Aranda, D. and Sánchez Navarro, J. (2010). Juventud y tecnologías digitales: Espacios de ocio, participación y aprendizaje. *Revista de estudios de juventud*, (88), 77-96.

Universidad Camila José Cela (2010). *Informe Generación 2.0 2010*. Hábitos de los adolescentes en el uso de las redes sociales. Estudio comparativo entre Comunidades Autónomas.

In: Virtual Environments
Editors: Stephanie Trautman and Francheska Julien ISBN: 978-1-62618-090-1
© 2013 Nova Science Publishers, Inc.

Chapter 8

BRINGING SKIN OBSERVATION TO THE HIGHER LEVEL WITH 3D IMMERSIVE VIRTUAL ENVIRONMENT

Marie-Danielle Vazquez-Duchêne [1,*], Christophe Mion[2], Solène Mine[1], Christine Jeanmaire[1], Olga Freis[1], Gilles Pauly[1] and Alain Denis[1]

[1]BASF Beauty Creations, BASF Beauty Care Solutions France SAS, France
[2]Scalable Graphics, France

ABSTRACT

Sectioning biopsies for confocal microscopy observation poses various difficulties to the user in the 3D volumetric reconstruction model such as distortions and warping during the cutting with cryostat and the labeling of sections with antibodies. It results in a misalignment between sections which corresponds to the major challenge that needs to be solved with accuracy and efficiency.

Computer-based visualization of large volume has led to the creation of 3D virtual skin models near to microscopic reality. To be at micrometer level and use a microscope system for observing histological sections automatically reduces the field of view.

Virtual environment (VE) enhances the user capacities and gives to him a skin interpretation. Most of the time, VE is developed for training tasks but, in cosmetic research the immersive SkinExplorer™ platform has been set up for observing 3D reconstructed data.

The aim of the platform is to give to the user the ability to reconstruct the 3D model intuitively, effectively and accurately and finally to explore the architectural organization of the 3D model components. The skin observation by virtual environment provides appropriate insights, allows exploration and understanding of the spatial arrangement and structural characteristics of complex serial histological sections.

---

* Email of corresponding author: marie-danielle.vazquez-duchene@basf.com.

The overall goal is to propose a novel approach for construction, display, manipulation, interaction and scientific visualization of skin components with volumetric data from confocal microscopy acquisitions.

The innovative immersive platform already permits researchers to visualize cutaneous structural changes in elastic fibers network during chronological aging and premature photo aging or after stretch marks formation. Some investigations also show the effect of cosmetic treatment. In this chapter, the SkinExplorer™ platform proposes to "enter" into the spatial organization of specific cells such as melanocytes responsible for skin pigmentation.

1. Introduction

Recently, Jennifer Khan has published an article on Jaron Lanier, a computer scientist and author who is often described as "the visionary". [1] In the nineteen-eighties, he strongly believed that "virtual reality (VR)– the creation of computer-simulated environments in which real people can interact – would precipitate an extraordinary revolution in art and communication". He was the first to sell VR products as the data gloves and other new VR devices. In particular, this device uses a computerized camera to match the movements of the user and this kind of technology becomes an expansion of what it means to "think". This research is coming far to an end. It is only a matter of time before virtual reality research generates environment and virtual models so realistic that the user can feel to be in his actual field of observation and to move in his imaginary world as an explorer.

Virtual environment (VE) tries to give to the user the feeling of being in a real environment with a visual sensory path. The sense of presence in VE can be enhanced, for example with 3D immersion and haptic feedback systems. The more sensory pathways used, the more realistic is the VE.

The virtual reality seems to be the most natural three-dimensional interface for the interpretation of reconstructed slicing biopsy. Recent innovations in the study of life with virtual reality technology contribute to perfect the knowledge of human or batrachian anatomy [2, 3 and 4].

Similar to the Visible Human Project which aids to study and apprehend the human anatomy, the V-Frog software, a virtual reality application which improves the organs dissection practices, by demonstrations on cutting, peeling off and exploring specimens. VE had become a standard tool for biology education.

Another approach is the "Virtopsies" or "Virtual Autopsies" which are non-invasive imaging of an entire corpse CT-scan. Their robot is called "Virtobot" and allows to determine the cause of death for each autopsy [4]. Effectively, with a few examples, the study of life sciences with VE can be considered a "biorealistic" domain in human anatomy, in legal medicine and also in skin morphology.

Fluorescence imaging of skin histological sections with multiphotonic microscopical systems, which is a method of reference in cosmetic research, brings so much promise in applications.

For instance, optical microscopy research of the skin drives on the user to collecting different signals by multiphotonic fluorescence and multimodal imaging. Intrinsic fluorescence and immunochemistry fluorescent probe allows the visualization of specific component.

Anyway, the photons flux is only able to combine two photons energies at the exact focal point. This precise focal point avoids overheating of targeted area and preserves the high definition of each scanned image.

For a long time we have used microscopical and histological techniques as tools to construct skin micro-reality. Actually, skin observation gets ready to ride the next "virtual" wave of its exploration by the development of the SkinExplorer™ platform.

2. Historic HMI Platform

Our approach of the HMI platform for skin visualization is to combine three technologies as H for histology, M for microscopy and I for imagery [5].

For many years we have been developing our expertise in all histological techniques for skin, like classical histology, histochemistry, histoenzymology and especially in immunohistochemistry on skin sections.

Specific antibodies are used in immunohistochemistry to identify and localize the desired targets. This particular histological technique works with cell cultures, reconstructed epidermis cultures or sections from biopsies skin. These histological techniques provide measurements and quantification of expression of markers at the protein level by image analysis.

In terms of new devices for image acquisition and quantification; we constantly strive to be at the peak of innovative technology. Microscopy imaging improves cosmetic investigations while now a growing number of technologies rooted in photonics area are available on market but expensive to acquire.

The diversity of our samples needs a range of microscopical devices and specific skills which direct us to the innovative optical technologies which become more and more complex to use. To get close to the subject of investigation, being aware of photonic technologies novelties is a necessity for empowering our active ingredients valorization. For all these reasons, the activity is directed towards diverse tools acquisitions; from conventional photonic microscopy, confocal microscopy and multiphotonic microscopy to macroscopy, these devices open up a powerful mixed source of data as signal processing, quantification and interpretation of images [6, 7, and 8].

Continual advances of industrial communication tools and new software tools focus efforts in 3D visualization use around us. 3D innovations are in the press daily from camera new high-tech, 3D HD camcorder, 3D TV, specific 3D graphic cards for computers, 3D smartphone, 3D theater movies, 3D game-simulator devices, real-time applications on website, 3D illusion programs, to decision tool during product life. These featured technologies are omnipresent in our environment and are becoming a breakthrough solution for industries competitiveness.

During the last ten years, the number of articles on 3D applications has considerably increased because of their success, high potential and pertinent results. Conversely, the high cost of functional use drives few industries in this discovery and challenge. In spite of all these difficulties, 3D histological visualizations and representations are prolific, showing cutaneous structures with a modern regard [9, 10 and 11].

Researchers in BASF Beauty Care Solutions are exploring the possibilities to "enter" inside the skin and they are working on a synergistic approach with the HMI platform and the new SkinExplorer™ platform.

3. The SkinExplorer™ Platform

The SkinExplorer™ platform rises up as a 3D exploration prototype [12]. This technology expands into an immersive virtual environment to visualize epidermal and dermal structures and to explore the microanatomy of theses cutaneous microstructures. Several serial histological sections from confocal laser scanning microscope can be matched by stacks, aligned in depth by use of a few sections and put together into a 3D volumetric data. All these reconstruction steps have been accelerated using adapted algorithms.

There are multiple gains including automatic matching, precise alignment, better data perception, lower memory requirement and high quantity of treated data. This tool offers numerous improvements (Table 1). The new technical assets were developed around rendering and lighting. Firstly, volumetric and isosurfacic renderings can be used, separately or together. Secondly, in terms of lighting and depth perception, some tools have been implemented such as "Sphere Mapping", "Ambient Occlusion", "Halo", and "Overlaying colour channels".

These methods are pillars in virtual immersive environment when the goal is searching to display models with high complexity in depth.

The platform should answer to four main objectives: to observe and explore 3D virtual models, interpret complex three-dimensional data, show the basic microanatomy structures and visualize the effects of cosmetic treatments on these microstructures [5].

Moreover, rendering the virtual skin needs 3 components: the virtual environment, the interface and the user. The platform SkinExplorer™ has been set up an immersive environment interface around the user (Figure 1).

In principle, cutting into slices an object and gathering slices as a white bread which is regularly sliced seems to be easy to putting together. At the microscopic level, we meet some difficulties with slicing a biopsy in histological sections that include the following:

- Difficulty to align serial sections linked to the cutting force with the cryostat knife and the ability to apply the section on the slide
- Different penetration of antibodies for each serial section
- Sometimes, the difficulties during the cutting and staining steps can lead to warping and slipping on the slide of the sections and occasionally to lose it.

Despite these technical problems, we reconstruct an alternative 3D virtual model of serial histological skin sections. SkinExplorer is a trademark of BASF Beauty Care Solutions France SAS. The SkinExplorer™ platform incorporates the advantages of automatic reconstruction and multimedia to provide 2D and 3D overviews, animations, movies and an interactive immersive environment.

Table 1. Comparison between previous manual method and the use of the SkinExplorer™ platform (⊘: no possibility, X: available, Bad: hard to obtain a result)

TECHNICAL ASSETS	MANUAL METHOD with different tools and softwares	AUTOMATIC METHOD with the SkinExplorer™ platform
RENDERING		
Volume rendering	X	X
Isosurfacic rendering	X	X
High quality rendering	⊘	X
Transparency	X	X
Slicing the skin	X	X
LIGHTING and DEPTH		
Sphere Mapping	⊘	X
Ambient Occlusion	⊘	X
Halo	⊘	X
Overlapping effect	X	X
Overlaying effect	⊘	X
RECONSTRUCTION		
Alignment	Bad	X
Complex matching	⊘	X
Interpolation	Bad	X
Big volumes	⊘	X
Drop shadow	X	⊘
VIRTUAL		
Stereoscopic view	X	X
3D interaction	⊘	X
3D immersion	⊘	X

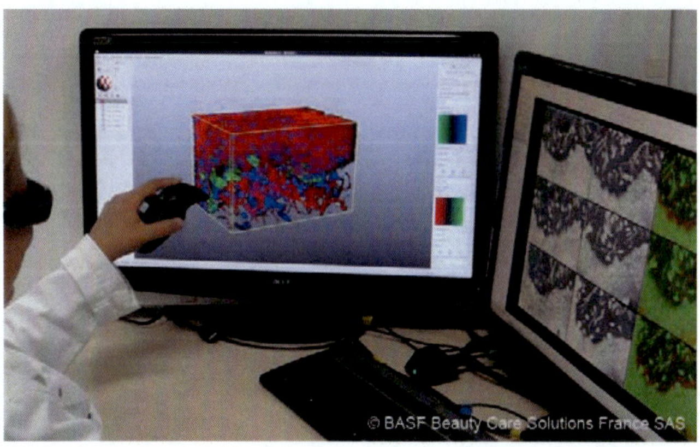

Figure 1. The platform SkinExplorer™ on 4 serial histological sections with alignment procedure and melanocytes organization (in green color) with its volumetric arrangement.

The platform offers a large choice of techniques. Many improvements have been driven since the creation of the SkinExplorer^{TM} platform at different technical assets (Table 1) and characteristics (Table 2). Experiments were conducted to work into rendering, lighting, reconstruction and virtual aspects [13].

The comparison between the previous method and the new SkinExplorer^{TM} platform shows obvious improvements in depth perception, in visual effect and in exploration mode.

Table 2. Roles of SkinExplorer^{TM} platform (⃠: no possibility, X: available)

CHARACTERISTICS	AUTOMATIC RECONSTRUCTION	MULTIMEDIA	SKINEXPLORER PLATFORM
BENEFITS			
Provides an authentic feedback experience	X	⃠	X
The user can freely manipulate the 3D model	X	⃠	X
Provides an exploratory based interaction	X	⃠	X
Provides an exploratory immersion	X	X	X
SAFETY CONCERNS			
No user exposure to chemicals	X	X	X
No user exposure to dangerous instruments	X	X	X
ISSUES			
Multiple uses of samples	X	⃠	X
Multiple representations	X	⃠	X
Multimode of immersion	X	X	X

4. Applying 3D Immersive Environment to the Skin World

Skin is a great organ with numerous components and complex activities as renewal, desquamation, protection and defense… The skin contains a multitude of cells and fibers. Many non-invasive technologies such as confocal in vivo, echography, and instrumental measurements allow us to study and observe the skin structures but not with the same accuracy and precision as the bi or multiphotonic confocal microscope images.

The counterpart of the highest quality of visual aspect is the necessity to cut a biopsy in serial histological sections and use specific antibodies for each protein. Even if the skin covers the entire body, it corresponds to a fine layer.

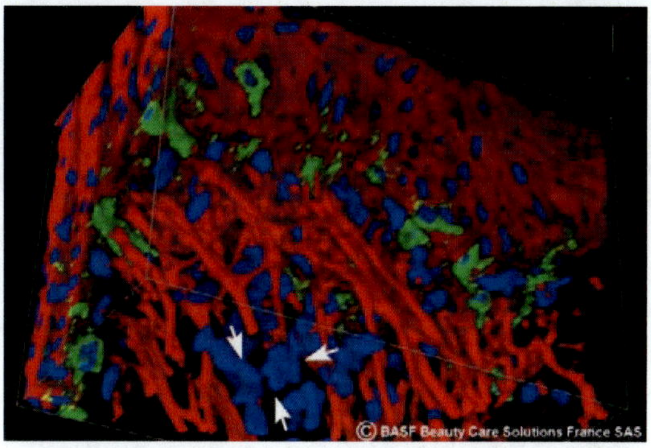

Figure 2. Bottom view of the histological volume.

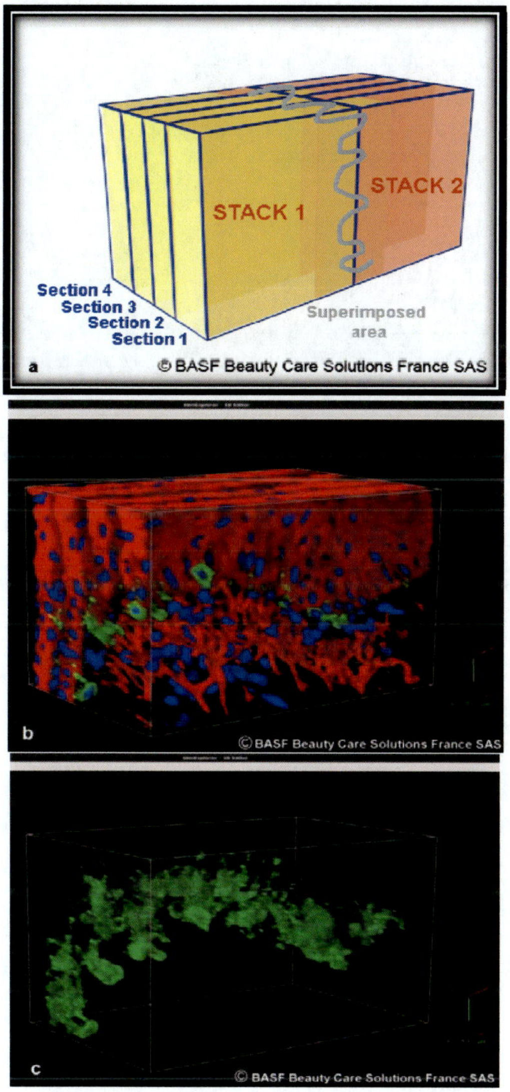

Figure 3. (Continued).

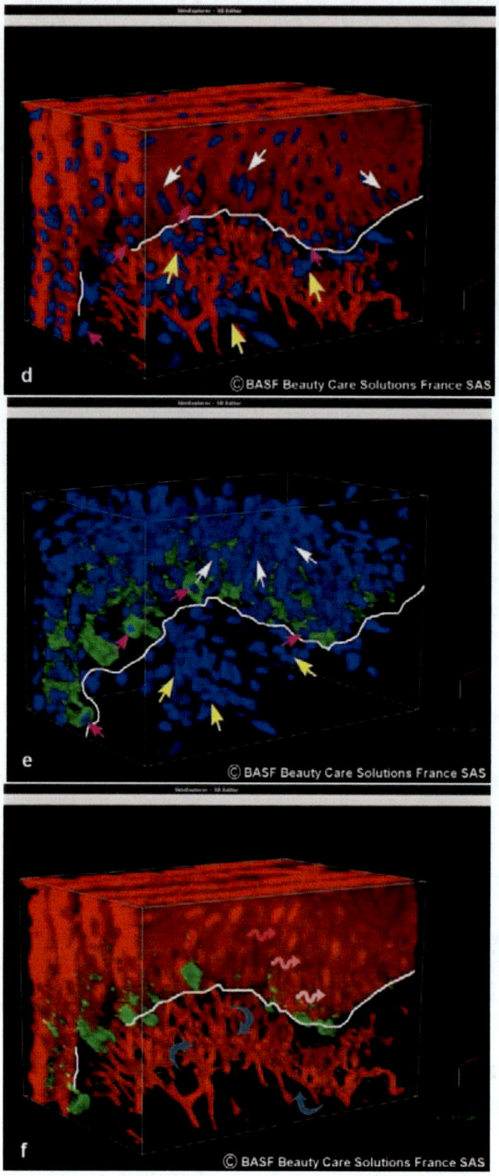

Figure 3. Profile view of the histological entire volume; visualization of the constitutive elements (a) with 2 stacks per section and with 4 sections per volume. The resulted volume of 3 color channels is reconstructed in b with its melanocytes stained in green (b). A white line in Figures 3d to 3f shows the dermo-epidermal junction that separates epidermis from dermis. Three kinds of nuclei are visible. In epidermis, the nuclei from keratinocytes are observable under white arrows (in d and e) and from melanocytes under pink arrows (in d and e). In dermis, the nuclei from fibroblasts are localized under yellow arrows (in d and e). Then, the red counterstaining corresponding to the blue Evans has no specificity. The Figure 3f shows the different keratinocytes layers (pink wave arrows) and the elastic fibers below (curved blue arrows).

This fine layer does not overpass a millimeter in thickness except for some particular body regions and reduces our field of study and the technological way and methods of exploration. For these reasons, we combine the capabilities of the HMI platform to the

SkinExplorer™ platform. In figure 2, four serial histological sections were realigned to give a bottom view where a whole heap of fibroblasts can be identified by the blue nuclei gathering (white arrows) inside an elastic fibers network and below a dermal papilla.

We are also interested in the intersection between creativity and technology for reconstructing 3D skin at the micrometer level (Figure 3). The Figure 3a summarizes the constitutive stacks of 4 sections with a superimposed area (gray zigzag) which gives us a global view of puzzle pieces (Figure 3b). On c, the melanocytes repartition at the dermal epidermal junction and then from d to f, we choose to mix two color channels. These 3 figures (d, e and f) show the relationships between keratinocytes and melanocytes and their localization. Turning around the dermal papilla in immersion offers observation in the spatial organization, as well as the quantity and the importance of melanocytes. Another relevant component such as elastic fibers, Langerhans cells, keratinocytes, corneocytes can be studied using this technique. This morphological exploration is an opportunity to model the next step such as precisely studying the morphological aspect, physiological or molecular mechanisms and being handled to cosmetic uses.

5. Applying a 3D Immersive Environment to Cosmetic Uses

Visualizing, observing, exploring and measuring features inside the skin are a general purpose. A diversity of reconstructed 3D cutaneous models [12 to 15] allows cosmetic researchers to explore volumetric data intuitively with powerful tools such as the platform SkinExplorer™. Different results have been presented on elastic fibers. We use this to work on various concepts:

- Morphological aspect of skin [13,14]
- Dynamic skin behaviors [15]
- Functional nutriments (in/out) of skin
- Cellular behaviors or localizations.

The main motivation is to deliver the possibility of visualizing cosmetic changes [16]. An example of cellular behavior or localizations on figures 4 to 6 shows that the visualization of our 3D confocal reconstructed models has an exceptionally high quality that takes care of a precise view at the level of one to three melanocytes with their dendrites around keratinocytes and an overview of serial sections.

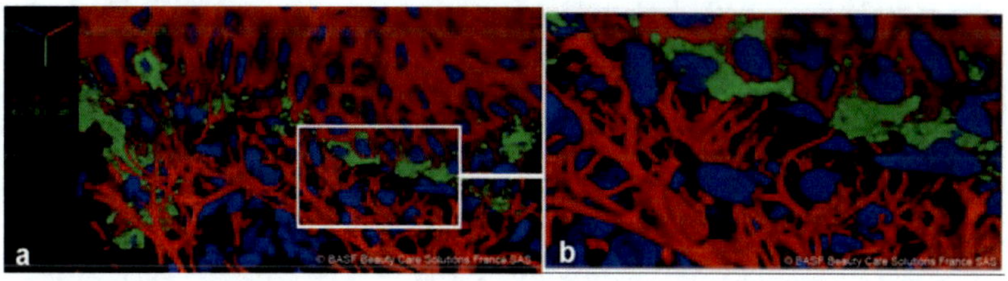

Figure 4. Front view (a) of the histological entire volume with a magnifying (b).

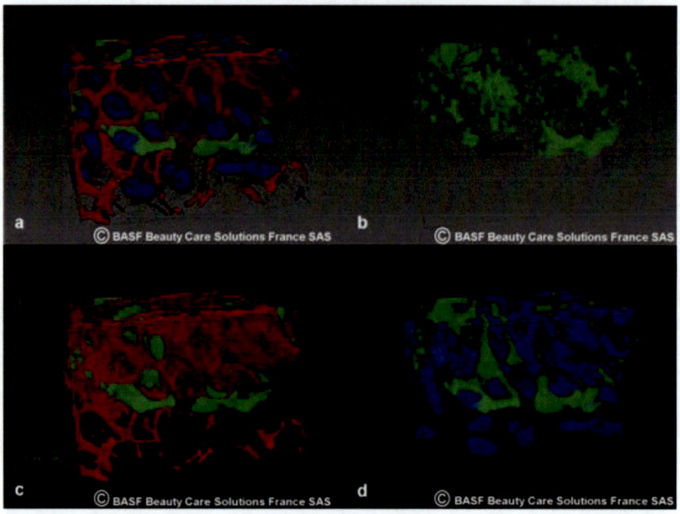

Figure 5. Several melanocytes at epidermal level cross 4 serial sections (a). Melanocytes are underlined with ambient occlusion on green channel which accentuates the depth perception (b). Their relationships with keratinocytes are presented with their cytoplasmic part (red, c) and their nuclear repartition (blue, d).

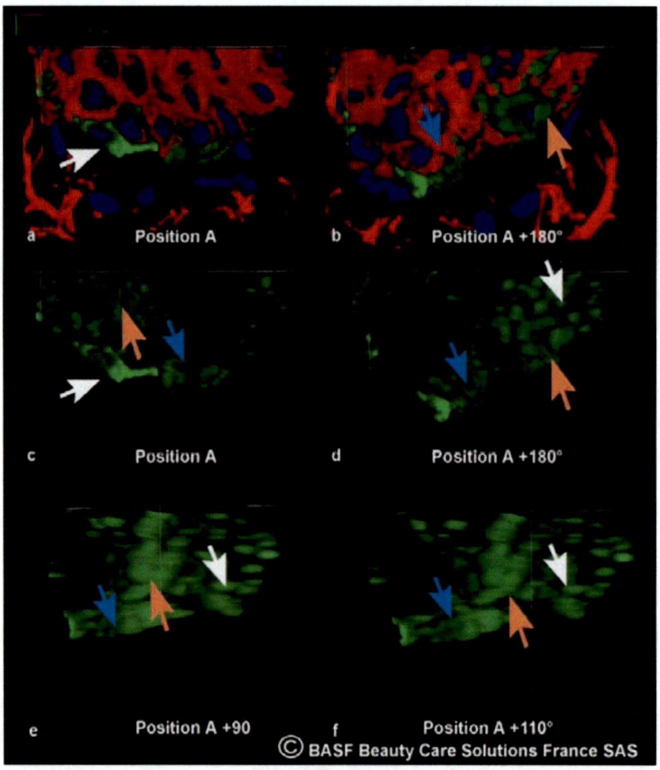

Figure 6. Focus on local area of the first section from the position A with the three (red, green and blue) color channels (a) and after u-turn (b). Three distinct melanocytes are differentiated by white, orange and blue arrows along 180° (c, d, e and f).

Figure 4 is a magnification of the frontal view of the entire volume where the melanocyte environment can be assessed with its nuclear part, including the elastic fibers and keratinocytes surroundings. The melanocytes are numerous and their relationships with keratinocytes are complex. In VE, figure 5 shows to the user changes such as the lighting with ambient occlusion (b) and the perception of the melanocytes spatial organization.

Figure 6 illustrates the possibility to turn around a specific melanocyte (white arrow) and follow how 2 neighboring melanocytes (orange and blue arrows b to f) are localized around a vertical axis. All these figures 2 to 6 promise a relevant cosmetic future in VE by offering to the users (researcher, customer, and seller) to physically interact, participate, explore, be present and touch the studied cutaneous structures. As all new technology, its life has a profile, Hype Cycle of Jackie Gartner, rising, growth with a peak of expectations, disillusion and finally a plateau of productivity. We focus on this plateau of productivity in relation with the market demands [17].

6. The Future of Virtual Environment in Cosmetic

Nowadays, VE is omnipresent in our life, at laboratory for scientists or physicians, at home with serious games, on web with "webdoc", and in companies for "websales". Progress in VE leads to become a common tool to study biological structures. The future is constructing now with our abilities and our expectations. For these reasons, perspectives can be done with reconstructed skin as reconstructed dermis, epidermis or both. If we perform this step, we can imagine interacting in an immersive world with such a thematic:

- Impact of active ingredients on skin morphology
- Impact of active ingredients on the skin functionalities [16, 18 and 19]
- Exploration of different kind of skins with a library of skin components
- Dynamic focus of specific interactions

To deny seeing the cosmetic interests of VE is like closing the door of new experiences.

Conclusion

For a successful experience in VE for researchers, customers and sellers, a lot of experts intervene to get the expected results. Histologists, biologists, experts in microscopy, specialized computerized scientists and other scientific people participate in this adventure. We can imagine what we would like to do with all these wonderful and powerful tools to explore subtle changes inside the cutaneous structures.

References

[1] Khan, J. The Visionary, The New Yorker, july 2011, 46-52.
[2] http://www.tactustech.com/vfrog/.

[3] Lalley, JP; Piotrowski, PS; Battaglia, B; Brophy, K; and Chugh, K. A comparison of V-Frog© to physical frog dissection, *International Journal of Environmental and Science Education,* 2010, 5, 2, 189-200.

[4] http://www.forim-x.com/virtobot.php.

[5] Pauly, G. When 3D invests the field of skin imaging, Expression Cosmétique, nov-dec 2011, 12, 144-145.

[6] Pauly, G; Jeanmaire, C; Danoux, L; Bardey, V; Freis, O; and Rathjens, A. New Approaches for Collagen and Elastic Tissue to Improve Skin Firmness and Elasticity, *IFSCC Magazine,* 2011, 10-11, 269-278.

[7] Pauly, G; Vazquez-Duchene, MD; Gauche, D; Contet-audonneau, J.L; Jeanmaire, C; Danoux, L; and Freis, O. Advanced histological technology and three-dimensional imaging: a fruitful partnership to visualize the human skin micro-anatomy and changes in cutaneous structures, *Journal of the society of cosmetic chemists,* 2004, 55, 2, 224-225.

[8] Pauly, G; Moussou, P; Contet-audonneau, J.L; Jeanmaire, C; Freis, O; Sabadotto, M; Danoux, L; Bardey, V; Benoit, I; Rathjens, A. Tetrapeptides targets epidermal cohesion, *Cosmetics and Toiletries,* 2008, 1, 75-86.

[9] Song, WC; Hu, KS; Kim, HJ; Koh, KS. A study of the secretion mechanism of the sebaceous gland using three-dimensional reconstruction to examine the morphological relationship between the sebaceous gland and the arrector pili muscle in the follicular unit, *British J. Dermatology,* Aug 2007, 157, 2, 325-330.

[10] Stern-Kiefer, M; Porwol, T; Acker, H; Altmeyer, P; Bacharach-Buhles, M; Dreidimensionale rekonstruktion in der dermatologie, *Hautarzt,* 2000, 51, 746-752.

[11] Rodriguez, A; Ehlenberger, D; Kelliher, K; Einstein, M; Henderson, SC; Morrison, JH; Hof, PR. Wearne, S. Automated reconstruction of three-dimensional neuronal morphology from laser scanning microscopy images, *Methods,* 2003, 30, 94-105.

[12] Vazquez-Duchêne, MD; Kraemer, P; Saugnier, N; Levy, B; Mine, S; Jeanmaire, C; Freis, O; Pauly, G; Rathjens, A. SkinExplorer™: a new high platform to interact inside the skin by immersive virtual 3D cutaneous environment, Skin Research and Technology, 2012, Online.

[13] Vazquez-Duchêne, MD; Mion, C; Cavin, X; Mine, S; Jeanmaire, C; Freis, O; Pauly, G; Rathjens, A; SkinExplorer™ platform: High quality visualization of skin components with 3D overlaying channels, Laval Virtual 28-30th March 2012, Laval-France.

[14] Vazquez-Duchêne, MD; Mion, C; Mine, S; Jeanmaire, C; Freis, O; Pauly, G; Rathjens, A. Skin interactive exploration in multi-resolution visualization, AFRV 28-30th October 2012, Strasbourg-France.

[15] Vazquez-Duchêne, MD; Kraemer, P; Mion, C; Mine, S; Lévy, B; Jeanmaire, C; Freis, O; Pauly, G; Rathjens, A. The platform SkinExplorer™ from full-size overview to dynamic skin visualization in S3D environment, ISBS 28-30th November 2012 Copenhagen- Danemark, 37.

[16] Pauly, G. New approach to improve skin firmness and elasticity, In Cosmetics 2-4 November 2010, Bangkok-Thailand.

[17] http://en.wikipedia.org/wiki/Hype_cycle.

[18] Rival, D; Bonnet, S; Sohm, B; Perrier, E; A Hibiscus Abelmoschus seed extract as a protective active ingredient to favour FGF-2 activity in skin, *International Journal of Cosmetic Science,* 2009, 31, 419-426.

[19] Kurdykowski, S; Mine, S; Bardey, V; Danoux, L; Jeanmaire, C; Pauly, G; Brabencova, E; Wegrowski, I; Maquart, FX. Ultraviolet-B irradiation induces epidermal up-regulation of heparanase expression and activity, *Photochemistry and Photobiology B: Biology,* 2012, 106, 107-112.

INDEX

A

B

C

D

E

F

G

H

I

J

K

L

M

N

O

P

Q

T

U

V

W

Y